CONTRACTING FOR HEALTH

CONTRACTING FOR HEALTH

Quasi-Markets and the National Health Service

Edited by

ROB FLYNN
and
GARETH WILLIAMS

OXFORD UNIVERSITY PRESS
1997

Oxford University Press, Great Clarendon Street, Oxford OX2 6DP
Oxford New York
Athens Auckland Bangkok Bombay
Buenos Aires Calcutta Cape Town Dar es Salaam
Delhi Florence Hong Kong Istanbul Karachi
Kuala Lumpur Madras Madrid Melbourne
Mexico City Nairobi Paris Singapore
Taipei Tokyo Toronto
and associated companies in
Berlin Ibadan

Oxford is a trade mark of Oxford University Press

Published in the United States
by Oxford University Press Inc., New York

British Library Cataloguing in Publication Data
Data available

Library of Congress Cataloging in Publication Data
Data available

ISBN 0–19–829022–5

1 3 5 7 9 10 8 6 4 2

Typeset by J&L Composition Ltd, Filey, North Yorkshire
Printed in Great Britain by
Biddles Ltd, Guildford & King's Lynn

FOREWORD

The National Health Service and Community Care Act of 1990 initiated a radical reform of the organization of health-care services in the UK, introducing market-style relations between the newly separated providers of health care (such as NHS Trusts and GP practices) and the purchasers (such as district health authorities and GP fundholders). The associated introduction of contracting in Britain's National Health Service—with the purchaser/provider split and the use of GP fundholding—brought new and often inexperienced players into the contracting arena. Negotiating skills and legal implications have been tested, often for the first time, and a diversity of contracts are being introduced.

What does this imply for patient care? Are market processes appropriate for delivering health services? This book reports the results of the most comprehensive research to date on such questions, resulting from a £2-million, five-year research programme funded by the UK's Economic and Social Research Council, on 'Contracts and Competition'. This programme set out to investigate the increasing use of contracts within both the public and private sectors—as well as across these sectors. The work sought to advance our understanding of the problems, processes, and outcomes associated with this trend. Seven of the twenty research teams looked at these questions with an explicit focus on the health sector.

The range of issues investigated by the research teams included the way in which purchaser/provider competition in the NHS operates, not only in general but also in the specific case of community health services; the way the general medical practitioners (GPs) have managed fundholding; the changing relationships between key occupational groupings; and a range of socio-legal issues, including the mechanics of dispute resolution, approaches to contract drafting and variation, and perceptions of the role of public and private law in these and related matters. The results include an evaluation of the effects of these various management changes and their implications for service delivery, and offer insights for the wider policy debate concerning the value of these policy and contractual changes.

While the focus of the research was on the reforms introduced in the National Health Service in Britain, the lessons are of more global significance. Many of the research teams worked closely with colleagues across the world in order to draw on relevant recent experience and to reflect on what the key lessons have been.

This book is the result of a truly interdisciplinary research effort. It has involved economists, lawyers, sociologists, and accountants. The research includes a rich mix of case-study work, theoretical reflection, and policy analysis. The results will contribute towards the development of theory in areas such as organizational change, as well as being of key political relevance for the development of the National Health Service.

The research arising from this ESRC research programme and reported in this book will therefore be of direct interest to academics in and students of economics, sociology, social policy, politics and public administration, law, and management and business studies. Professionals and practitioners will find it an invaluable analysis of the changes they have been living through. And it will be vital reading for all those interested in public policy. It provides a unique opportunity to reflect on the regulatory changes which have been introduced over the past few years, to learn the lessons from that experience, and to chart a way forward for developing improved public health-care services in the future.

Jonathan Michie
Cambridge
June 1996

CONTENTS

viii　　　　　　　　　　*Contents*

LIST OF CONTRIBUTORS

KIT BARKER is Lecturer in Law, Faculty of Law, University of Southampton.

WILL BARTLETT is Reader in Social Economics, School for Policy Studies, University of Bristol.

JANE BROADBENT is Reader in Accounting, Department of Accounting, Finance, and Management, University of Essex.

MARTIN CHALKLEY is Lecturer in Economics, Department of Economics, University of Southampton.

PETER CHECKLAND is Professor of Systems, The Management School, University of Lancaster.

NICHOLAS DEAKIN is Professor of Social Policy, Department of Social Policy and Social Work, University of Birmingham.

ROB FLYNN is Senior Lecturer in Sociology, Department of Sociology and Institute for Social Research, University of Salford.

LESLEY GRIFFITHS is Lecturer in Health Policy, Department of Nursing, Midwifery, and Healthcare, University College of Swansea.

DAVID HUGHES is Reader in Social Policy, Department of Nursing, Midwifery, and Healthcare, University College of Swansea.

IRVINE LAPSLEY is Professor of Accounting and Director of the Institute of Public Sector Accounting Research, University of Edinburgh.

RICHARD LAUGHLIN is Professor of Accounting, Department of Accounting, Finance, and Management, University of Essex.

SUE LLEWELLYN is Senior Lecturer in Accounting, Department of Accounting and Business Method, University of Edinburgh.

JEAN MCHALE is Lecturer in Law, Faculty of Law, University of Manchester.

JAMES M. MALCOMSON is Professor of Economics, Department of Economics, University of Southampton.

JONATHAN MICHIE is Programme Director for the ESRC 'Contracts and Competition Programme', and Lecturer in the Judge Institute of Management, University of Cambridge.

JONATHAN MONTGOMERY is Senior Lecturer in Law, Faculty of Law, University of Southampton.

Susan Pickard is Lecturer in Health Services Management, Health Services Management Centre, University of Birmingham.

Carol Propper is Professor of Economics of Public Policy, Department of Economics and School for Policy Studies, University of Bristol.

Paula Smith is Research Fellow, Institute of Local Government Studies, University of Birmingham.

Peter Spurgeon is Director of Research and Consultancy, Health Services Management Centre, University of Birmingham.

Mary Straker is Research Fellow, Health Services Management Centre, University of Birmingham.

Neil Thomas is Lecturer in Social Policy, Department of Social Policy and Social Work, University of Birmingham.

Kieron Walsh was (until his death in 1995) Professor of Local Government Studies, Institute of Local Government Studies, University of Birmingham.

Gareth Williams is Reader in Sociology, and Deputy Director, Public Health Research and Resource Centre, University of Salford.

1

CONTRACTING FOR HEALTH

ROB FLYNN AND GARETH WILLIAMS

This book presents analysis of, and evidence about, contracting in the British
National Health Service (NHS) internal market. It comprises chapters by
authors working in different social science disciplines who have all carried
out recent empirical research funded by the Economic and Social Research
Council on different aspects of contracting theory, policy, and practice. This
introduction describes the context within which NHS contracting developed,
and reviews briefly some of the important themes which have emerged from
recent debates about contracting as a particular type of economic and social
action.

Contracting in the NHS evolved as part of a fundamental restructuring of the
welfare state. Its functions are central to the internal market and so-called
purchaser/provider split. However, there have been significant changes in the
environment and form of contracting adopted, and there is considerable uncertainty about its impact. Assessing the *overall* effect of these developments is
almost certainly impractical; rather, analysis must focus on selected features of
institutional and behavioural change. The selection of issues depends on prior
theoretical assumptions, since there are important differences in conceptual
and methodological approaches between disciplines—as will become evident
in the chapters which follow. Empirically, there are variations in modes and
contexts of contracting, and different degrees of endorsement for 'soft' versus
'hard' styles of contracting. The following sections discuss these themes and
outline the contents of the chapters.

RESTRUCTURING THE WELFARE STATE

The present volume cannot review the history and organization of the health
service or of the welfare state in which it exists, but it is important to place the
NHS in its social and political context (Deakin 1994; Timms 1995). There is
no single, universal history of the welfare state which can be described from a
position of value neutrality; there are a number of theoretical and empirical
examinations which attempt to make sense of the complex processes involved.
What we now refer to holistically as 'the welfare state', and associate nostal-
gically with the name of Beveridge, is in fact the outcome of incremental

in the relationship between the state and society which stretch back to
d beyond.

welfare state was founded upon a political and civic acceptance of
services funded by the state and provided by paid professional workers.
Teachers, doctors, nurses, and social workers were all part of an expanding
population of public sector, state-financed professionals employed in the
schools, hospitals, and social services departments which were part of the
post-war reconstruction of British society. Universal primary and secondary
education, wider access to university and college, universal health care, and
access to social services in times of need were all part of the post-war
developments which became staple features of social life in Britain. The period
from the end of the Second World War until the mid-1970s saw what has been
referred to as the rise of professional or corporate society (Perkin 1989). The
principles of this society were that health and welfare should be distributed
according to need rather than the ability to pay, and that the quantity and
quality of provision was best determined by professional judgement.

Within the NHS a vast range of professional workers deployed the fruits of
state funding and channelled the rapid technological developments taking
place in health care. Doctors, nurses, therapists, and a variety of technical
support workers occupied defined roles in an increasingly complex division of
labour in health care (Stacey 1988). With a growing armoury of drugs and
surgical techniques at their disposal, effective treatment of many previously
intractable illnesses became available and there was a growing expectation that
other diseases would be dealt with in the same way. Those working in the
health service, probably more than any other occupational groups in the
professionalizing society, were seen to be engaged in an activity that was
both scientific and ethical, as well as making a contribution to the post-war
economy and society.

Prior to the 1960s the professionalization of society was seen to be almost
wholly benign. While the competence and ethical judgement of individual
doctors or nurses might be questioned, scarcely anyone doubted the moral value
and political legitimacy *per se* of the institutions of the health service and its
professional workers. However, from the 1960s onwards criticisms of the
medical profession became more vocal and doubts about the benefits of
medical science became more unsettling. Critics questioned the altruism of
health professionals, the effectiveness of their interventions, and the cost
efficiency of the whole system of health service organization. Challenges to
the legitimacy of professional power in general, and medical dominance in
particular, are now heard from both inside and outside the health-care system
(Gabe *et al.* 1994).

During the last two decades governments in most industrialized countries
have been faced with fiscal crises and political conflicts linked with the post-
war expansion of the welfare state and subsequent attempts to reform it. In
order to contain rising public expenditure and also to make public services

more accountable to those who use them, attempts have been made to introduce elements of the private sector—the disciplines of the market—into what
were formerly nationalized and bureaucratic systems of allocation and service
delivery (Saltman and Von Otter 1992). In Britain, attempts were made during
the 1980s to 'roll back the state' in order to reinvigorate the economy. This
'privatization' was a multifaceted programme: various measures applied in
different ways across local government, the civil service, public housing,
education, and transport, and most clearly in the de-nationalization of formerly
state-owned industries (Gamble 1900, Hills 1990).

The meaning and form of privatization has varied. For example, some
industries became wholly privately owned for-profit enterprises, whereas other
public services (education and health) remained state-owned and tax-funded
but were required to make organizational changes which emulated the private
sector and introduced forms of quasi-market competition. The new watch-
words for the public sector became competitiveness, efficiency, consumer
choice, and value-for-money, while other values embedded in the history of
the welfare state—access, equity, need, and universalism—were ideologically
discredited (Taylor-Gooby 1991). The post-war institutions of the welfare state
were thus subjected to a radical overhaul, amounting to a transformation not
only of the public sector but of the 'public sphere' as a whole (Edgell *et al.*
1995). While these institutions maintained many of their functions, their
structure and operation were reformed. This was most conspicuous in the
reforms of the British National Health Service (NHS) and the related reforms
of the local authority social services with regard to their responsibilities for
community care, both of which were implemented after 1991.

THE NHS PURCHASER/PROVIDER SPLIT AND INTERNAL MARKET

The recurrent and worsening budget crises presented the government with a
dilemma: in view of the enormous political support for the publicly owned,
tax-financed health system, tighter fiscal controls could be imposed only at the
risk of alienating voters. As a way out of this dilemma the government
attempted to increase managerial control over doctors and other health professions. There were three strands to this strategy: general management, clinical
budgets, and the separation of purchasers and providers (Harrison and Pollitt
1994). The 'internal market', as the latter came to be known, was believed to
combine the virtues of private sector discipline with welfare values, and would
thus limit potential political damage to the government. Essentially it involved
the creation of a quasi-market in which *providers*—such as semi-autonomous
hospital and community Trusts—would compete with each other for the
'business' demanded for patients by primary-care doctors (GP fundholders
and GPs) and local health authority *purchasers*. The central idea was that since

ls' and other providers' revenue was dependent on meeting purchasers'
ments, they would have very clear incentives to increase efficiency,
___ l costs, and improve quality.

In this new system, *contracts* were regarded as the main instrument for
bringing about change, and a complex system of commissioning and contracting was established. For all involved, not only did this represent a new method
of working which entailed significant administrative and organizational turbulence, it also required a new set of values and the evolution of a new organizational culture—the culture of competition and contract negotiation, business
planning, and marketing.

It is widely accepted by commentators, practitioners, and politicians that the
creation of an internal market within the NHS constituted the most fundamental change in organization and culture since its inception in 1948. Prior to
1990, responsibility for planning, financing, and managing secondary hospital
care was vested in all-purpose health authorities, while primary care was
essentially the function of independent GPs who were funded and regulated
by local Family Health Service Authorities. The NHS internal market (like
other quasi-market reforms in the public sector), was premised on the division
of purchasing from provision, so health authorities effectively lost direct
managerial control over local hospitals, and larger GP practices were enabled
to obtain their own budget to buy services from a range of suppliers. Provider
units (hospitals and community services) were required to become 'self-governing' Trusts, whose funding depended on obtaining contract revenue from
health authority and GP fundholder purchasers.

This separation of roles and functions was intended to stimulate greater
competition, and thus increase cost efficiency and improve quality. Purchasers
who sought new or different forms of care, or were dissatisfied with waiting
times or treatment received by their patients, could use the mechanism of
contracts to persuade providers to change and improve their performance, and
they could also consider moving contracts to alternative providers. In its
original guidance, the Department of Health stated that the aim of both
purchasers and providers 'should be to maximize the total quality and quantity
of service', and they were warned to avoid cartels or abuse of monopoly
position (Department of Health 1989*a*: 16). Later advice stressed that the
objective of negotiating contracts was to 'reach a clear and explicit allocation
of risks and responsibilities between parties'. This was seen as a *management*
process, and purchasers and providers were warned that contracting should not
be undertaken in an 'adversarial' or 'legalistic' way, but rather they should
regard the contracting exercise as an opportunity to agree how improvements
to patient care could be secured. An identity of purpose was assumed: 'In the
end, both parties have the same objective: better health services for patients'
(Department of Health 1990: 25).

THE CONTRACTING ENVIRONMENT

The early years of implementing this new system were preoccupied with setting up provider Trusts, establishing GP fundholding, and reorganizing health authorities in line with their new tasks of health needs assessment and purchasing. It is generally accepted that the purchasing function was inadequately developed and received less attention from national policy-makers than issues associated with service provision (Ham 1994*a*; Hunter 1993). During this period an entirely new machinery of NHS contracting had to be invented to deal with fundamental issues of costing and prices, information systems, and quality monitoring. Hospitals and community units had to be converted from being 'directly managed units' to autonomous NHS Trusts. Health authority managers had to learn new skills in contract specification, negotiation, and performance monitoring. Sensitive to potential political criticism and practical problems in establishing the internal market, the government anticipated a so-called 'steady state' for the first year of the reforms—which broadly meant that pre-existing arrangements were to be maintained and no major changes in the pattern of hospital services were expected.

From 1992 onwards, however, competitive forces were expected to come into effect, especially as GP fundholders exercised their new powers. It soon became evident that the continued viability of some hospitals and specialties was no longer certain and that emergent competition between acute Trusts in particular conurbations had prompted moves towards 'rationalization' of services. In some areas this resulted in local political opposition, further fuelled nationally by criticism of an alleged inequity produced by the GP fundholding scheme. There were claims that a 'two-tier' service was developing, with patients of GP fundholders obtaining hospital consultations and treatment more quickly than patients of non-fundholding GPs (for discussions of inconclusive evidence about this, see Glennerster *et al.* (1994*a*, 1994*b*); Whitehead (1994); and Chapters 2, 3, and 6, this volume). To avoid or minimize the possible disruptive effects of evolving competition, the Department of Health continued to exert firm budgetary control over costs and prices and regulated the effects of local contracting.

From the outset, therefore, there have been inherent contradictions in the 'managed market' (Ham 1994*b*; Maynard 1993; Spurgeon 1993), as policy-makers and local managers have sought to reconcile the objectives of competitive efficiency with other NHS strategic goals such as access and equity. By the end of 1994, after carrying out a major review of the administrative structure and organization of the recently 'reformed' NHS, the Department of Health urged the need for 'constructive cooperation between different parts of the NHS as well as the beneficial impact of competition . . . We have to find the appropriate balance between the two' (Department of Health 1994: foreword). This document exhorted the virtues of competition, but also acknowledged the pragmatic advantages of *contestability*—that is, even where there were reasons for permitting a sole supplier, that provider's behaviour should be stimulated by the possibility that other providers might displace it in the contracting process. The internal market was therefore expected to be both efficient and responsive to patients' needs; competition was the *sine qua non* for both, but there would be a necessary degree of central intervention.

THE EFFECTS OF NHS CONTRACTING

The overall impact of these changes is extremely difficult to assess, largely because the confounding effects of concurrent financial, organizational, and policy changes make it impossible to isolate the specific features of quasi-market competition. Numerous analysts have noted that there have been no large-scale national evaluations of the implementation of the internal market, and most still argue for more detailed research to be carried out (Appleby 1994*a*; Ham 1994*b*; Le Grand 1994; Robinson and Le Grand 1994; Tilley 1993). It is also the case that there is much local and regional variation in market structures and thus the environment for contracting is highly complex. Changes in the national financial allocation formulae (per capita funding) and thus the purchasing power of health authorities, have added to this variability and complexity.

The Kings Fund Institute (Robinson and Le Grand 1994) evaluation of the first phase of the NHS reforms demonstrated the methodological problems of impact assessment and gave only a provisional and tentative endorsement of the internal market's success when measured against criteria of choice, efficiency, equity, responsiveness, and quality. A national survey of purchasers and providers in the 1994 contracting round concluded that there had been significant developments in the sophistication of contracts—but despite this, modified block contracts still comprised nearly half of the value of purchaser spending and there was widespread dissatisfaction with information, which was inadequate to carry out performance monitoring (NAHAT 1994). Another NAHAT-sponsored longitudinal case study of the reforms found that purchasers and providers in the West Midlands had attempted to develop a 'relational' market (discussed further below). Contracting had been problematic owing to deficiencies in information, asymmetry of information, disagreements about measuring quality, and high transaction costs in drafting, negotiating, and monitoring contracts (Ranade 1995). A National Audit Office study of contracting for acute care (1995) suggested that progress in developing more complex forms of contracts had been slow and constrained by inadequate information and difficulties in categorizing diagnoses and treatments for costing purposes. It also observed that purchasers and providers had been encouraged to develop relationships characterized by 'creative tension' and that the regions and the NHS Executive believed that health authorities and hospitals were principally concerned with their own, *separate*, objectives rather than jointly beneficial agreements. The NAO concluded that implementing the contracting system was an immense task and that contracting for acute care was still undergoing change.

CONCEPTUAL AND THEORETICAL APPROACHES TO CONTRACTING

While there has been no large-scale comprehensive evaluation of the implementation of the internal market, there has been a large and growing literature debating its merits and defects. The contributions to this volume reflect the diversity of theoretical approaches and themes found in these larger debates. Very broadly, studies of contracting and the quasi-market tend to have been based on predominantly *economic* and *socio-legal* arguments about the nature and impact of contracts.

For some economists (for example, Bartlett 1991; Chalkley and Malcomson 1994; Le Grand 1990; Maynard 1993; Propper 1993*a*, 1993*b*) the issues concern fundamental and long-standing problems about the behaviour of actors in different types of market. Many of these basic issues revolve around incentives to secure efficient exchanges, questions about the effects of monopolistic or opportunistic behaviour, and whether contracts can be designed to make the supplier or seller of the goods or services comply fully with the buyer's wishes.

One important economic approach—principal-agent theory—lays great stress on the motives and strategies employed by actors in a relationship where the principal contracts with the agent to perform a task for a fee. It is assumed that actors are self-interested and that the agent may 'shirk', mainly because principals and agents may not have identical or congruent goals. The principal, of course, is aware of this risk and may seek to monitor task performance closely: the main problem here is information asymmetry and its effect on contract compliance. Criticisms of this model challenge the basic assumption of self-interest, and its highly abstract level of conceptualization; it has also been questioned as to its applicability in public sector non-profit organizations (Broadbent *et al.* 1993*a*; Noorderhaven 1992; Perrow 1990). None the less, principal-agent theory emphasizes the significance of control over task performance and the centrality of information in a contractual relationship.

The other very influential paradigm for analysis of these problems is that which has developed from Williamson's (1983, 1985) 'transaction cost economics'. In a highly abbreviated and simplified form, this approach argues that business firms (and by extension other organizations) confront a choice about whether to produce goods through a vertically integrated (hierarchical) production process, or to buy in components or services from specialized suppliers through contracts in the competitive market. Williamson argued that markets and hierarchies were alternative means of dealing with transactions. Where contracts were difficult to specify, because of complexity, uncertainty, and insufficient or inadequate information, then it might be more economically efficient for firms to use bureaucratic methods to organize production. He argued that organizations will want to minimize the costs of transactions while also seeking to reduce the risk of opportunism.

There are many criticisms of this theory (see Francis *et al.* 1983; Thompson *et al.* 1991) but it has been highly successful in focusing attention on the nature of the contracting process and governance structures within organizations. In particular, in analysing the NHS internal market, there has been much interest in Williamson's stress on the difficulties of writing complex contingent claims contracts and problems in monitoring performance (Bartlett 1991).

These economic debates inevitably connect with socio-legal discussions about the character of regulation in market exchanges, and the effectiveness (or even relevance) of contract law in dispute resolution. Usually, legal contracts entail duties and obligations, based on voluntary agreement, about future actions by contracting parties. They contain stipulations about conditions attached to the exchange, standards of performance, and remedies for failure or cancellation. There is an assumption that contracts can ultimately be *enforced* through judicial decision, on appeal by either party. In fact, however, in commercial and industrial exchanges, there is often reluctance to invoke legal remedies, there is often considerable vagueness in the contracts, and cooperative business relations are frequently maintained through informal understandings based on 'gentlemen's agreements' (Macaulay 1992).

Despite the rhetoric of the contract culture within the public sector, NHS internal market contracts are *not* legally enforceable. There are important features which limit the application of contract law to the NHS quasi-market: the parties are not limited companies or private actors; there is often a monopoly supplier; disputes cannot be referred to the courts but are the subject of administrative arbitration; and above all, the basic terms and conditions of NHS 'contracts' are heavily determined by statutory regulation (see Allen 1995; Hughes *et al.* 1994; Jost *et al.* 1995). Formal legal machinery, therefore, does not seem to have much relevance for the operation of NHS contracts (as Chapter 7 shows)—a situation which is unwelcome for those who favour a strengthening of public accountability through constitutional and legal mechanisms (Harden 1992).

TRUST, NETWORKS, AND RELATIONAL CONTRACTING

Clearly what economists and socio-legal scholars have focused on are the inextricably connected questions of competition and regulation, control and cooperation, risk and trust. There has been a recent convergence among the social sciences about the centrality of collaborative relationships within markets and the importance of reputation and trust in maintaining long-term contracts (Fukuyama 1995). This has affinities with sociological discussion of the social *embeddedness* of economic action (Granovetter 1985, 1992; Granovetter and Swedberg 1992). Granovetter has argued cogently that economic action is socially constructed and socially situated: it is 'embedded' in personal relationships and ongoing networks, rather than being the outcome of atomized individuals' decisions. Consequently, economic institutions are created, modified, sustained, and regulated culturally and socially. For Granovetter, there is thus a need to move beyond the formal rationality of Williamson's 'new institutional economics' to examine empirically actors' values and actions and their influence on the pattern of relationships (and the mobilization of resources) within and between organizations.

This type of approach has also been promoted in the 'new institutionalism' in political science and organization studies. A common theme is the necessity of recognizing that organizations and institutions do matter in explaining policy. Drawing on sociological theory (for example phenomenology, and Giddens's structuration theory) there has been a revived attempt to examine the contingent and dynamic relationship between actors' beliefs, values, and actions, and their role in constituting the institutional and organizational 'environment' (see Ham and Hill 1993; DiMaggio and Powell 1991). There is also a direct link between this analytical framework and more recent 'postmodernist' arguments about the importance of understanding discourses and practices when trying to explain organizational life (Reed 1993).

These coalescent theoretical debates have both a methodological and substantive significance. First, they emphasize the necessity for detailed empirical and processual accounts of economic and organizational action. Secondly, they focus our attention on the social construction of networks and rationalities which themselves comprise the 'infrastructure' of both cooperation and competition. Many contemporary economists, in seeking to explain market exchanges and patterns of contracting in commercial and industrial companies, stress the fundamental value of inter-firm cooperation and trust, and observe the prevalence of long-term collaborative relationships. Where there are strategic alliances between firms, or partnerships or franchises, there is mutual dependency, so their contractual behaviour is likely to be 'relational'. This requires a high degree of reciprocal trust and high levels of investment in maintaining inter-organizational networks. Such networks do not necessarily preclude or eliminate conflict, and they may not be long-lasting, but they are relatively stable depending on wider market conditions and the commitment of key actors (Larson 1992; Powell 1991; Ring and Van de Ven 1992).

There is, therefore, considerable disciplinary and theoretical convergence about the centrality of social networks in economic exchanges, about the importance of trust in collaborative business relationships, and about the significance of the cultural and institutional context in which contracts are embedded.

The extent to which these ideas are also reflected in the theory and practice of NHS contracting is problematic, as the chapters which follow indicate. Certainly there are some indications that attempts at relational contracting have been made by some NHS purchasers and providers (see Chapters 4, 5, and 9 this volume; Ferlie 1994; Ranade 1995) but there are also signs that both competitive *and* hierarchical imperatives stressing regulation and control may be having contradictory effects (see Rea 1995, and many of the chapters in this volume). The challenges of *managing* the contracts in both health and social services place considerable strain on purchaser–provider relationships (Challis *et al.* 1994; see also Chapters 5, 6, and 7). In a comparative study of contracting across different public sector services, Walsh (1995*a*, 1995*b*) found that most health agencies saw contracts as generating conflict (especially because of an undue stress on default and sanctions) and increasing management complexity. Equally, however, there was much diversity in the form and content of NHS contracts, and the extent of (and mechanisms for) monitoring and regulation varied (see also Spurgeon and Smith 1995; Smith 1994). These researchers have also found that, comparatively, local government contracting displayed the most obvious attempts at long-term trust relationships; social care contracts were very varied but the lowest support for the principle of contracting was found among social services (Deakin and Walsh 1994; Smith and Thomas 1993; Walsh 1995*b*).

Given that there is differentiation and heterogeneity—reflecting both the complexity of the services involved and the effects of quasi-market competition, it is unlikely that there will be any single consistent pattern in the mode of contracting. Indeed this volume illustrates some of the diversity which characterizes the real experience of contracting in the NHS and in the public sector generally. It also indicates that it is valuable to think beyond the official rhetoric surrounding contracts, and examine concrete practices. Clearly the process of contracting is a set of technical procedures which may dominate the work of certain managers and professionals in purchaser and provider organizations. However, contracts are not formed in a vacuum— the contracting process is only one part of a much larger set of relationships and is influenced by the prehistory of inter-agency relationships as well as the current financial and political constraints and dominant policy issues. As Jost *et al.* (1995) (following a much earlier Durkheimian precept) have observed, contracts do not comprise the totality of the relationship between contracting parties.

Further, contracts may be 'soft' and function symbolically as general statements of intent—providing a legitimating framework for collaborative work.
But contracts can also be 'hard' and prescriptive, embodying close surveillance and sanctions. Contracts have substantive effects on decisions about
resources and services, but those decisions may not be exclusively explained
as the outcome of the contract negotiations *per se*. There may be struggles
about the meaning and purpose of contracts *within* purchasing and providing
agencies, as well as disagreements between them. Contracts, therefore, must be
analysed in context, and must be understood not simply as formal documents
for economic exchange between a principal and an agent, but as socially
constructed, bargained, and contested 'treaties' (Williamson 1990) embedded
in a complex nexus of constantly changing organizational (and, in the NHS,
political) relationships.

THE ORGANIZATION OF CHAPTERS

There is a need, therefore, for empirically grounded analysis of the practice of
contracting for health. The present volume presents recent findings from a
series of research projects about NHS and related forms of contracting, and
examines various dimensions of the commissioning and contracting process in
detail. The chapters refer to a number of sectors of the health-care system, and
discuss analytically separate but empirically interlinked issues. While each
chapter presents evidence about specific features of the NHS and particular
project findings, a number of common questions are addressed.

This is a multidisciplinary book which illustrates the value of working
between and across disciplines in addressing complex and fast-changing areas
of policy, while also indicating the importance of the concepts and practices of
different disciplines as the basis for the interpretive policy analysis. Not only
do the chapters illustrate the different methods disciplines employ, they also
highlight the very different theories, and ways of thinking, which characterize
the work of different disciplines. Lawyers, economists, sociologists, anthro-
pologists, management scientists, and others are all here, each making a
contribution to our understanding of the complex issue of contracting in the
public sector.

This interdisciplinarity was stimulated by the organization of the projects on
which the chapters are based within a large programme of research commissioned by the Economic and Social Research Council on contracts and competition which began in 1992. The origin and rationale for this programme are
discussed in the Foreword by Jonathan Michie. The work presented here is
based on projects which have been undertaken with a view to enhancing our
understanding of key areas of public policy and practice. We hope that the

collection will therefore be of interest beyond the world of academic research, and help to make a contribution to health policy and practice.

In Chapter 2, Bartlett and Propper analyse the motivations and behaviour of acute hospital trusts and their contract negotiations with GP fundholders and health authorities through case studies using quantitative and qualitative data. They examine the relationship between prices and competition in local quasi-markets, the role of financial incentives, and the constraints on NHS Trusts imposed by the Trusts' financial regime. In Chapter 3, Broadbent and Laughlin explore some of the similarities and differences in the social and organizational effects of recent wide-ranging contractual changes on GP fundholding practices and schools. Particular emphasis is given to the effects of the 1990 GP contract and the Local Management of Schools (LMS) initiative enacted through the 1988 Education Reform Act.

In Chapter 4, Flynn, Williams, and Pickard analyse one important component of health care in which the contracting process is proving difficult to implement—community health services. They discuss the problems of contracting in CHS, and argue that there are inherent features of those services which are incompatible with a competitive quasi-market.

In Chapter 5 Lapsley and Llewellyn examine the contract-setting and negotiation process in social services, particularly the quasi-market in residential care for the elderly. They discuss evidence from case studies of relationships between social services purchasers and voluntary sector providers in Scotland, and stress the importance of 'soft' or relational contracting.

In the next two chapters, some of the legal issues surrounding contracts are discussed. In Chapter 6, Barker and colleagues provide a detailed analysis of legal and economic problems in the design and use of NHS contracts. They discuss the economic theory of contracts and consider some of the legal issues which arise in their enforcement in the NHS. In Chapter 7, Hughes and his colleagues explore the role of formal and informal mechanisms for dispute resolution in the internal market. They describe alternative pathways of statutory arbitration, agreed arbitration, and conciliation, noting that these distinctions are not preserved in practice.

The following two chapters examine, in very different ways, aspects of the culture of the contracting process. In Chapter 8, Checkland discusses evidence about the management of the contract process. Using management development theory, action research, and case studies of organizational development and learning, he examines the influence of intra- and inter-organizational relationships on contracting. In Chapter 9 the team of researchers from Birmingham University presents a comparative analysis of different types of public sector contracts (NHS, local government, and social care). This chapter explores the ways in which the contracting process has entered the culture and functioning of the different organizations.

In the final chapter, the editors provide concluding comments and a brief overview of the main themes from the previous chapters. The relationship between (quasi-) markets and other forms of economic organization, and the role of contracts in mediating aspects of social relationships, are issues of very great importance at the present time. In the context of developments in British health and welfare services, the contributions to this volume indicate some of the major strengths and limitations of contracting for health, and explore empirically aspects of the unfolding relationship between contracting processes and the complexity of the organization and functioning of health services.

2

THE IMPACT OF COMPETITION ON THE BEHAVIOUR OF NATIONAL HEALTH SERVICE TRUSTS

CAROL PROPPER AND WILL BARTLETT

INTRODUCTION

This chapter focuses on the behaviour of providers, specifically NHS Trusts in the newly created quasi-market for health services. The quasi-market was set up with the intention that NHS providers would compete with each other and with the private sector to secure contracts from purchasers (district health authorities (DHAs) and general practice fundholders (GPFHs)). At the time of the reforms it was argued that such supply-side competition would result in a more responsive and efficient service, while the maintenance of tax finance and the allocation of funds to purchasing agents on the basis of need would ensure that NHS equity goals would continue to be met (Department of Health 1990). In the new contract system financial incentives are given a key role in improving the quality and quantity of health service provision. However, these effects may vary depending on the competitive situation in which NHS Trusts are located, and on their internal organization and aims. In addition, while it was argued that market forces would help deliver more efficient services, NHS providers were also subject to direct regulation by the Department of Health. If regulation is sufficiently high the impact of market forces as an engine for change may be considerably limited.

This chapter examines the extent to which competition appears to affect the behaviour of Trusts. We begin with an analysis of the incentives set by the Trust regulatory regime. In the second section we examine the pricing behaviour of Trusts located in markets with different numbers of potential competitors with respect to DHA and GPFH purchasers. In the third section we supplement this quantitative analysis with a set of qualitative case studies of three NHS Trusts to provide an insight into the variety of responses to the introduction of competition for health services. We conclude with an assessment of the impact of the new contract system on the behaviour of Trusts.

NHS TRUST REGULATION

The aim of the reforms on the supply side of the NHS quasi-market was to improve the productive efficiency of provider units (in other words, to bring about an improvement in either or both the quantity and quality of services obtained from the available resources). As part of this process, the separation of providers and purchasers was intended to harden the budget constraint of providers. Freed from the need to meet NHS equity goals by the creation of the purchasing role, a Trust's budget constraint was to be set by the income earned from selling services to purchasers. Management was given the right to exercise greater discretion over labour and capital inputs. Ownership of the physical assets of hospitals remains with central government and implicitly, since the state owns the assets, it has rights to any residual surplus accruing from those assets. In contrast with the explicit licences drawn up in recent UK utility privatizations, the rights to use these assets, and to surpluses from their use, were not explicitly defined as part of the reforms. Nor, in contrast to the franchise methods sometimes used to allocate other state assets (such as the radio spectrum), was there any competition for the management of these assets. The rights to manage these assets were given to the existing provider unit managers (sometimes after merger with other units).

In this structure, managers have to operate within the regulatory framework defined by the Trust financial regime. Officially, Trusts have the freedom to retain surpluses, borrow funds for new or replacement assets, and set local pay and conditions of service. However, these freedoms are exercised within a regime which regulates the return on capital assets, the level and structure of prices, and access to capital markets. Trusts are required to break even on their income and expenditure account taking 'one year with another'; neither over- nor under-spend their allowed borrowing on capital projects; and set prices such that the revenues earned on NHS contracts are neither more nor less than that required to cover all costs including depreciation plus a 6 per cent return on net assets. In addition, cross-subsidization between activities is not permitted, so that price is supposed to equal average total cost on all services sold to the NHS. In theory, Trusts are permitted access to private capital markets, and the recently introduced Private Finance Initiative will in future see more assets leased from the private sector. However, until July 1994 they operated under the constraint that borrowing from the private sector had to be at an interest rate no higher than that charged by the government. This means that in practice almost all borrowing has been from the public sector.

Essentially, this regime imposes a 'not-for-profit' model on Trusts along with a 'no reserves' condition (Propper 1995). This implicitly gives all the rights to any residual which is not spent within year to the owner of the assets—central government. We argue that the long-run properties of such a regime probably bias expenditure towards current expenditure and decrease the incentives for long-term productive efficiency gains.

The lack of an explicit savings mechanism increases the incentives to spend surpluses within year. Within-year expenditure may not be the most efficient use of such funds, since such expenditures tend to be expenditure on staff and on small amounts of capital. Large capital expenditure can be easily detected and is therefore less likely to be undertaken. It is often argued that not-for-profit organizations spend too much on staff remuneration because they have no owner with residual rights over surpluses (Furobotn and Pejovich 1972; Preston 1988). Such tendencies for Trusts to spend too heavily on staff or capital equipment arising from this not-for-profit status are likely to be further exacerbated in NHS Trusts by the lack of a savings mechanism.

The lack of a savings mechanism also means that one of the signals of the long-term level of demand for a Trust's services is absent. Accumulated reserves (or lack thereof) can provide a signal, albeit an imperfect one, of financial viability. Lack of such a signal means that other data must be collected when assessments of viability are needed—in particular, for the investment and disinvestment decisions that are required in a quasi-market. To make such decisions, the Department of Health has to gather relatively large amounts of information from each Trust. This has a cost in terms of time and effort. It may also have other more long-term effects. First, it may result in 'regulator capture', as government regulator and the regulated Trust become closer in order to minimize the costs of information gathering. Secondly, since there are more pieces of information to collect, there is greater scope for disagreement over the weight to attach to each signal. This leads to delay in decisions over whether a Trust is viable. This in turn leads to market blight and creates a gap in which political, rather than economic, considerations can once again become important. Trusts may therefore put energy into persuading purchasers and the Department of Health of their long-term viability. Such 'rent-seeking' activities (Chalkley and Malcomson 1995a) can be very costly. By late 1995 there had been a review of service provision in almost all major conurbations in England. In all such reviews disinvestment decisions (exit) have been protracted (for example, the implementation of the restructuring of hospitals in London) and open to political pressures. Such forces are likely to soften the individual provider budget constraint (Kornai 1989), although it may still remain firmer than under the pre-reform regime.

The pricing rules are designed so that Trusts recover full costs (and no more) on all NHS intra-marginal activities. The purpose of the rules is that Trusts should not make a loss by underpricing activities, should not make a profit from NHS activity, and should not exploit monopoly power. However, there are grounds for believing that these rules may be broken, may encourage inefficient use of resources, and may hinder the ability of Trusts to develop new markets. Moreover, the definition of full costs is open to interpretation. This is not only because a high proportion of costs are perceived as fixed (which they may or may not be), but because the nature of health services production is such that many costs are joint. In this case their allocation to different services is open to interpretation. This means that it is difficult to verify whether the regulations are being followed. Rogerson (1990) argued that in the US defence industry, even with heavy monitoring, firms paid on an average cost basis are able to shift costs onto outputs for which there is less competition in sales because the allocation of joint costs may be manipulated. This is separate from any incentives to cost-pad (i.e. to increase costs through hidden inflation). The extent of competition for different services provided by a single Trust is likely to vary since some services are more location-specific than others. Trusts therefore have the ability to shift costs whilst remaining within the pricing rules.

The pricing rules limit the gains from entrepreneurial behaviour by a Trust. If the rules are followed Trusts cannot exploit new opportunities through sales of 'loss leaders' or by undercutting rivals. In addition, Trusts may fail to price contracts to reflect risk. In consequence few short-term gains can be realized from entrepreneurial behaviour. There is clearly a trade-off between the short-term social gains from market-seeking behaviour and the possible longer term social losses from monopoly. The current rules appear to embody the belief that the possible emergence of monopoly is so likely, or its effects so detrimental, that any profit-seeking should be discouraged.

Initially Trusts were also subject to regulations (an efficiency index) which determined the annual rate of reduction in operating costs. However, the replacement of a surplus accumulation motive by a regulatory tool to increase productive efficiency may not have the desired effect. The efficiency index, as applied to most Trusts, is a target based on own past performance. Trusts have to achieve a reduction in target expenditure in each year that is a function of the previous year's performance. This is a backward-looking rule. Weitzman (1980) has shown that under such passive forms of target-setting, a firm may undertake lower effort than it would do if the regulator did not use past performance in the contract. Essentially, a Trust has an incentive to under-perform in the current year as it knows that good performance will make future schemes more demanding.

In addition, the efficiency index is likely to affect the nature of the services provided because if the regulator cannot observe all characteristics of the good produced Trusts have an incentive to increase production of the characteristics which are measured and will count most towards the target to be achieved. The efficiency index is a cost-weighted activity index, in which over 70 per cent of the costs are achieved by in-patient activity. It therefore provides an incentive both to over-record such activity and, more damaging, to change the nature of output so that more in-patient activity is undertaken. There is currently considerable anecdotal evidence of manipulation of both data and activity to meet targets (Appleby and Little 1993). There is also anecdotal evidence of manipulation of waiting list targets. The efficiency index, along with a waiting list target, are now both set as annual targets for DHA purchasers. However, purchasers use them in their negotiation with Trusts, and so Trusts are still subject to such regulations, albeit indirectly.

In summary, the long-run effects of the Trust financial regime are likely to weaken the intended strengthening of the budget constraint. The lack of clearly defined property rights encourages short-term hiding of surpluses and within-year expenditures and probably discourages effort. Similarly, the attempt to appropriate all efficiency gains through the operation of the efficiency index probably also discourages effort. The lack of a residual surplus means there is no clear signal of Trust long-term financial viability, which in turn is likely to permit the return of political interference in investment decisions.

While the long-run properties of the regulatory regime would appear to give little incentive for dynamic efficiency, the short-run properties may be some-what different. Over 70 per cent of costs are staff costs, most of which are fixed within the year. Capital costs are more fixed than staff costs. Contracts with purchasers run only for one year. Thus, on an annual basis providers have a relatively fixed set of costs but an uncertain revenue stream. Since they are not allowed to hold reserves, any shortfall of income as compared with costs means the provider will be 'loss-making'. Within a climate in which the Department of Health argues that there is excess capacity in the secondary and acute sector and that resources should be switched to the primary sector, individual Trusts with short-term deficits may be perceived (and perceive themselves) as being vulnerable to closure, even though they might have been viable entities in the absence of such regulation.

THE EFFECT OF COMPETITION ON TRUST PRICING BEHAVIOUR

Using a large-scale empirical analysis we have sought to establish whether market forces have any discernible impact on the pricing behaviour of Trusts given the financial regime identified above. Our aim was to establish the extent to which greater competition on the supply side of the market was associated with lower prices to either DHA or GPFH purchasers. In other health-care markets, competition has not always resulted in lower prices. Evidence from the USA (the only market in which there has been competition for a number of years) indicated that when purchasers of health care had soft budget con-straints, competition was associated with higher quality, higher costs, and generally higher prices (Culyer and Posnett 1990). Recent changes which have made purchasers' budget constraints harder appear to show that competi-tion is associated with lower prices or lower price increases (Gruber 1992, Melnick *et al.* 1992, Zwanziger and Melnick 1988). We have sought to establish whether this pattern of association is evident in the quasi-market in the UK.

To investigate the impact of competition it is necessary to establish whether there is scope for competition and whether providers and purchasers have incentives to respond to this competition by lowering price (if a seller), or asking for lower price (if a buyer).

The Extent of Competition and the Incentives of Purchasers and Providers

Although the quasi-market was created from an existing health-care system in which hospital location was planned, the existing configuration of Trusts is such that there seems to be scope for competition on the supply side. It is a stylized fact that health care has a locational dimension. Unless there is a great deal of excess capacity, most hospitals will have some measure of monopoly power. But this monopoly power will not extend to all services. For example, while emergency services must be provided within a certain time, for other services patients may be prepared to trade off travel time against other costs. Thus for certain services, particularly those bought by GPFHs, competition may be provided by hospitals located at some distance from the patient. An examination of the distribution of hospitals in the UK indicates that while this distribution reflects population density, hospital catchment areas do overlap. Relatively few providers do not have another provider located within a thirty-minute travel distance.[1] This (and our case studies) suggest there is potential for competition. Indeed, one of the reasons for the introduction of the internal market was the existence of cross-boundary flows—the provision of services by a hospital that was not part of the DHA.

Do providers have incentives to respond to this competition by lowering prices in more competitive markets? In theory, providers are not meant to price according to market conditions. However, we have argued the price equals cost rule cannot be monitored and the case-study discussions suggest that providers are well aware of this. In addition, providers face a different elasticity of demand from two purchasers. There is growing evidence to suggest that GPFHs have been more active in 'shopping' between providers than DHAs. Glennerster *et al.* (1994*a*) and Mahon *et al.* (1994) found that GPFHs were prepared to choose new suppliers and/or change the nature of the product that they bought. DHAs on the other hand seem to have been less ready to change patterns of purchase. This may be because of inertia, or because of a concern that the effect of moving large quantities of services will lead to the closure of the local hospital, or to poor incentives to be active purchasers. DHAs therefore have less elastic demand than GPFHs. Our case studies also suggested that providers see the DHA as less able to change purchasing patterns. Given this different elasticity of demand, providers in competitive markets may attempt to attract GPFHs by offering lower prices, whilst raising prices to DHAs in order to keep within the price-equals-cost regulations at the hospital level (where violations may be more easily observed). If the short-term vulnerability argument advanced above holds, providers have an incentive to do this (as long as the marginal benefit of sales outweighs the marginal cost). Do DHAs and GPFHs have an incentive to switch between providers on the basis of price? DHAs are allocated annual budgets and have to spend these within the year. While they may not keep surpluses nor make losses, they do have hard budget constraints. In addition, they have targets for waiting lists and efficiency indices. Given this, they are likely to be interested in price reductions (for a given quality of output).

GPFHs, on the other hand, may keep the surpluses from their budgets (though these are supposed to be 'ring-fenced' and spent on secondary care or for future practice investment). However, monitoring of the GPFHs' use of surpluses has been limited (and is difficult as GPFHs are self-employed contractors with the NHS) and GPFHs have made surpluses on their funds. To the extent that they are interested in making such surpluses they may seek price discounts. However, the nature of the budget and the internal aims of GPFHs may limit the extent to which the shopping between providers by GPFHs is determined by price. GPFHs are allocated budgets on the basis of historical cost—their expenditure during the year of entry into the scheme. Such an allocation formula appears to give limited incentives for patient selection (Glennerster *et al.* 1994*a*). If the formula is generous, the budget constraint is softened in practice, and this may limit the extent to which GPFHs are interested in price competition as distinct from quality competition. It has been argued that the lack of a hard budget constraint in the US has led to the 'quality competition' experienced prior to the introduction of selective competition (Robinson and Luft 1985). In a detailed study of GPFHs' purchasing intentions Whynes *et al.* (1995) found that price played a relatively small role for fundholders and the most important factors were aspects of quality. However, price and competition may still be negatively correlated, if the impact of competition is such that providers in competitive markets have both to lower prices and raise quality. If this is the case, for any given quality, price will be lower in more competitive markets.

Factors other than market structure and bargaining power may affect price. A hospital may be able to charge more because it provides a superior service. In the US market both teaching status and provision of high-tech services have been hypothesized to affect the ability of hospitals to charge premium prices (Dranove *et al.* 1993; Gruber 1992). A hospital may charge more because it is located in a more costly region.

Methods of Analysis

On the basis of these arguments we hypothesized that prices would be lower where the market is more competitive, higher where the Trust has more bargaining power, and higher where the hospital is seen as higher quality. We investigated this for two sets of prices. The first set were a subset of the extra-contractual referral (ECR) prices which are charged by Trusts to DHAs.

The second set were a subset of the GPFH prices charged by Trusts to their GPFHs. Both these prices are 'spot market' prices, prices charged to purchasers who are buying small quantities of a specific treatment. In addition, all the prices we were able to examine are 'posted prices'—prices from the price lists published by Trusts. Ideally, we might like to observe contract prices, since most services sold to DHAs are by means of annual contracts. However, these are currently (late 1996) not in the public domain, and ECR prices are the best guide we have to these prices implicit in the contracts negotiated between DHAs and Trusts, and GPFH prices are the best guide to contract prices negotiated between Trusts and GPFHs. In fact, to the extent that discounts from posted prices may be higher in more competitive markets, our analysis may underestimate the impact of the relationship between price and competition.

We examined ECR prices for four specialties—general surgery, orthopaedics, ENT (ear, nose, and throat), and gynaecology; and we examined specific procedure prices charged to GPFHs for the same four specialties. The specific procedures examined were varicose vein removal, hip replacement, tonsillectomy, and dilatation and curettage (D and C). Every attempt was made to ensure that the prices were comparable across hospitals and years. The ECR prices are for the financial years 1992/3 and 1993/4 and the GPFH prices are for 1992/3–1994/5. It is not possible to compare directly prices charged to DHAs with those charged to GPFHs, since ECRs are a price for a specialty, whereas GPFH prices are a price for a particular procedure. These prices were collected for 118 acute hospitals in England in eight of the then fourteen regions.

We defined market competitiveness by identifying a thirty-minute travel zone round each provider and either counting the number of providers in this zone who provided the speciality whose price we examined, or the total number of patients in the relevant specialty treated by all hospitals located in this travel zone. We defined bargaining power as the share of total income received from DHAs in the year prior to that for which prices are posted. We defined a hospital as higher quality if it was a teaching hospital or provided certain high-tech services. In the analysis we also used measures of regional location, measures of the morbidity in the district in which the hospital was located, and measures of the average speciality costs for each of the four specialities. We undertook econometric analysis of this data and subjected our results to a variety of tests for robustness. The details are provided in Propper (1996) and Propper and Wilson (1995).

Key Findings

The results of our analysis show that prices are not completely determined by the regulatory regime and that there does appear to be some role for market forces. First, for none of the ECR prices did the price-equals-cost regulation appear to be followed. Secondly, for two of the four ECR prices (ENT and gynaecology) and one of the GPFH prices (general surgery), the total size of the local quasi-market (our proxy for greater supply-side competition) was significantly associated with lower prices. For none of the prices was greater competition significantly associated with higher prices. Thirdly, for two of the ECR prices (orthopaedics and gynaecology), a greater bargaining power of the Trust with respect to its DHA purchasers was significantly associated with higher prices charged to DHA purchasers. For one of the GPFH prices (general surgery), greater bargaining power with respect to DHA purchasers decreased the prices charged to GPFHs. On the other hand, at this aggregate level, none of the measures of quality, all of which can be easily observed by potential purchasers, appeared to be systematically associated with prices.

These findings are limited by the size of our sample (only four out of seventy GPFH prices, only four ECR prices), by the proxies for quality and bargaining power that we had to use, and by newness of the market.[2] They are therefore suggestive, rather than definitive. Nevertheless, they do give some support to our hypotheses that greater competition will be associated with lower prices, and that the effect of the regulatory regime may be to allow sellers to increase prices to purchasers with lower price elasticity (the DHAs) whilst lowering them to the demander with more elastic demand. In addition, the lack of a systematic relationship between price and easily observed measures of quality also suggests that a price–quality spiral of the kind seen in the US market in the 1970s and early 1980s has not emerged to date. However, this does not mean that quality does not play a part in purchasing decisions; and other, non-measured dimensions may do so too.

The lack of impact of competition on price suggests that price may not be an important dimension of GPFHs' trade with NHS hospitals. Only for general surgery is there a negative relationship between the extent of competition in the local market and GPFH price. If this is so, it raises the question of whether GPFHs are currently not interested in price because they have generous budgets. Trusts in competitive areas responding to this competition might increase quality rather than reducing price. However, the number of GPFHs is rising. As GPFHs become responsible for larger proportions of the budget for secondary care, price may come to play a larger role.

THE EFFECT OF CONTRACTING ON TRUSTS: CASE STUDIES

In the previous section we discussed the results from a quantitative analysis of the effect of competition on pricing behaviour. These results showed that competition appeared to have varying effects in different segments of the market and for different clinical specialties. This suggests that the impact of competition is sensitive to some unobserved features of the organizational and behavioural characteristics of Trusts. Specific models of hospitals as not-for-profit firms in a market setting provide a clue as to why this may be so. The predictions of these models are sensitive to the underlying assumptions which are made concerning the goals and levels of influence of the main decision-makers in not-for-profit hospitals. Some models stress the interests of hospital managers in the decision-making process (Newhouse 1971), whilst others stress the role of clinicians as key decision-makers (Pauly and Redisch 1973). In practice it is likely that a combination of both groups exert some influence (Harris 1977). Differences in the balance of interest between the different groups in different hospitals will give rise to a different balance of aims and objectives as between patient throughput, the quality of services provided, and the working conditions and levels of remuneration of employees. Different combinations of such objectives will in turn give rise to differences in behaviour of hospitals which otherwise face similar market conditions (Bartlett and Le Grand 1994). In this section we report on the findings of case studies of three NHS Trusts in different local quasi-market settings, with differing degrees of market competition, and differing systems of internal organization and decision-making.[3] These provide a qualitative picture of the variety of effects of such differences which are difficult to capture through the more widely based, but less in-depth analysis of the previous section.

Information was gathered from interviews carried out with chief executive officers (CEOs), finance managers, business managers, and development directors in late 1994 and early 1995. The interviews covered the managers' perceptions of the impact of contracts and competition on Trust performance, the role of differing management methods and systems of internal organization, and a balance of advantages and disadvantages of the contract system. The findings from these case studies illustrate in detail many of the problems experienced by NHS Trusts operating within the over-regulated NHS quasi-market. They show how a variety of management structures have emerged in different localities, partly in response to new opportunities, but also embedded in the previously existing structures with which the newly established Trusts were endowed.

Trust A

The first Trust, established in 1992, is situated in a local quasi-market with a relatively low level of competition on both the provider and purchaser sides of the market. Over 85 per cent of its patient services are funded by a single local DHA purchaser and only 4 per cent comes from GPFHs. It is a general hospital located in a suburban area, providing a wide range of services including acute services, community services, and mental health services. There is a dominant DHA and relatively few of the local GPs operate on a fundholding basis. The Trust operates a system of internal organization in which professional managers have the greatest say in decision-making.

Internal Organization

In 1992 the Trust failed to meet its financial targets, and in response to this it increased managerial control by replacing the system of clinical directorates with a system of service management. These group together specialties which are headed by a professional manager. The service manager works in collaboration with a 'lead clinician' but the service manager is the head of the section. These, together with the headquarters services (personnel, information, finance, nursing, medical, and development) and the CEO, form the Trust's management team. This group meets to determine the overall policy of the Trust, and clinicians are not directly involved in management. The main objectives of the Trust are determined by the management team. The views of clinicians are taken into account, but the service managers are firmly in charge of planning and do not collect 'wish lists' of new activities from clinicians as happened under the previous clinical directorate model and, in the view of the CEO, nearly led the Trust to bankruptcy.

Impact of New System

The CEO saw the following advantages of the specialty management system. First, a greater focus upon the cost consequence of decisions has led to a much greater interest in the real costs of services. Secondly, a predominantly inward-looking provider orientation has given way to an outward-looking consumer orientation as a result of the reforms. Thirdly, the management skills have been sharpened. Management is now quite strongly driven by economic factors, and there is an overriding concern to deliver services at cost and to meet financial targets.

Trust B

Trust *B* is situated in a local quasi-market which also has a rather low level of competition among purchasers although with a gradually increasing exposure to GPFH purchasers. The Trust has contracts with twelve main DHA purchasers and fifty GPFHs. However, the latter only accounted for 5 per cent of in-patient services, 20 per cent of day-case services and 26 per cent of out-patient services by 1994/5. Unlike the system of internal organization in Trust *A*, the hospital clinicians have an important role in decision-making within the Trust.

Internal Organization

The internal organization is structured through a system of clinical directorates headed by clinicians, which are directly accountable to the CEO. The clinical directors are supported by professional managers including a finance adviser and an information specialist, but they are responsible for presenting the business plan for any new service they want to introduce. The management team (the clinical directors, the CEO, and other senior managers) debate all new proposals, and make decisions about the overall Trust priorities and priorities between new proposals once a year. The clinical director makes long-term strategy and is responsible for contract fulfilment. The CEO sets the overall objectives of the Trust and the clinical directors have to fit their objectives into her scheme. The main objective is quality, and this is enforced by setting minimum quality standards; and by a rule that emergency cases must never be refused treatment.

The management team has a strategy meeting every three months, at which the clinical directors must produce a monitoring report and explain the reasons for any underspend or overspend. This is an effective means of managerial control which makes clinical directors responsible for any financial deficits, but also rewards success with a share in any surplus. The sharp edge of such arrangements is modified by the use of a central risk fund which is managed by the CEO, and used to develop new services and to bail out clinical directorates which face unavoidable losses. The CEO regards this as a system in which clinicians are much more accountable than in other organizational structures.

Internally, clinical directorates compete against each other for distribution of surpluses. Any surpluses arising from ECRs are distributed equally between the clinical directorate responsible, the central management, and other clinical directorates which are not in a position to benefit from ECRs. Therefore, internally, the Trust operates a system of surplus distribution which is likely to be effective in creating incentives for efficiency.

Impact of the New System

In the view of the CEO the predominant objective of the Trust is its commitment to quality. This is interpreted in a way that is sometimes in conflict with other goals such as financial viability. For example the Trust will not refuse to treat patients for which there is no contract funding, which may occur either because the contract volume has been exceeded or because a treatment has not been specified in a contract. For example, in the year prior to the interview neurosurgery cases exceeded the stipulated contract volume by 35 per cent. However, the local DHA refused to adjust the contract to take account of this and the negotiated block contract contains no provision for cost overruns. This has meant that the contract risk is taken entirely by the Trust and often means the Trust has to subsidize the provision of some services. The new system has however provided opportunities and strong incentives to consultants to be innovative in the provision of services. However, incentives to innovate tend to be stronger under contracts with GPFHs than under contracts with DHAs, since the local DHA purchaser is reluctant to invest in the overheads which new services sometimes require.

Trust C

This was a second-wave Trust, which was in financial crisis in 1993. It is located in a highly competitive quasi-market with three major DHA purchasers and a large number of GP fundholders. Within the Trust's DHA area 56 per cent of the value of contracts are made by GPFHs, and in line with this about 50 per cent of the Trust's contract revenue derives from GPFH contracts. This diversity of purchasers means that Trust C is quite exposed to market changes. It operates a highly devolved system of internal organization and management which provides a high level of influence in the decision-making process to clinicians, but also flexibility in response to changing market demands.

Internal Organization

In June–October 1993 Trust *C* was restructured by a new CEO, who established fourteen clinical directorates, with a high degree of devolved responsibility. The clinical directors are clinicians who can however call on the services of professional business managers employed centrally by the Trust, and each clinical director has his or her own administrator, personnel manager, and accountant. Central management sets overall corporate objectives in the light of a market analysis and discussions with purchasers about their wishes, but on an operational level the clinical directorates are highly autonomous, and so the Trust operates a clinician-led system. Clinical directors can retain surpluses they earn above set target levels of activity, and these can be used to buy better equipment or employ more staff. The main motivation was perceived not to be financial gain as such, but rather wishing to preserve jobs. This emphasis on employment reflects the influence of clinicians in decision-making and suggests that the Trust operates along the lines of a labour-managed firm in which the interests of employees are an important consideration in decision-making.

Impact of New System

Most of the Trust's GPFH contracts are already negotiated directly with the Trust's clinical directors and in the future clinical directors are likely to become even more involved in consultations with business managers in drawing up contracts with DHAs. The business plan is used as an active tool in drawing up GP contracts, and clinical directors discuss the contract with GPs on the basis of the business plan and on the basis of GP priorities. Under this system many GPs are willing to talk about long-term contracts and are keen to monitor health outcomes on a long-term basis. In addition, the clinical directors' strategy groups have a GP member, and they develop market forecasts together. Trust *C* is one of the few Trusts to do this, and one perceived advantage is that it has led to a number of innovations including one-stop shops for patient care and a marked increase in the number of day cases treated.

The new system has led to some real improvements in health service delivery. In the year prior to the interviews the Trust achieved one of the largest reductions in waiting lists in the country. Overall, in the view of the CEO the devolved management structure has been beneficial because it has provided the hospital with the flexibility needed to take action to correct its problems. The diversity of purchasers has also helped because this flexibility can be used in a creative way to provide innovative services.

In summary the findings from the three case studies indicate that a variety of management structures and styles can be observed in NHS Trusts. Whilst we are not able to establish conclusively that these differences account for the variability of the effects of quasi-market competition on economic behaviour such as pricing decisions, the evidence does lead us to speculate that such differences are likely to have important effects on the performance of Trusts in a number of key dimensions. Broadly, one may expect that, where management has more influence over decision-making, Trusts' performance will be more oriented to meeting the financial targets embodied in contracts. Where clinicians' influence is relatively important however, other goals such as quality, throughput, and employment are likely to be given greater weight. In addition there is some evidence that there may be greater internal incentives for innovation in service provision under more decentralized forms of management structure.

DISCUSSION

The aim of the quasi-market reforms in the NHS has been to provide market participants with greater incentives to improve efficiency and responsiveness to patients' needs. NHS Trusts have become autonomous units responsible for managing their own business activity. Decision-making in areas such as pricing, employment, and the level and mix of service provision has been decentralized to local level. But these reforms have been accompanied by a high degree of regulation, intended to deal with possible monopoly pricing and the potential problem of financial non-viability confronting managers unused to these freedoms. The new regulatory regime has attempted to limit the freedoms of Trusts by imposing central controls over their ability to earn surpluses, over their investment and disinvestment decisions, and over their freedom to set prices to meet market demand.

In the first section of the chapter we argued that such regulatory controls are likely to blunt the potential incentive properties of the quasi-market reforms and limit the gains to efficiency-improving entrepreneurial behaviour. Moreover, the regulatory regime may give rise to perverse effects. For example, the pricing rules, which require Trusts to price at average cost, may inhibit the development of new markets, and may induce Trusts to shift activity to areas where there is less competition. Moreover, the imposition of a backward-looking efficiency index may induce Trusts to perform below their potential operating capacity, and induce an artificial shift towards in-patient activity.

However, as in other industries, autonomous units operating in their own self-interest may attempt to evade such regulations, and so market forces may have real effects on Trust behaviour. In the second section we reported the findings of our research designed to test this hypothesis through an empirical investigation of the relationship between price and competition. That competitive forces were indeed making themselves felt was indicated by the strong evidence that Trusts were generally managing to evade the average-cost pricing regulations. However, the relationship between price and competition was not straightforward. The research indicated that in some but not all specialty sub-markets competition did have an effect on prices, leading to lower pricing of services in more competitive markets. In other sub-markets, prices were also influenced by the Trusts' bargaining power *vis-à-vis* purchasers.

The lack of consistency in these results led us to speculate whether differences among not-for-profit Trusts in their internal organization and management decision-making arrangements and goal-setting were responsible for differences in observed behaviour. In the third section we reported the findings from a small number of in-depth case studies which focused on this issue. These revealed a variety of different systems of managerial control within Trusts, ranging from a high degree of managerial control (under a system of specialty management), to different degrees of clinician control ranging from moderate degrees of clinician influence to more fully fledged devolution reminiscent of labour-managed control mechanisms (under systems of clinical directorates). The different mixes of managerial and clinician control in different Trusts were associated with different emphases on goals such as financial control, quality, patient throughput, and preservation of employment levels. Moreover, although the evidence is limited, and should be treated with caution, the case studies also indicate that Trusts which operate with a more devolved system of managerial control appear to be more innovative and more responsive to the demands of GPFHs. Given such differences in internal organizational and decision-making structures it is not surprising that market competition has an ambiguous effect on performance.

In summary, our findings indicate that market forces have real, though variable, effects on the provision of health services in the NHS quasi-market. Under some circumstances patient interests may be well served by the introduction of efficiency-improving competitive markets which undermine the 'vested interests' of the medical profession, while in other circumstances Trusts may be able to exploit their monopoly power at the expense of consumers. The Department of Health's attempt to minimize the potentially adverse impact of the quasi-market on levels of health service provision, and to minimize some of the more inequitable effects of markets appear to have been only partially successful. However, attempts to regulate the market may be ineffective where Trusts can effectively evade regulation, and probably give rise to perverse and unintended incentive effects. In addition, in the absence of a fuller understanding of the effects of market competition on not-for-profit Trusts with different forms of internal organization, the design of appropriate forms of regulation may be difficult to achieve.

We are grateful to Deborah Wilson for her excellent research assistance and to the ESRC for providing funding under grant no. 114251005 in their Contracts and Competition research programme.

NOTES

1. Definition of hospital markets in terms of geographical location is standard (see e.g. Dranove *et al.* (1993), Gruber (1992), Noether (1988)). In the empirical analysis discussed here, we calculated a thirty-minute travel-time radius for each hospital for each of the four specialties examined. The average share a hospital had of general surgery activity was 31%, orthopaedics activity 30%, ENT activity 36%, and gynaecology 37%. The range was from 3–100%. The proportion of providers in the sample without any competitors in any of the four specialties in a thirty-minute travel zone was 8%.
2. The newness of the market has the advantage that cost structures are less likely to be endogenous than in a more established market.
3. This is similar to the studies reported by Ball (1994) on the operation of the local quasi-markets for secondary education.

3

CONTRACTUAL CHANGES IN SCHOOLS AND GENERAL PRACTICES: PROFESSIONAL RESISTANCE AND THE ROLE OF ABSORPTION AND ABSORBING GROUPS

JANE BROADBENT AND RICHARD LAUGHLIN

INTRODUCTION

The 'new public management' (Hood 1991, 1995) in the public sector is now well established in the UK. The central features of this revolution are thoughtfully captured by Hood (1995: 94): 'lessening or removing differences between the public and the private sector and shifting the emphasis from process accountability towards a greater element of accountability in terms of results'. It is this programming of tasks through changes in contractual relationships, in which accounting and accountability systems are inextricably linked, which is at the heart of the 'new public management' reforms with consequent ramifications for the role of professionals. The nature of these contractual changes and their effects is the core concern of this chapter.

This chapter is one outcome of previous and continuing work examining the effects of the new public management on schools and GP practices (for earlier work on the schools research see: Broadbent 1995; Broadbent et al. 1992, 1993b, 1993c, 1994; Shearn et al. 1995a, 1995b; for earlier insights into the research on GP practices see: Broadbent 1994; Laughlin et al. 1992, 1994). The overall conclusion from this body of literature is that the new public management changes are seen as an unwelcome intrusion into the definition of professional activities and that rather than allow these new requirements to impinge and redefine the perceived rightful indetermination of task, various forms of organizational resistance have been instituted. The primary form of resistance has been the formation of informal and formal 'absorption' processes to counteract and 'mute' the changes.

This chapter develops these themes in two interconnected ways: first, by providing a comparative study of these absorption processes in both GP practices and schools and secondly, by extending the analysis to show how these absorption processes change, as the nature of the technical 'disturbances' of the new public management shift and develop. The reason for the latter is that the new public management is not a static set of requirements but a constantly changing round of realignments and adjustments which, in the main, require ever more subtle forms of professional absorption.

The chapter has three major sections. The first section summarizes the nature of the contractual changes with regard to GP practices and schools and how these have developed over time. The second section presents a 'middle-range' (Laughlin 1995) language of organizational change which helps to inform and articulate the data that follow. The third and final section draws from data collected from twenty-four schools and thirty-four GP practices over the last few years to amplify the nature of the absorption processes involved and how they have changed over time.

CONTRACTUAL CHANGES IN SCHOOLS AND GENERAL PRACTICES

In both health and education policy the organizational arrangements have been changed primarily through the National Health Service and Community Care Act of 1990 and the Education Reform Act of 1988, allowing a new contractual set of relationships to emerge. New 'principals/purchasers' have been created to act as custodians and directors of the actions and activities of direct service units who, in this new world, are 'agents' of, and 'providers' for, these new masters. Previously in both the health and education areas, district health authorities, family practitioner committees, and local education authorities (LEAs hereafter) were the administrative and financial enablers of the independent practitioners and professionals. In the new order professionals still perform the services yet the administrative bodies are no longer there to be a simple supplier of resources to enable these services to be performed according to the dictates of the professions; they are there to direct and, in some cases, redefine professional action and activities using financial contracts to ensure compliance.

Since the nature of these financial contracts differs across and within the health and education sectors, the explication that follows will concentrate on the primary focus of this chapter—the contracts between family health service authorities (FHSAs hereafter) and GP practices, and between LEAs and schools. It is important to note that our interest is not centred on either GP fundholding practices (those which have responsibility for some secondary care) or grant maintained schools (those opting out of LEA control). The reason is that in both cases this change in status is a *chosen* option. With regard to the remaining GP practices and schools the financial contractual requirements have been imposed on them without their choosing. It is the nature of these required contractual changes which is the focus of the following.

With regard to GP practices there have been three key contractual changes. These relate to the prescribing behaviour of GPs, their medical care via medical audit, and the nature of their more general, contractually defined,

and actions. To date it is the third of these—the new GP Contract—
been the most dominant. We will, therefore, concentrate only on this
the following.

The 1990 Contract is traceable to the 1987 White Paper, 'Promoting Better Health', yet the contents of the actual Contract are markedly different from this original source. It was intended to replace the original Contract which had not been changed since 1966 and which, whilst portrayed as a 'revision' to this original set of requirements, has a markedly different emphasis. Unlike the 1966 Contract, which was graphically portrayed by Scott and Maynard (1991) as the 'John Wayne Contract' (i.e. 'a GP's got to do what a GP's got to do'!), the 1990 Contract specified in considerable detail 'the services GPs are expected to provide', making plain and emphasizing that 'health promotion and disease prevention fall within the definition of General Medical Services' (1990 Contract: 7). A central aim of the changes is to reduce the amount of block grants and revenue per item of service to financial flows which can be linked to particular definable concerns and activities. Nevertheless up to 60 per cent of the remuneration of a 'normal' GP is still (even after the changes) linked directly to the number of patients under his or her care.

However, to receive this, certain requirements must be met. Paragraph 13 of the Contract lists the provision of advice on general health, the offering of consultations and physical examinations including those 'aimed at reducing the risk of illness', arranging referrals, and giving advice on how to obtain help from social services, as key obligations. This reflects the central emphasis of the contract on prevention rather than curative medicine as a key, if not *the* key, part of the work of a GP. Other specific requirements of the contract are that GPs have to offer to all patients who are 75 or over the opportunity of a home visit and consultation (which is intended to include an assessment of health and social standing) as well as to offer a health check to all those aged between 16 and 74 who had not seen a doctor within the previous three years. A further requirement, which, unlike the above, attracts a specific financial reward, is to offer all new patients a health check within twenty-eight days of joining a practice. There are other non-remunerated accountability require- ments which involve making plain the times and places when GPs will be available, producing a practice leaflet for patients about services available, and, finally, the need to produce an annual report for the FHSAs to contain information about actions and activities over the previous year.

The optional elements of the contract are a mixture of preventative and specialist elements with definable financial rewards and accountability expec- tations. Childhood immunizations and cervical cytology are of central concern: both have attached target ranges. For childhood immunizations, 70 per cent of the eligible list is the minimum point at which remuneration starts with the maximum reward for those who have given immunizations to 90 per cent or above of eligible children. For cervical cytology, the minimum payment is made when 50 per cent of all eligible women are tested for cervical cancer, with the maximum reward granted for those who have offered screening to 80 per cent or more of the eligible list. Financial returns were also offered in the Contract to those practices which run specialist clinics (for ten patients or more) for different types of health promotion and disease prevention (e.g. well person, hypertension, asthma, diabetes, and so on), child surveillance for the under-fives, and for minor surgery. Finally, further financial rewards were also offered in the Contract to those GPs who undertake their own night visits, and to those who attend postgraduate training workshops and conferences. Whilst these are optional elements of the Contract the financial incentives involved and the heightened accountability give great emphasis to these activities. Not to undertake them involves a financial penalty but also a possible categorization as a 'poor' GP.

Following considerable pressure from GPs two substantive changes have been made to the nature of the Contract. The first has been the abandonment of the requirement to offer a health check to all those patients who have not seen their doctor in the last few years. A rather more questionable change, certainly to the GPs, is the abandonment of health promotion and disease prevention clinics. On the one hand, GP practices became extraordinarily able at running clinics and making a great deal of money. The financial cost of this to the Government was beyond acceptable limits. On the other hand it was clear that GPs could see no medical value in these clinics. The result of this set of conflicting messages was the change from clinics to placing GP practices into three health promotion bands with varying levels of annual financial rewards as well as additionally rewarding those who make provision for asthma and diabetes care.

Whilst the contractual links between activities and finance for GP practices are clear, they are somewhat decoupled for schools. The 1988 Education Reform Act (ERA) has two distinct parts to it. The first involves a requirement for all schools to teach a defined National Curriculum. This was defined to a certain extent in ERA but has been developed and refined over the years causing the teaching profession more and more difficulties. This reached breaking-point during 1993 following constant protests by the teaching profession. This led to a marked reduction in the demands of the prescribed National Curriculum, now restricted to the basic subjects of English, mathematics, and science, with greater flexibility in the design of other subjects. In addition there was a proposed reduction in the testing requirements for younger school children and the amount of information about tests that had to be made public. The second change, enacted through ERA, requires the delegation of certain financial responsibilities to all primary and secondary schools of over 200 pupils. Allocations were and are based on a defined formula which is primarily driven by age-weighted pupil numbers with further allowances for certain definable characteristics of the schools (small schools, split sites, and so on). Here too refinements were made to the nature of the formula and to those activities and finances which were to be delegated to school level. However, the direct linkage between the finances received through the formula and the achievements of the schools remains unspecified even though it is indirectly linked through the 'market' for students and consequent per capita money received through the formula.

There is also a link in terms of the increasing demands for accountability. The primary focus for this increased 'visibility' on schools is contained in the 1991 Parents Charter. To reinforce and develop the accountability requirements of the Parents Charter two aspects have been the subject of further refinement and regulation.

First, the publication of performance measures for schools has been the focus of a range of Education (School Information) Regulations from 1991 onwards. These Regulations provide requirements for a school to declare publicly how well it has performed over a range of areas. The primary focus is on GCSE and A level results but also includes details of 'avoidable and unavoidable' absences and the hours spent on teaching. The second aspect comes through the reports from a four-yearly inspection by the newly created Office for Standards in Education (OFSTED). The 1992 Education (Schools) Act and Circular 7/93 created OFSTED, which came into existence on 1 September 1992. OFSTED is required to conduct four-yearly reviews of all schools and report publicly on 'the quality of education provided by the school; the education standards achieved in schools; whether the financial resources made available to the school are managed efficiently; and the spiritual, moral, social and cultural development of pupils at the school' (Circular 7/93: paragraph 22).

A 'MIDDLE RANGE' THEORETICAL LANGUAGE FOR UNDERSTANDING THE
EFFECTS OF THE CONTRACTUAL CHANGES

Following Laughlin (1995), the 'middle range' theoretical language which we have adopted for understanding the organizational effects of the contractual changes is derived from the analysis of organizational change processes. Organizational change is perceived to be generated by 'environmental impetus' (Bartunek 1984), 'kicks' (Morgan 1986), 'environmental noise' (Smith 1982), or 'disturbances' (Laughlin 1991). Organizational life has a tendency towards an equilibrial, entropic state; thus any disturbance is initially, and possibly permanently, seen as an unwelcome intrusion. It is the possible 'tracks' (Hinings and Greenwood 1988) these disturbances could follow through an organization which provide the important 'skeletal' language which can inform, but not completely define, the empirical detail which, in the context of this chapter, concern schools and GP practices.

These 'tracks' appear to be of two major types, broadly described as 'first order' and 'second order' (cf. Levy 1986; Laughlin 1991; Broadbent 1992). In the case of 'second order' change the 'disturbance' leads to major shifts in the core value systems or 'interpretative schemes' (Laughlin 1991; Broadbent 1992; Giddens 1979) of the organization. This will have lasting effects on the 'genetic code' (Smith 1982) of the organization in the future. 'First order' change involves shifts in the managerial arrangements and more tangible systems in the organization but in such a way that the interpretative schemes remain largely untouched and undisturbed.

Laughlin (1991) refines these tracks into four different possible pathways, two of which are 'first order' and two 'second order'. The 'first order' pathways he refers to as 'rebuttal' (rebutting the disturbance) and 'reorientation' (taking on board the disturbance by reorienting the organization in such a way that the interpretative schemes are unaffected). The 'second order' pathways are termed 'colonization' (where the disturbance leads to a forced change in the organization's interpretative schemes) and 'evolution' (where the disturbance leads to chosen change, by all stakeholders, in the interpretative schemes). These broad pathways, and the amplifications provided by Laughlin (1991) as to the oscillations and 'stopping points' along the routes, are intended to provide an exhaustive and dynamic set of possibilities. However, whilst any one of these four pathways is a logical possibility, it is impossible to predict which one will be operative. As a 'middle-range' language it provides a way to articulate what is happening in actual empirical situations but does not either predetermine the process or detract from the importance of recounting the detail as an important complement to the theoretical, 'skeletal' language.

The other important theme which is developed by Laughlin (1991) and further extended in Laughlin *et al.* (1994) is the position and role of the 'design archetype' in the pathway followed. The concept of the 'design archetype' is derived from the work of Hinings and Greenwood (1988) and Greenwood and Hinings (1988), building on the work of Miller and Friesen (1984). They define a design archetype as 'compositions of structures and (management) systems given coherence and orientation by an underlying set of values and beliefs' (Hinings and Greenwood 1988: 4). The design archetype shapes 'prevailing conceptions of what an organization should be doing, of how it should be doing it and how it should be judged, *combined with* structures and processes that serve to implement and reinforce those ideas' (Greenwood and Hinings 1988: 295). The design archetype is the important decision and communication system which is expressed in and through actual organizational, structural, and processual arrangements. The design archetype becomes the first 'port of call' for any disturbance and it is how it reacts that in large measure determines the pathway that is followed.

Central to the design archetype is the presence of what organizational psychoanalysts refer to as 'specialized work groups'. Bion (1968)—whose theory of group behaviour still dominates thinking in this area—maintains that within all group core activities there are 'basic assumptions' which are shared by all about the need to be protected from unwanted intrusions (fight/flight), the need for leadership (dependency), and the need for continuity and 'reproduction' of core values, concerns, and activities (pairing). Someone or a small group always arises in each and every organization to manage these basic anxieties and concerns so that the core activities can continue unhindered. These 'specialized work groups' have a unique position in any and all organizations. They, in effect, filter environmental disturbances, ensure systems are in place to provide leadership for the organization, as well as providing the direction for the full expression of the values or interpretative schemes in the actual and future workings of the organization.

Whilst they are all-pervading, how exactly they work and what means they use to perform their intended protective and proactive function will vary. One thing is sure: they are in a unique position to mould the behaviour of the organization. They are instrumental, as Greenwood and Hinings (1988: 295) make plain, in creating the 'prevailing conceptions of what an organization should be doing, of how it should be doing it and how it should be judged'.

Bion (1968) always saw these groups as having a defending or 'absorbing' role, yet because of their unique position within the organization they can always run the risk of becoming a 'colonizing' force. They are there to defend the value base and continuity of the group/organization. Their function is to absorb any disturbances, filtering through creative elements, and 'soaking up' destructive ones. In addition to protecting their unique position, they also have the opportunity to attempt to change the 'genetic code' of the organization fundamentally.

It is for this reason that the design archetype and, more especially, the specialist work group is seen as crucial in all four possible pathways in determining the way a disturbance tracks its way through an organization. For the rebuttal and reorientation pathways the specialist work group acts as defender exercising primarily the flight/fight assumption role. In this case the group becomes an 'absorber' of the disturbances so that the core activities of the organization can go on unhindered. In relation to the colonization, but also the evolution pathways, the specialist work group acts as a proactive-change agent—in the colonization case this is through force and in the evolution alternative through discourse and more gentle persuasion. In both these 'second-order' change models, however, the specialist work group goes beyond its protective role to use its unique position within the organization to exercise real change. In the colonization pathway it enables the disturbances to infiltrate and affect core activities by changing and redefining norms of behaviour, it unlocks and puts in place different forms of leadership, and, finally and more significantly of all, uses its understanding to shift and change the genetic code which defines the very essence of the organization as it is known and understood.

The change in the specialist work group from an absorbing to a colonizing force is not, however, the only danger facing any organization experiencing either deliberately generated or unintentional disturbances. The other danger is when the actual disturbances are such that they cannot be retained or absorbed by the specialist work group. Sometimes there is 'satiation' of the specialist core activities (as with an overfull sponge) and in these cases the disturbances spill over into the work group. This inevitably leads to those involved in core activities having to devote time and effort to address this 'spillage'. In other cases the disturbances are such that their very design prevents them from being able to be fully retained by the specialist work (absorbing) group. In both these cases the dangers of colonization are considerably increased unless those who are actively undertaking core activities can come up with a strategy to expand the absorbing capacities of the specialist work group in the first case or find different ways to cope with the disturbances in the second case.

Even where, by their very nature, the disturbances cannot be retained by the absorbing group, they will initially be lodged with these groups. As a result, how they are passed on to other organizational actors will make a difference as to the levels of aggravation experienced by these bodies. It is not impossible to envisage at least three different scenarios for this. A 'fully committed' absorbing specialist work group will attempt to pass on these disturbances in a way which tries to minimize the intrusion into the core activities. For the more 'agnostic', verging on the colonizing, absorbing, specialist work group, the very act of passing on the requirements may amplify the nature of the original disturbance and the fundamental change in the definition of core activities. Finally, for the 'colonizing' specialist work group, the presence of disturbances which can and should be legitimately passed on to other organizational actors provides a welcome opportunity for engendering and hastening the levels of change intended.

THE NATURE OF SPECIALIZED WORK GROUPS IN GENERAL PRACTICES AND SCHOOLS

The empirical evidence discussed below is drawn primarily from interview data from 24 schools and 34 GP practices. In addition to these sites the authors have also been extensively involved with 4 schools and 6 GP practices and it is the insights from these which have formed the basis for interviews with key individuals in the 24 schools and 34 GP practices.

The 24 schools, of which 10 are primary and 14 secondary, range in pupil numbers from 150 to 1,500. The schools serve areas with a range of socio-economic profiles in three different local education authorities (LEAs). Interviews were conducted with a headteacher, teacher, and chair of governors in 1991 and 1994. To allow consistency and comparison between the findings already published in Laughlin *et al.* (1994), quotations in the following will continue to use the descriptors used in this original publication (i.e. P1 to P10 to refer to the primary schools and S11 to S24 for the secondary schools).

In the 34 GP practices patient numbers range from 2,218 to 11,822 in single-handed through to seven-partner practices. Of the 34, 12 are small practices (with 1 or 2 GPs), 15 are medium sized (with 3 or 4 GPs) and 7 are large (with more than 4 GPs). The GP practices are drawn from different locations within one Family Health Service Authority (FHSA). Interviews with a GP, a nurse, and the practice manager were conducted in 1993 and 1994. All quotations in the following will use the same descriptors as in Broadbent (1994), namely, GP1–34, PN1–34, and PM1–34 to refer to GPs, practice nurses, and practice managers respectively.

Of key importance in managing the reforms in schools and GP practices are the headteachers and senior GPs respectively. It is they who are the initial butt of all environmental disturbances. It is they who constitute the foundation and base of the absorbing 'specialized work group' and who decide how best to handle any past, present, or future disturbance. Institutionally, however, their role is not only to be a 'specialized work group' but also to be the leader and definer of what constitutes the core activities of the school and GP practice. That this is an almost intolerable burden to handle without allowing other individuals to share the load, given the immense disturbances that are occurring, is one of the central themes which will become apparent in the following. How this works out in practice is dependent, to a considerable extent, upon the attitudes of headteachers and senior GPs to the managerial changes.

In general the attitude of headteachers to the initial Local Management of Schools Initiative (LMS) was one of limited short-term enthusiasm followed by varying levels of disillusionment connected primarily with the opportunity cost of the time involved in managing what increasingly became apparent as an administrative nightmare. LMS, as originally constituted, has turned into a heavy administrative workload connected with budget and contract management which has possibilities for discretion where resources are uncommitted but which, with a continuing and almost universal decline in the budget that is available, has considerable potential anxiety-inducing elements. These anxieties have increased with the introduction of league tables and OFSTED inspections except that, in these cases, the worry is in relation to the coupling between finance and education activity which is an important ingredient of these changes.

What we have, therefore, is a set of headteachers who are fundamentally happy with how to cope with the demands of LMS but troubled, to varying degrees, by the situation where resource pressures are present and by the ramifications that come through increased accountability via OFSTED and the league tables. The common threads in this set of attitudes are to do with control. Where the reform package is simply delegation of resources which are managed in the interests of the school then there is little problem—control of this, in effect, administrative burden becomes possible through a reasonably simply structured absorbing 'specialist work group'. How this works will become clearer in the following. Increasing problems emerge where the demands are such that their control and containment has, of necessity, to spill over into the functioning of core activities whether through having to exercise budget cuts, as a result of the requirements of the national curriculum, through gearing education processes to examination performance, or through being required to follow OFSTED inspection reports produced by people who may have an administrative axe to grind. How this is 'managed' becomes rather complicated.

Nothing similar to the introduction of LMS, with its decoupled connection to the national curriculum requirements, has occurred in the reform of GP practices. As indicated previously the most significant vehicle for change in GP practices has been the 1990 GP Contract (with its 1993 changes). These requirements are primarily related to the introduction of some quite specific health promotion and disease prevention requirements. From the outset this has been resented by GPs. The dilemma is nicely portrayed by GP5 when he made plain that 'population medicine is about preventative care . . . it has led to a split in doctors either to be there for the population or to be there for the individual'. Whilst it is always difficult to generalize, Broadbent (1994) highlights the fact that GPs have a much greater tendency to see their role in different ways—in clinical terms, caring for the individual in and through the one-to-one consultation process, rather than achieving target goals on health promotion for populations as a whole. As GP1 put the matter: 'health promotion is not our role . . . most of us are trained as diagnosticians and manipulators of medicine'. Or as GP6 made plain: 'health promotion was ill-thought-out; doctors are the wrong people to do it'. Similarly as GP27 points out, in relation to health promotion: 'I feel these are social not medical problems'; and, by way of an echo, GP20 stated: 'we're not trained to do a social worker's job'.

This antagonism has been accentuated with the introduction of banding. What the banding did was to create great financial pressure for GPs and start to actively impinge on the area which is at the heart of biographical or biopsychosocial medicine (i.e. the individual consultation time). Neither of these are as easily manageable as the original contract requirements.

How GPs and headteachers have managed these changes is, in general, to develop an 'absorbing group' (Laughlin *et al.* 1994)—a 'specialist work group' which can 'absorb' the requirements without interfering with the core activities of GP practices and schools. How these 'absorbing groups', and the changing levels of involvement of headteachers and GPs in them, have worked over time varies. The changes in these ways of working are influenced by and can be understood through two different sets of common forces at work in GP practices and schools. The first concerns the way the changes have been absorbed—through the creation of definable formalized positions and the resourcing arrangements and implications of this process. The second—given the shifting and more demanding nature of the requirements—concerns the activities and mechanisms used to buffer these requirements as far as possible from affecting the core activities of schools and GP practices. We will explore each of these themes in turn below.

Where possible GPs and headteachers have tried to involve others in the management of the reforms although the opportunity for this has been considerably greater for GP practices than for schools. As indicated above GPs and headteachers were and are in a unique position being part of the absorbing group as well as involved in core activities. Both already had a full work schedule before the introduction of LMS and the new GP Contract. The changes involved new tasks which were *additional* to their activities as educational managers and medics. Where possible both headteachers and GPs wanted to involve others in the management of these new tasks but the GP practices were at a considerable advantage in this respect. At the time of the introduction of the new Contract, GPs could receive 70 per cent of the ongoing salary costs of employing assistants (particularly practice managers and nurses) from the FHSAs. This financial supplement has now decreased adding to the financial pressures on GP practices, yet the take-up of the original offer was considerable. Such financial support was not available from local education authorities for schools.

Although among GPs there was universal condemnation of the GP Contract in its original form, the necessity to meet its requirements for financial reasons effectively involved a splitting of tasks into 'financial' and 'operational' control—with the work involved in the latter being delegated in total, and with a more cautious delegation of the former in particular circumstances. GPs have always been independent contractors and thus involved in 'financial' control—using the term loosely to refer to ensuring the GP practice is viable financially, covering its costs from the revenue it receives, and taking strategic action where this is not the case—although medical care offered to patients has been and continues to be free at the point of delivery. The difference with the Contract is the much closer linkage between finance and activities to be performed. As Laughlin *et al.* (1994) and Broadbent (1994) have made plain, the GPs have employed practice managers, (the 'housekeepers' as we described them) to handle the 'operational' administrative requirements and, in some cases, a more proactive set which we called 'managers' who started to extend their activities into some aspects of what we have referred to as 'financial control'. The GPs have also employed practice nurses to handle the more sensitive (in terms of being more challenging to the core activities of GP practices) 'operational' tasks which come with the health promotion and disease prevention requirements of the GP Contract. So successful have GPs been in delegating these requirements that we have expressed the view that this is not so much a GP as a practice-manager and practice-nurse Contract! The important point for the current argument is that GPs have been in a unique position to call on a resource base to employ these new assistants and have exercised this power with considerable alacrity—nationally, practice nurses, for instance, increased from 1,921 in 1984 to 7,520 in 1990 (Atkin and Lunt 1993).

The situation in schools is rather different. LMS was imposed without any additional resources being made available to meet the costs of managing what has turned out to be a major administrative workload. As we have pointed out elsewhere (Laughlin *et al.* 1994), because of this lack of resources headteachers, from the outset, played a key role in shouldering these administrative burdens. They were, of necessity, involved in the 'operational' as well as overall 'financial' control aspects of these delegated budget responsibilities. They were keen to have overall control of the finances of the school as distinct from allowing this to lodge with the governors as the legislation originally intended (see Shearn *et al.* (1995*a*) for more details on this dynamic), yet the operational aspects of managing a large budget and the extensive contractual relationships which came with it were something headteachers would have preferred to avoid but found it difficult to pass on to others. How much of this burden was absorbed by the headteachers depended a good deal on their personal characteristics and what other teaching and non-teaching staff were available at the time to share the responsibilities. The greatest pressure was and is apparent in the primary sector because these invariably are small schools with few staff available to involve, whether the headteachers wanted to delegate or not. It was in the primary sector where we found all of what we referred to as 'soaker-sinker' headteachers who took the entire burden upon themselves and either could not or would not delegate any responsibilities to others and were rapidly 'going under' with the strain. In the secondary sector the situation was rather different. There was much more active involvement of other staff, often deputy headteachers, with attempts to involve bursars and registrars who were in place in earlier eras when budgets were more closely related to dinner money than staff salaries. The only time when headteachers played no part in the administrative tasks was when they were what Laughlin *et al.* (1994) referred to as 'managerial (pastoral) headteachers' who wanted nothing to do with the financial aspects of LMS and chose to remain as they had always been—involved in the pastoral care of the children and staff. In these cases the whole burden of LMS, both the more strategic 'financial' control aspects as well as the more 'operational' administrative management tasks, fell on the shoulders of hard-pressed deputy headteachers.

Since those early days all of the schools have in some way or other actively tried to bring non-teaching staff into the administrative tasks involved in managing LMS. In the primary sector there has been a marked change in the role and position of previously employed secretaries or clerks. They have been either replaced or retrained to take on more of the 'operational', administrative aspects of the changes. Many primary headteachers no doubt would concur with the views of the headteacher P6 (a former 'soaker-sinker' according to our classification) when she said: 'former worries over LMS are much improved thanks to my new clerk. If I hadn't had a change of clerk I would have gone under . . . I couldn't understand it alone'. In a number of secondary schools the role of deputies has expanded considerably and the descriptor of 'finance' deputy has been used on occasions. In addition, in a rather more exaggerated form than the primary sector, there has been a considerable expansion of the role of some administrative staff into roles variously referred to as financial administrators, budget managers, administrative directors, senior administration officers, as well as the more customary bursars and registrars. Some of these secondary schools are now looking towards the possibility of taking on an additional full-time staff member who can take even more responsibility away from the headteachers and deputies. The logic for this change and the way the cost of this has to be covered primarily by reducing the number of active teaching staff is portrayed by the headteacher of S21 when he said:

We are assessing the role of deputies . . . are shedding one deputy . . . have now created a non-teaching administrative post of Administrative Director . . . responsible for policy development, health and safety, financial planning, personnel management, IT development . . . in fact anything of lower priority . . . the deputies are then in a position to be free to plan, support, and evaluate . . . playing a more strategic role . . . the core of the development plan is the curriculum plan . . . time needed on that.

Other headteachers have been actively looking at this possibility. Thus, for instance, a 'managerial-pastoral' type headteacher, who had totally delegated the administrative responsibilities to his deputy, rather than sharing these responsibilities with him, made plain, when referring to the deputy, that: 'the rest of his job has suffered since he's taken over the budget role . . . his health has suffered . . . he works himself into the ground . . . he is not a happy man . . . we need to do something about it . . . I feel a bursar might be better for us'. The difficulty with this in most schools seems to be the cost factor. There is an awareness that this is a role which needs filling but the expense of providing this professional assistance is something that frightens many schools, yet it is being faced, as in the case of S21 mentioned above, in the context of looking very seriously at the role and number of deputy head-teachers. One thing is certain, schools do not have the resourcing for assistants which is available to GP practices.

For schools the emphasis on examination league tables and the OFSTED inspections and for GP practices the move to banding and allied resource constraints are very intrusive requirements which cannot be displaced in a simple fashion onto the absorption processes/groups already in place. Practice managers and nurses and secretaries and bursars were permanent roles created to absorb the original reforms and have managed very successfully to protect GPs and headteachers and the core activities of GP practices and schools from intrusion. Yet the new set of required activities are rather more demanding and pervasive and have considerable colonizing potential. Headteachers and GPs have little alternative but to be actively involved in 'managing' these changes.

How they have done this is critical to understanding how colonizing these changes have been and will be.

With regard to the banding and accompanying financial constraints in GP practices, there is a sense in which even though these are impinging on the behaviour of GPs yet in the majority of cases they are finding ways to prevent too much intrusion, again by looking to practice nurses and managers to absorb the new set of responsibilities. Some GPs have found that there is no escape from having to take over responsibility for collecting the data for the banding and have had to accept its impact on the time available for seeing patients. These doctors may have some considerable sympathy with the concerns of GP21 when he made plain: 'the banding has made a difference to the consultation'. Other GPs expressed levels of despair with regard to the financial strains and stresses. This was most poignantly expressed by GP20 when he said rather desperately, 'eventually they'll control me through my pocket'. These GPs, however, were the exception rather than the rule.

The level of dissatisfaction and strain was apparent in all GPs interviewed, though most were trying to innovate. Some went for 'binges where we have to weigh and measure people in order to make up the numbers' (GP3). Others have passed all responsibilities for collecting the data for banding to nurses. These would probably concur with the views of GP27 when he said: 'most of the banding is done by nurses . . . I don't get too involved . . . I will try and complement it . . . if we see any benefit then we don't mind doing it'. The financial strains and stresses are rather more complex to handle but there is still an air of confident hope and many GPs would probably share the views of GP15 when he said: 'I'll keep going . . . I'll get the funding to do what I want to do from somewhere so the practice won't suffer . . . I won't be forced to be a different kind of doctor from the one I want to be'. A number of others were looking towards travel clinics as a way to help make ends meet where a cost-per-item reimbursement could be received. A limited number of others, however, were somewhat desperately looking towards greater involvement of practice managers in partnership with GPs to help manage the financial control problem. GP1 put this view succinctly when he pointed out: 'what I'd like to do is delegate it all and discuss it as equals with the practice/fundholding manager . . . I'd pull the money in from some other sources and leave the rest to the competent manager'.

Whilst the GPs were managing to prevent the banding and allied financial pressures from impinging on the core activities of GPs, OFSTED inspections and examination league tables are having rather more significant effects on the headteachers and their schools. Even those who were desperate to protect their school from the effect of these changes could see real dangers. Take, for instance, the headteacher of P4 who maintained that 'if the trend continues there won't be a primary system . . . OFSTED will impose a principle of secondary system on it . . . most important will be to have pristine documents, evidence, timetables etc . . . it's a downward spiral they can't get off

. . . so teachers will collapse . . . and then, hopefully, they will have to change the system'. Or as the headteacher of S17 made plain: 'what puts staff under pressure is the National Curriculum plus possibly OFSTED . . . being constantly dictated to . . . the fun has gone out of teaching . . . what I came into teaching for was to pass on my enthusiasm'. Other headteachers, admittedly in the minority, have seen OFSTED inspections as a way of reinforcing an expanding managerial emphasis. For instance, the headteacher of S18 emphasized: 'I have used OFSTED to pull staff up'. On the question of examination results and league tables even those headteachers who were sceptical about their worth were also aware of their power. Thus as the headteacher of S23 observed:

we don't have a fixation on league tables . . . [we] are proud of the achievements of our pupils and the school . . . but we're not a football team . . . so we would never stop a child from entering an examination in order to boost our results . . . [we] are not into massaging figures to look good on paper . . . but it's hard to remain committed to that ethos . . . but it's never been easy to have integrity, feel you have to stick to your principles . . . the legislation sets school against school . . . it's vicious.

There were other headteachers, however, who were also using this new requirement to put pressure on teaching staff to fall into line. Thus the headteacher of S16 made plain how he had 'put staff under more pressure to get kids through exams . . . talked to people individually and set them targets . . . [and] will discuss their performance when the exam results come out'.

CONCLUSIONS

The key argument of this chapter is the role of and need for 'absorption' of perceived unwelcome contractual changes in schools and GP practices through the workings and changing nature of an absorbing, 'specialist work group'. Headteachers and GPs, being the initial butt of these contractual changes, have looked towards making key appointments of either existing or new personnel to absorb as much as possible of the 'operational' implications of the changes to allow core activities to continue unaffected. GP practices have been considerably more successful at this than schools thanks to the resource base upon which they can call. The employment of practice managers and practice nurses has been the solution to the operational handling of the administrative and health promotion changes with which GPs and their practices have had to cope over the last few years. Much of the financial as well as administrative, operational workload involved in the devolved responsibilities coming from the LMS initiative were originally undertaken by headteachers but involving, where possible, either established teaching (usually deputies) and non-teaching staff to assist. More recently there has been a tendency for headteachers to look towards offloading these administrative responsibilities to others (as GPs have done). At one extreme, there is an increasing tendency towards employing full-time bursars to 'manage', and consequently absorb, the administrative responsibilities, but this is invariably at the expense of having to reduce the teaching staff to pay for these new appointments.

Whilst many of the changes can be absorbed by these new key members of the 'specialist work group', some of the more recent government requirements are rather harder to handle in this way. We postulated the theoretical possibility that some disturbances would be too much to absorb, leading to a range of different effects both on the absorbing strategies and on the core activities. The banding change and allied financial pressures for GP practices have this potential as do OFSTED inspections and examination league tables for schools.

To date GPs are continuing to prevent this level of change through continuing delegation, yet the case of schools is less clear-cut. This potential for the changes not to be absorbed in schools is a constant reminder of the volatility of the situation. As we have seen some headteachers are actively using their position and the intrusiveness of the reforms, to make some initial moves towards pursuing more fundamental 'second-order' change. Using our theoretical terms they become 'colonizers' and not 'absorbers'. Similar changes are possible when any headteacher or GP sees the reforms as an opportunity and not a threat. The new members of the absorbing, 'specialist work group' have the possibility of acting as change-agents if they become real 'believers' in what they are doing and would like to move from being 'absorbers to being colonizers'. Unlike headteachers and GPs, however, they have to gain a position of power. In GP practices the difficulties of this for practice managers and practice nurses, which takes us into the realm of gender issues, is discussed at length in Broadbent (1994). In schools the establishment of bursars is only just starting and their influence is uncertain at the moment. The greatest 'danger' to the schools, at the time of writing, is the very nature of the reforms themselves and the amplification that is possible if certain headteachers become increasingly 'managerial' in their emphasis.

In conclusion it is important to reflect on the question of whether the reforms can be justified. Was the government right to impose such wide-ranging changes on schools and GP practices and continue to exert ever more intrusive pressure? Has there been 'value for money' for taxpayers in implementing the changes? Are schools and GP practices right in reacting so strongly against the changes? Is the coping strategy they are adopting in terms of the creation of formal absorbing 'specialist work groups' a strategy that makes sense—and how can sense be defined? These and other evaluatory questions and concerns are not being addressed by the government as they continue to pour ever more money into making the changes 'work'. Our view is that now is the time to subject the reforms and their effects to a critical, creative debate between *all* stakeholders using an open and adaptive evaluatory model (see Laughlin and Broadbent (1996*a*; 1996*b*) for more details). We hope this chapter will strengthen the argument that such evaluation is not only necessary but part of the duty of a democratic government.

The financial support of the Economic and Social Research Council (Contracts and Competition Programme; project no. L114251004) is gratefully acknowledged.

4

QUASI-MARKETS AND QUASI-TRUST: THE SOCIAL CONSTRUCTION OF CONTRACTS FOR COMMUNITY HEALTH SERVICES

ROB FLYNN, GARETH WILLIAMS, AND SUSAN PICKARD

INTRODUCTION

Much of the debate about the emergence and impact of the NHS internal market has focused on acute hospital services and the effects of GP fundholding (see Chapters 2 and 6, this volume). However, as this chapter, and those by Lapsley and Llewellyn (Chapter 5) and Spurgeon *et al.* (Chapter 9) show, there are *other* components of health and social care which are increasingly important, and in which the experience of contracting may be different. This chapter examines the particular features of community health services (CHS), and argues that their attributes render contracting highly problematic. After a brief definitional and methodological introduction, the significance of relational contracting, networks, and trust in community health services is outlined. Next, qualitative evidence from case studies is reviewed about the process of conceptualizing and specifying CHS; health authority and Trust contract negotiations; and attitudes of GP fundholders. Finally, we conclude by arguing that the contingencies and contradictions of contracting in the NHS quasi-market—and the elusive and contested nature of trust—are displayed very clearly in community health services.

'Community health services' comprise a variety of different forms of health care, delivered by a multiplicity of professionals and practitioners through several types of agency and modes of organization outside of hospitals. Briefly, they consist of district nursing, health visiting, and community-based health promotion and surveillance, as well as specialist therapies (such as counselling, physiotherapy, palliative care, speech therapy). NHS revenue expenditure on CHS was almost £3 million (13 per cent of total NHS spending) in 1994–5 (NHS Executive 1996a). In England, there were 15,641 district nurses and 10,135 health visitors, who, with other community paramedical staff, carried out 122-million patient contacts in 1995–6 (Health and Personal Social Services Statistics 1995). These staff are mainly based in sixty specialized CHS Trusts, twenty-three combined acute and community Trusts, and sixty Trusts combining CHS with services for those with mental illness and learning disabilities. Their work has become increasingly significant with the rise in hospital throughput, reduced lengths of stay, and greater demand for, and use of, primary and community-based treatment and rehabilitation of patients with chronic illness, disability, or mental illness.

In order to study the development and experience of contracting in CHS, case studies of purchasers and providers in three different districts were carried out over two contracting 'rounds' (1993/4 and 1994/5). Using a combination of fieldwork observation, interviews, and documentary analysis, qualitative data were collected about, *inter alia*, health needs assessment, the formulation of purchasing plans, contract negotiations, Trust business planning, and quality assurance and monitoring. The areas—comprising large metropolitan districts in one English NHS region—were selected primarily because they contained different commissioning and purchasing configurations. The provider Trusts ranged in size from those employing 750 to 1,000 community staff, with health authority annual contract values of between £13 million and £29 million (for details of methodology, see Flynn, Williams, and Pickard 1996). In the discussion which follows, the case study sites are referred to as Areas 1, 2, and 3. Given the crucial role of GP fundholding in the NHS internal market (see Chapters 2 and 3, this volume) it is essential to assess their importance for CHS. Consequently as part of the project described here, we draw upon findings from semi-structured interviews carried out with a purposive sample of ten GP fundholders from the three case study areas.

QUASI-MARKETS, CONTRACTS AND RELATIONAL CONTRACTING IN COMMUNITY HEALTH SERVICES

As noted in Chapter 1, the evolution of the internal market entailed a shift from an initial 'steady state' towards more managed competition, and a parallel move from simple block contracts to more complex and sophisticated contracts. During the early phases, almost all district health authority (DHA) contracts with CHS provider Trusts were block, and similarly GP fundholder contracts for community nursing were 'fixed price non-attributable' (i.e. not linked to individual patients). More recently, there have been attempts to devise more sophisticated contracts (with stipulated case-load minima and maxima, and quality indicators), and GP fundholders have secured some cost and volume and/or cost-per-case contracts, especially for specialist community therapies. In practice, most community services are still covered by varying types of block contract (NHS Management Executive 1994) and are placed predominantly with 'local' providers. There appear to be several reasons for this: first, the very locality-boundedness of *community* services places constraints on the possibility of competition from non-local suppliers; secondly, inherent coding, measurement, and information problems (discussed further below, and in Flynn, Pickard, and Williams 1995) and underdeveloped IT systems; thirdly, recognition of the interdependence and interrelationship of different aspects of CHS and primary care, which is linked with a preference for a complete 'package' rather than an assemblage of subcontracts with several suppliers.

Even (or rather, especially) with sophisticated block contracts, there are fundamental problems in defining the 'currency'—activity is a notoriously unreliable measure in most community services—and there are uncertainties about cost apportionment and outcome measures. These features, while not unique to CHS, are particularly significant, as they manifest some of the limitations of a commodified and formalized approach to contracting, and illustrate some of the reasons why there has been debate about how competitive the NHS quasi-market could or should be. Those who support a vigorous commissioning strategy in which purchasers stimulate provider competition to secure lower costs and improve quality may favour a type of adversarial contracting and penal sanctions for non-compliance. Those who regard this as impractical may observe that CHS cannot be straightforwardly encapsulated in precise categories, have complex cost structures, and deal in-patient outcomes which are difficult to identify and evaluate. Consequently, there is a necessary reliance on collaborative working, a high premium placed on reputation and interprofessional trust, and a predisposition to adopt a relational form of contracting.

This echoes similar discussions about experience in commercial and industrial contracting (see also Chapters 2 and 6). Williamson (1983; 1985; 1991) observed that constraints of bounded rationality and uncertainty, and the high transaction costs created by complex contingent-claims contracts tend to lead to either bureaucratic approaches or quasi-market relationships based on 'private ordering'. Similarly, other economists have stressed the prevalence of collaborative alliances and reciprocity among networks of ostensibly competing firms, in which cooperation and mutual loyalties lead to long-term obligation, expressed through relational contracts (Bradach and Eccles 1991; Powell 1991). Further, as Ouchi (1991) argues, where it is difficult or impossible to specify contract conditions in advance, where performance is difficult to monitor and determine, and where there is a need for coordination through cooperation, 'soft' or relational contracting within a 'clan' system has advantages over both market and bureaucratic approaches.

It is now recognized that in quasi-markets where there are few buyers and sellers, where exchanges are expected to be long-term, and where there is a common identification with goals of reliability and quality, soft or relational contracting is appropriate—and that this applies to the NHS internal market (Ferlie 1994). It is especially relevant in connection with CHS, precisely because their network structure (linking hospital and GP primary care, as well as personal social services and voluntary agencies), the heterogeneity of their functions, and substantial discretion in task performance require a clan structure and demand high levels of trust. However, as we shall see in the following sections, our case study evidence shows considerable variation in the capacity and willingness of purchasers to trust local CHS providers. In all three areas there were oscillations between hard and soft styles of contracting, and while some DHA purchasers professed a commitment to collaborative working, contract negotiations revealed the limited extent and precariousness of relationships of trust. Equally, a small purposive sample of GP fundholders paradoxically expressed their contract demands in an adversarial way yet also voiced satisfaction with (and in practice remained loyal to) their local provider. To examine some of the reasons for these patterns, we will first present findings about differences in purchasers' and providers' perceptions of the nature of CHS, then describe contract negotiations concerning specifications, finance, and monitoring, and finally consider the position of GP fundholders.

CONCEPTUALIZING COMMUNITY HEALTH SERVICES

The features that make community services what they are: their closeness to the lay sector of informal care, their locality orientation, and the diffuse, non-acute health needs which form a large part of their workload, make CHS difficult to define and measure with the kind of precision necessary for the setting of formal contracts between purchasers and providers. Moreover, in contrast to many forms of acute provision within hospitals, CHS deal with the less clearly defined forms of ill health for which people require help and support in their own homes; health problems which lie on the confused and shifting boundary between health and social or community care. The focus of this section is the way in which CHS are defined, and the difficulties and conflicts that were encountered in doing so.

In all our fieldwork areas, purchasers and providers recognized the importance of moving towards a conceptualization of CHS in terms of outcomes, but they also saw that this would be difficult: 'We are having difficulty with information' was a continual refrain from the providers in early 1993, and the purchasers were always having to say: 'you need to give us more data'. The problem of defining and conceptualizing what CHS were, and what activities comprised the work of different CHS professionals, was therefore partly a reflection of lack of information. For purchasers the problem of information about what CHS are and do was very far-reaching. As one purchaser Public Health Consultant argued:

We have no way of knowing what is going on in the community. When they refer to health visitor contacts, for example, that may involve talking to the parents of the child about a whole range of things, about family planning, about safety, about lifestyle, about all kinds of things, we have no idea.

Part of the difficulty involved in providing more information derived from the lack of the necessary systems for the collation and presentation of the appropriate information. However, it became clear from our data that producing information for the purposes of setting contracts between purchasers and providers was dependent upon a set of prior questions about what CHS were. The problem of CHS was not just an informational question, but a conceptual one, and for providers this gave rise to a problem of identity. As one contracts manager in a provider Trust put it:

Really we're trying to *redefine* what we are. We may provide some highly specialized services (e.g. learning disabilities), some managed agencies (e.g. therapists) sold back to hospitals and GPs, and then some core work, bread-and-butter services (like district nursing), sold to the HA purchaser.

For many people in the provider organizations, therefore, the services they were contracted to provide consisted of such a 'variety of forms of provision and split responsibilities', that the specification of services for contracting purposes gave rise to a high degree of uncertainty.

This led some on the provider side in particular to argue that CHS were almost different *in kind* from acute services, arguing that the 'localness' of CHS made it difficult to describe the content of services without reference to the broader context, and this was not something which could easily be conveyed in the terms of a contract. One purchasing manager argued that even if it were possible to contract meaningfully for CHS, the paperwork required often got in the way of the kind of collaborative relationship with local providers necessary for the delivery of effective and appropriate services. The problem was less one of information and contracts, and more about relationships and cultures: 'changing the way in which services are delivered is as much about changing professional practice and professional mind-sets as it is about any sort of contract or anything which is written down on paper'.

A prevalent view, therefore, amongst some purchasers and providers, was that the information to contract meaningfully for CHS was not available and that this was partly a function of the nature of the services. While the solution to this problem was, in part, to provide more and better information, it was recognized that the nature of the services made them difficult to measure, that any measure would distort the nature of the services, and that an over-concentration on contracts would limit the collaborative relationship that the provision of good local services would require. In the words of one Trust director of contracting: 'The concept of CHS is very different from other types of health—it's about an ethos or culture'.

This view of the special qualities of CHS was by no means universally held by either providers or purchasers. Even where the problems of measurement and information were recognized as posing particular difficulties, many managers took the view that it was important to begin the process of defining and measuring what could be measured, in order to move towards some kind of meaningful contract currency for CHS. As one provider director of contracting argued:

I think there are a lot of things that can be measured in community, and I think we should start with those and get good data on that . . . You can measure a reduction in hospital beds to correspond with increased activity in community. You can measure the uptake of vaccinations. You can measure the number of children detected before a certain age with difficulties. There is a whole range of things you can measure.

Taking a similar position, a purchaser director of contracting argued that the process of contracting transcended any substantive differences that might be said to exist between different kinds of services or different sectors of service delivery. He could see no difference, for example, between contracts with the voluntary and the statutory sectors. As far as he was concerned: 'We are interested in health problems and health care, not CHS *per se*. The organizational boundaries between primary/community/secondary are *irrelevant* from the point of view of us as purchasers'.

Moreover, in view of the standardization brought about by the contracting process, he did not think that there was any difference in principle between CHS and acute hospital services. Community services are not distinctive because they have multiple clients, needs, and professionals, he argued— look at general medicine or surgery—and there is no qualitative difference between acute and community health services. For this reason: 'It is not intrinsically difficult to specify CHS. It is the lack of information, data, that is the key problem. It is an informational issue, *not* a conceptual issue about the nature of the service'.

While both purchasers and providers recognized that CHS posed problems for contracting greater than those faced in the acute sector, the order of magnitude varied, with two different perspectives emerging. The first view was that CHS were not in principle more difficult for the contract mechanism than any other kind of services. It was not a conceptual but an informational problem. The second view was that these services were different, and were posing difficulties for purchasers at this time. These services were culturally distinct, and for this reason they posed difficulties of conceptualization and definition which were not open to an easy technical solution. As the chief executive of an integrated hospital and community Trust argued: 'CHS are not really in a competitive environment. The nature of the services is such that they've got to be local'.

The purchasers' response to this problem varied depending on which view they held. For those who defined the problem as one of information, the solution was to negotiate harder and to specify contracts more tightly. For those who took the second view, it was best to see the contract as a necessary piece of paper, but not to spend too much time on it, concentrating instead on the development of collaborative relationships, as it were, 'outside' the contracting process.

On both views, however, there was an understanding that the heterogeneity of the services collected under the rubric CHS meant that problems of conceptualization and measurement would differ from one service to another. Many, but not all, CHS were seen to pose problems for the contracting process because of difficulties in specifying activity:

It is for health visiting, not for district nursing . . . you can almost itemize the activities of district nursing . . . They've got activity codes to record their activity against objectives . . . Health visiting is very much more difficult to specify in terms of activities. (provider clinical director)

It was also seen to be difficult because of the multi-agency working that necessarily took place around managing complex health problems in the community. For the community nursing services there was a limit based on more than the weaknesses of the information base:

I think in most of the areas it's going to be difficult to see any real competition. If you think about our elderly service . . . children's services, most mothers don't want to take their children long distances, they want to go somewhere locally . . . Community services [too], again you're going to want somebody that is local and can provide a fast service. (provider director of finance)

Purchasers also recognized that 'localness' (purchaser director of finance and contracting) was an important quality of CHS, something that was almost intrinsic to a definition of them. While this did not mean that they would always contract with the main provider, it did mean that the only factor that would lead them to contract with another provider was where they are geographically closer to residents living at the edges of the health authority's territory. One purchaser had five years' data from the acute sector, and this meant that they were able to 'go to five or six different suppliers'. But 'it's not really appropriate to do it in a community environment . . . As a general principle it has to be community-based'. In this area there was a model of collaboration with the local community service, but with competition 'at the edges', and an emphasis on moving towards developing a strategic model based on linking needs, resources, and outcomes, while also developing 'a much sharper contract'.

The degree of conflict between purchasers and providers over the issues of what CHS were, and how difficult they were to specify in contracts, depended, of course, on many features of the local policy and political context which we explore in detail elsewhere (see Flynn, Williams, and Pickard 1996). However, one aspect of the conflict which appeared in all our fieldwork areas was the way in which purchasers were keen to develop a strategic framework for health gain and health outcomes into which CHS had to fit, whereas CHS providers were, inevitably, more concerned with the operational definition of the services as such. For this reason the providers were more urgently concerned about the nature of their services whereas purchasers were more interested in what they would be able to show they were achieving with those services at the population level. In order to break down the gap between the global concept of 'health gain' on the one hand and on the other the reality of defining, measuring, and contracting for numerous services provided from different sites, one purchaser attempted to develop a dual purchasing strategy based on care groups to reflect operational interests and 'locality-sensitive purchasing' focused on population health needs and health gain.

The problem of conceptualizing CHS, therefore, is more than a technical aspect of contracting. It raises fundamental questions about the philosophy and values of care, and about appropriate organizational forms for services so deeply embedded within the networks of local relationships. It is also profoundly affected by the varying political relationships and turbulence in each of the areas we studied. The relationship between the political economy of resources and the semiotics of CHS varied between our fieldwork areas. None the less, the problem of conceptualization exerted a profound influence on the process of specifying and implementing contracts. During numerous meetings between purchasers and providers, discussions about resources and cash became the vehicle through which differences in definitions of community, measures of activity, and the nature of information were strongly debated, sometimes with no apparent resolution of the difficulties. As one purchaser director of contracting declared in a particularly fraught meeting: 'I'm coming to the humble realization that you don't know what you're selling us, and we don't know what we are buying. We're all just pretending'. It is the effect of this on the process of contract negotiation to which we now turn.

'GAPS IN UNDERSTANDING AND SUBSTANCE': CONTRACT NEGOTIATIONS IN COMMUNITY HEALTH SERVICES

District health authority purchasers encountered substantial problems in negotiating contracts with CHS providers in the two annual rounds which were observed. There were two major sources of difficulty—first, as the previous section has indicated, defining the detailed content and form of various services (specifications), and secondly, reaching agreements about finance (price) and resources (volume).

Specifications

Broadly, in Area 1, there was little disagreement between the DHA and Trust about service specifications, and there was a shared perception that this work was collaborative and continuous. According to a senior purchasing manager, it was necessary for the DHA and Trust to do *joint* work on specifications, and for there to be a cooperative relationship. Thus:

We want to get clinicians involved in contracting . . . really to give them a degree of ownership in the actual documentation, that they've actually participated in drawing up. It's not that the purchaser is seen to impose this specification and [say] 'This is what they will do'.

The main obstacles to developing outcome-related contracts were seen as technical and especially informational problems in identifying and measuring outputs and outcomes. While by 1994–5 there was some frustration among the purchasers about the apparent lack of progress in devising more complex specifications and quality indicators, it was also acknowledged that the pursuit of more detail might be spurious and, moreover, undermine the collaborative relationship. As the purchaser director of contracting noted:

If you start raising the question—'This isn't in the contract'—then you are destroying the relationship, because we're buying a *package*. We're specifying the main elements of a package: we're not specifying the nuts and bolts and the detail. If you start doing that, then you just build up a bureaucracy.

Within the Trust, very similar sentiments prevailed, but there was also a strong emphasis on the inherent difficulties of specifying numerous aspects of community nursing work.

In Area 2 purchasers saw CHS as no more difficult to specify than acute services, wanted to achieve a better fit between their purchasing plan objectives and patterns of services, but tended to regard the provider Trust as being reluctant to make both information available and standards more explicit. From the Trust's perspective, the DHA was seen to misunderstand the nature of community health services and to be unrealistic in their approach—requiring unnecessary detail which would be impractical to implement.

Over the two contracting rounds, discussions about specifications were often contentious, further exacerbated by disagreements about funding levels and cost reductions. A special group of senior managers from the DHA and Trust was established to overcome some of the problems, and at a series of meetings there were repeated attempts by the purchasers to obtain the Trust's commitment to devise detailed service descriptions and outcome indicators. Trust managers objected on the grounds of inadequate information systems, administrative workloads, methodological concerns, and structural issues resulting from the current reorganization of the Trust itself. Eventually, over a long period, agreements were finally reached about which specifications could be produced, and compromises were made about the content of those specifications. From the purchasers' viewpoint there was an overriding need to justify the commitment of resources, but also an awareness that there had to be (as one informant expressed it) 'shared understanding'. However, from the Trust's position, the slow progress reflected the purchasers' perceived unwillingness to understand not only the special nature of CHS work but also the particular transitional organizational difficulties being experienced by the Trust.

In Area 3 the purchaser had adopted a positive approach to 'commissioning for health gain' and sought rapid moves towards 'outcome-related' contracts in line with purchasing plan priorities and 'targeted' investments. The providers seemed to accept this as a philosophy and worked cooperatively with DHA managers on specifications, information, and quality indicators. However, their acceptance became severely strained in both rounds of contract negotiations as disputes about finance spilled over into these other discussions.

At various meetings, purchasers demanded increasingly detailed service descriptions and reappraisals of current patterns of provision. At one meeting the purchaser director of finance stressed that 'We are pushed to show how we are buying more health gain, but we don't know what we are buying at the moment, so we can't demonstrate health gain'. Trust managers queried the criteria used to select the services 'targeted' by the DHA, emphasized the organizational and technical complexities of disaggregating information in the ways suggested, and insisted that ultimately it was for the Trust itself to decide what it wanted to provide. Following the 1994–5 round of negotiations, Trust managers still felt that the DHA did not understand the special features of CHS, and were highly critical of attempts to devise complex specifications, especially when they found that contract decisions were largely determined by finance. As the Trust director of contracting noted: 'We could spend ages working up a specification and it not mean anything because contracts are about numbers essentially'. Among senior purchasers too there was a recognition (and apparent disappointment) that specifications as such had played only a marginal role in shaping the contract: money had dominated negotiations.

Finance

Throughout both contracting rounds, financial and resource issues dominated all the discussions in all three case study areas. They were the source of continuing and far-reaching disagreement in all areas, although the severity of conflicts varied—partly reflecting the differential impact of reductions in NHS per capita funding, and partly reflecting pre-existing inter-organizational (and personal) relationships between purchasers and providers.

Area 1 had a strategy of investing in particular priorities and disinvesting in others, and requiring providers to alter some of their current patterns of provision. The CHS Trust (along with others) had to demonstrate that their services conformed with the purchaser's objectives, but they were also requested to draw up cost savings schemes and reinvestment plans. During 1993–4, the Trust argued that they were experiencing rising demand across various services, and that this increased activity was under-resourced. Purchasers asked for detailed evidence, queried whether possible staff restrictive practices had been removed, and suggested varying the staff skill-mix in order to manage the workload more efficiently.

Arguments about finance continued throughout 1994 and into 1995, with provider managers criticizing the DHA strategy of selective disinvestment while purchaser managers sought a 'redirection' of the Trust's resources. Eventually, after intense negotiations, the contract for 1995/6 was agreed in principle, but this agreement was subsequently suspended by the Trust when it learned that the health authority had allocated additional finance to acute hospitals to reduce waiting lists. The Trust argued forcibly that this was a decision affecting the totality of resources available, and should have formed part of the contract negotiations. Consequently they revoked their earlier agreement, and threatened to seek Department of Health arbitration, on the grounds that the DHA had given inequitable preference in funding to already overspent hospital budgets. After a spate of further intensive negotiations, additional finance was allocated to the CHS Trust, but the purchasers' initial action had led to a sense of grievance and distrust among provider staff, and was believed to have weakened what had previously been a mutually cooperative relationship.

Area 2 was suffering from a chronic and worsening financial situation because of reductions in per capita funding, but the purchasers had a strategy of increasing resources available for primary and community services. However, during the 1993–4 negotiations, it emerged that the DHA was expecting real increases in CHS activity to be funded largely from savings from the Trust, through service rationalizations. The Trust rejected this approach, claiming that the rising demand for their services required additional resources, and that the purchasers were not fulfilling their strategic and purchasing plan objective of shifting resources into CHS. Numerous meetings were held to consider possible cost savings schemes, and to discuss Trust plans for service reductions. The Trust managers maintained that they could not secure the gains in efficiency being demanded by the DHA without adversely affecting front-line services. The purchasers repeatedly asked the Trust to justify their assertions with evidence and to give details of expected service losses. A situation of stalemate was reached—which was only resolved through arbitration by the regional health authority, so that a contract for activity and finance could be signed.

In the next year's negotiations this dispiriting experience still loomed large, and a special joint group of purchaser and provider senior managers met regularly to resolve outstanding and emerging financial issues. The purchaser adopted an even more robust stance about funding in the second round and sought lower prices, increased activity, *and* further efficiency savings from the Trust. Provider managers told purchasers that there was still serious underfunding, despite their programme of 'rationalizations'. Purchasers constantly asked for documentation about these claims, only to be met with Trust objections that they lacked investment in reliable information systems to generate the degree of detail required. This, and other responses, elicited the view among purchasers that the Trust were being obstinate and uncooperative, refusing to 'share' problems: as the DHA chief executive put it 'You expect us to trust you about the alleged underfunding, but you need to *show* us'.

Further meetings took place to try and identify common ground, and some of the difficulties were lessened by a higher than expected regional expenditure allocation. However, progress in negotiations was slow and occasionally conflictual. Another impasse had been reached with the deadline for signing contracts approaching. Trust managers reminded the purchasers that more services would have to be cut unless extra money was forthcoming. Purchaser representatives affirmed that there was no more money available, and that the Trust would have to find internal sources to make good the shortfall. As the purchaser director of contracting put it in a phrase which seemed to characterize the entire negotiation process: 'There is a gap in understanding between us, and a gap in substance'.

Intensive activity then followed inside the Trust to identify more cost-saving measures and to close the gap between the money offered and the resources required to fulfil the contract. Purchasers considered various proposals, and insisted that they wanted *explicit* assurances about what services they were buying, complete compliance with quality standards, and no service reductions. They offered some more money to help the Trust. Yet more protracted negotiations took place which resulted in a 'last minute' compromise. Representatives from both parties acknowledged in interviews that negotiations over finance had been 'a battle', 'very difficult', 'entrenched', and most felt that relationships and discussions had become *adversarial*. Moreover, managers on both sides felt that disputes about activity and money had obscured other discussions and had led to mutual distrust and suspicion.

The purchasing plan and strategic policy in Area 3 also proclaimed a shift in resources away from the acute sector into community and primary services, but again, financial negotiations revealed some of the limitations of this approach. In 1993–4, the DHA made a financial offer which was substantially below what the Trust expected, and there was a series of inconclusive meetings in which a large area of disagreement remained. The final decision to sign the contract was not reached within the formal negotiating teams, but taken by respective chief executives after the threat of going to arbitration appeared imminent. Provider managers felt that purchasers had 'reneged' on earlier commitments to enhance CHS provision, and they lost all faith in the credibility of purchasing plan statements.

This affected the negotiations in 1994/5, which commenced with purchasers proposing the withdrawal of money from certain services and selective reinvestment in other priorities. Trust managers argued that they already suffered chronic underfunding and stressed that it was demoralizing for their staff to be asked to undertake plans for service developments which had a remote possibility of funding *and* at the same time identify more cost savings and service reductions. Purchasers wanted to be completely satisfied that the Trust was implementing 'genuine' efficiency measures. As one of the key negotiators put it: 'You produce a plan to show how you can fund the service priorities you have, and then show the pain [from cash withdrawals by the purchaser] and *then* we can negotiate'.

Purchasers persisted in demanding that the Trust provide detailed evidence of internal cost savings, while providers maintained that they were unable to achieve the scale of reduction in costs required by the DHA. Another stalemate was reached, negotiations were temporarily suspended, and once more right on the deadline, a compromise was 'brokered' outside the negotiating teams by chief executives, and the contract was signed. Subsequently, informants in both the purchaser and provider described the negotiations as having become antagonistic and (according to one respondent) 'truly adversarial' to the extent that financial disagreements had a detrimental effect on otherwise cooperative discussions about joint development of services. Within the Trust there was a widespread belief that the conduct and result of the contract negotiations had been unsatisfactory, leading to some bitterness and distrust, and damaging working relationships.

Evidently, in all three case study areas, the experience of contract negotiations—especially concerning the content of services and the financial resources entailed—was generally similar, despite quite different organizational structures, budget conditions, and varied approaches to commissioning and purchasing. There were, beneath a surface commitment to principles of collaboration, numerous instances of disagreement and occasionally outright conflict. There appeared to be a determination by all three DHA purchasers to become assertive and directive in their commissioning while at the same time expressing their endorsement of collaborative contracting modes. In practice, providers' experience prompted them to complain about the *adversarial* character of contract negotiations and to bemoan the lack of understanding of CHS among purchasers. The cumulative and long-term effect of this seems to have been an ebb and flow of trust between the parties, in which cooperation and mutually acceptable progress on some issues (for example the monitoring of activity data and development of outcome indicators or quality standards) were undermined by disputes over money and what was perceived by providers as unnecessary and intrusive attempts by purchasers to inspect and evaluate the running of Trust business. The overall significance of this pattern is discussed in our concluding section, but the position of GP fundholders must now be reviewed.

PARADOXES OF GENERAL PRACTITIONER FUNDHOLDING

Prior to the report from the Audit Commission (1996) the only detailed exploration of GP fundholding was that undertaken by Glennerster and his colleagues (1994), where it was observed that, in acute services, GPs have had the motivation and the information to seek better contracts. They have switched to more effective providers, or have improved the performance of the same provider. Although concentrating on the relationship between fund-holders and acute services, they also noted that this operation of effective choice did not appear to be available in anything like the same degree for the purchasing of community health services.

In our study we explored the attitudes to and expectations of CHS held by a small number of fundholders. The various opinions of these GP fundholders coalesced around an expression of strong commitment to the population in the immediate locality along with a high degree of trust in existing primary health-care team relationships. Their present local CHS Trusts were preferred, pro-vided that the quality of their services was deemed to be satisfactory—which in every case it was. Indeed, although the concept of 'quality' is nebulous in community health services, *all* the fundholders stressed that they were gen-erally satisfied with service quality.

The view expressed by many of the fundholding GPs was that fewer changes were likely to be instituted with community health services, as opposed to acute services, because those services needed a locally based provider. As one doctor observed: 'One always considers the options, looks at it, evaluates it. But community services, by their nature, are basically area-based aren't they? I think it would be silly to get another provider to come in'. While they were willing to make competitive choices in what they described as fringe services, such as physiotherapy, psychotherapy, counselling, and speech therapy, this was never taken too far—'At the end of the day, if the morale down there is bad amongst the staff, then that can lead to bad care for patients,' as one fundholder put it.

This is not to say that GPFHs were simply content with what they had, and the respondents were willing to express a number of frustrations in their relationship with providers. These centred on the paucity of patient-based information available (generally considered to be an intrinsic problem in CHS, as noted previously) and their resulting inability to monitor services accurately; and on the lack of room for negotiation over prices of district nursing and health visiting services in the context of block contracts. However, despite these frustrations, poor information on services and rigidity of prices were fairly minor factors in the broader scheme of things. As one fundholder explained, 'There would be a lot of other factors—team building, continuity, and experienced members of staff would be very high on the list. The staff . . . are really appreciated. If the standard of the service went down, then we'd be looking somewhere else I suppose.'

Although there was little sense of GPFHs actively using the contracting process to impose changes on services with which they were largely satisfied, overall it was also believed that the fundholders' relationships with providers had improved directly as a result of fundholding. All respondents replied that there had been significant changes although they varied in identifying the type and impact of changes. One fundholder said that he now had 'more say' in how the services were provided: the Trust was 'more responsive' and had been more helpful than the local acute hospital Trust. Another fundholder observed that the services themselves had broadly stayed the same but there were some new services and she was getting more feedback from the community staff— there was now a much better flow and exchange of information between professionals. Another doctor pointed out that the provider 'will listen to us, do what we want when they can'; he gave the example of providing practice-based physiotherapy which had not been possible before fundholding.

There was no doubt that the process of contracting gave GPFHs some power over the provider. 'I think it makes everybody more aware and it means that GPs particularly think they've got a right to ask for information, whereas before maybe they felt they hadn't', as one fund manager explained. Similarly, for another doctor: 'You get more dialogue, more analysis, more effort on all sides to try and improve the services and look at their efficiency.'

Contracts did not appear to be valued because they stimulated supplier competition or large-scale shifts in services *per se*. Rather, they were seen (and used) as vehicles through which the fundholder could articulate a demand for information and influence quality in a way they were unable to do before holding their own budget, something which had been a long-held aim. The purchasing process had intensified this interest and facilitated its achievement; as one fundholder expressed it, the fact that they were now buying services made them more concerned that they were getting what they paid for. Fund-holders were anxious to receive as much information as possible, in order to know what exactly they were getting for their money.

As health policy increasingly emphasizes the development of primary-care-led purchasing, there is recognition that cooperation between fundholders and DHAs will be necessary if long-term DHA priorities in planning and health needs assessment for a large population are not to be subverted by the individualistic behaviour of fundholders responding to the demands of their small practice population. If competitive, adversarial contracting is an indicator of individualistic behaviour, then our data suggest that this concern about the likely subversive effect of GPFHs may be exaggerated.

In fact, our qualitative data suggest that, compared with DHAs, GP fund-holders displayed, if anything, a greater commitment to relational contracting in their purchasing of CHS, placing a high value on local networks, trust, and loyalty with regard to members of the primary health-care team. Although GP fundholding within the internal market had clearly produced greater clarity and definition in GPs' relationships with CHS, this had not led our respondents to 'play' the market and exchange money for services on some simple calculation of price and quality. While the contracting framework encourages GPFHs to take on an assertive role in purchasing, in community health services they are reluctant to destroy their long-term relationship with CHS professionals, and their contracting behaviour reflects this ambiguity.

In summary, a paradoxical situation is evident which reflects the tensions created in attempts to introduce the quasi-market into CHS. This paradox essentially reflects the conflict between the market and the clan model of organization. While the contracting system and the experience of bargaining and negotiation seem to permit or even encourage adversarial (and occasionally confrontational) modes of relating to each other, underlying this both parties agreed on the priority of maintaining local relationships within CHS. In practice, the value of preserving local networks was recognized as having a greater priority for GPFHs than exploiting the possibilities open to them in a quasi-competitive market. Thus, the model favoured by GPFHs as purchasers is that of limited contestability—the potential, but remote, threat of moving a contract to a different supplier—rather than 'free-market' or price-oriented competition.

CONCLUSION

The case study evidence indicates that health authority purchasers' styles of contracting for CHS veered between hard and soft approaches, and that GP fundholders, while occasionally invoking the rhetoric of adversarial competition, in practice endorsed relational forms of contracting. In general, health authority purchasers expressed aspirations to develop collaborative relationships with providers, but in bargaining and negotiations over financial resources—as well as over aspects like information—frequently engaged in adversarial behaviour.

For CHS Trusts, their experience in constructing contracts elicited two basic responses. First a belief that DHA purchasers often failed to understand the distinctive attributes and problems of community health services. Secondly, profound disillusionment that purchasers had consistently failed to honour their strategic commitment to expand and support community health services through real increases in resources. In contrast, despite some minor difficulties, Trusts appeared to have developed a pragmatic and mutually acceptable set of understandings with GP fundholders.

It appears that the experience of contract negotiation itself often evoked antagonistic or even confrontational attitudes among the parties, and led to (or exacerbated) mutual suspicion especially over finance and resources. This may be directly related to the particular nature of local inter-organizational relationships between purchasers and providers, but it is also a reflection of contradictory imperatives within the NHS about a purchaser-driven market and injunctions to achieve increased cost efficiency and 'health gain' while simultaneously promoting the virtues of cooperation in 'health alliances'. This is, of course, one of the several contradictions of the managed market discussed in other chapters.

There is a further broader issue raised by these findings, concerning the fragile and precarious nature of trust even within relational contracting. As noted in Chapter 1 and elsewhere in this volume, commercial contracting necessarily requires substantial degrees of trust, and this is especially true where long-term relationships are regarded as crucial to the exchange, where absolute precision in specification and monitoring are not feasible, and where interdependence in a network is high. Contingency, uncertainty, and lack of information are fundamental problems requiring purchasers to develop work-ing relationships which minimize the risks of opportunistic exploitation by suppliers but also safeguard collaboration, loyalty, and reciprocity. These general features are clearly also relevant when applied to health care and particularly to community health services, where trust at numerous levels seems to be a prerequisite given its clan and network form.

Following Giddens (1991) and Luhmann (1979), trust must be regarded as a 'project' to be constantly worked at, as an elusive and *variable* property of personal and institutional relations. Clearly, if a purchaser lacks confidence in the capacity of a provider to carry out a contract competently and reliably; or if the provider perceives that the purchaser does not subscribe to a shared definition of the task and lacks faith in their professional expertise and values—then mistrust may flourish and impinge on many other aspects of their relationship. Arguably, competitive contracting intensifies the risk of such mistrust occurring.

Here, Fox's (1974) cogent analysis of 'high trust' and 'low trust' syndromes in employment relationships can be usefully extended to NHS contracting. In high trust relationships, parties have similar goals and values, feel obliged to support each other, have long-term perspectives, share information freely, and do not regard problems as due to ill will. Low trust relationships, in contrast, evolve where parties have different goals and interests, expect constantly balanced exchanges, calculate costs and benefits carefully, guard information, minimize their dependence on the other, and blame mistakes on malice or incompetence, leading to sanctions. Fox argued that the expansion of calcu-lative market exchanges inevitably undermined diffuse obligations and high trust relationships, and threatened complex services involving high levels of professional discretion.

This model, while undoubtedly having direct relevance for the analysis of NHS contracting, should not be seen as implying a rigid dichotomy. Rather it suggests that although actors and organizations may gravitate towards oppos-ing 'poles' of trust/distrust, this is not irreversible, and there is the possibility of constructing relationships and contracts which maximize either 'high' or 'low' trust. At the same time, actions taken in some elements of the NHS contracting process (for example, collaborative work in connection with the development of quality indicators in CHS) may be jeopardized by action taken on others (for example, surveillance and sanctions). Even where relational contracting is sought after and emerges, trust is precarious and volatile. In the NHS quasi-market for community health services, purchasing has resulted in only limited and partial forms of relational contracting. Constructing contracts in the CHS quasi-market has revealed the difficulties of creating and sustaining high trust relationships between purchasers and providers. So far, it seems that quasi-markets have only produced quasi-trust.

The financial support of the Economic and Social Research Council (Contracts and Competition Programme: project no. L114241003) is gratefully acknowledged. The authors would also like to thank the many NHS staff who enabled us to carry out the case studies.

5

STATEMENTS OF MUTUAL FAITH: SOFT CONTRACTS IN SOCIAL CARE

IRVINE LAPSLEY AND SUE LLEWELLYN

INTRODUCTION

In this chapter, we examine contracting for social care in action, employing a perspective which allows us to study the emergence of contracting processes. Two benchmarks are employed to evaluate these processes: first, the arguments of proponents for market solutions to public sector problems (the origins of the impetus for contracts as mechanisms for the rationing of health and social care) and secondly, the commentaries and guidance (official and unofficial) which has followed. This study reveals a tension between, on the one hand, the convictions of proponents of market solutions and, on the other, the emerging modes of contract-setting. For market proponents, there is a certainty implicit in the various dimensions of contracting, that is, over the setting (the market-place), the activity (bargaining over prices paid, negotiating over detailed specifications), the mechanism (arms-length relationships), and the outcome (the contract). However, when we examine this idea of the contract from the perspective of the concepts underpinning it (in particular trust, but also expectations about trust and mistrust), we show that the instruments and processes by which contracts are implemented are not passive, neutral, and unable to influence events. Indeed it has already been suggested that introducing contracting into health and social care leads to some redefinition of contracting processes (Wistow *et al.* 1992). Where market expectations are not met and redefinitions occur, questions are raised as to what alternative purposes contracting may be fulfilling.

This chapter aims to outline such alternative functions by drawing on empirical evidence from a research project on contracting in the social services which explored the dynamics of contracting from the perspective of purchasers in the social services. In particular we observe that contracts for social care are more statements of mutual faith than of mutual trust. This, we argue, is because of the manner in which the market has emerged, with a lack of any substantive prior relationship between purchasers (social service departments) and *independent* providers of social care.

The findings of this study indicate that 'soft' contracting is the norm in the social services. Based on data from this study, we define soft contracting as follows: *soft* contracting is the obverse of formal contracts which have detailed specifications (including detailed procedural arrangements, costs of contracts) and contingencies extending to penalty clauses. The *soft* contract may also entail rules and procedures but is predicated on trust. In this sense (of *implementation*), such contracts can be related to professional values and distinguished from litigation as the arbiter of exchange or contractual relationships.

This accords with the findings of the classic study of contracting in business by Macaulay (1963), which demonstrated a reluctance to enter into formal contracts in the business world. Macaulay writes of reliance on one's word, or on a brief letter, a handshake, or 'common honesty and decency'—even when the transaction involves exposure to serious risks (Macaulay 1963: 58). This reveals a reluctance to grapple with the bureaucracy—the 'battle of the forms' (Macaulay 1963: 59). It also underpins Granovetter's (1985) perspective of the relational context of business relationships in general. This soft contracting is being used, first, to establish closer working relationships between purchasers in the social services and providers in the independent sector, secondly, to clarify the nature of the service, and, thirdly, to focus on enhancing the quality of the service. Such soft contracting works through partnership, relies on collaborative arrangements, and is predicated on trust. The extent to which such dynamics are realized is explored below. But first we examine and reflect further on these differing concepts of contract—the formal and 'soft' (or tacit)—and their implications.

FORMAL VERSUS TACIT OR 'SOFT' CONTRACTS

This section identifies some of the key ideas emanating from the libertarian school of thought which have proved influential in the emergence of 'contracts' as a pivotal mechanism in the blueprint for the quasi-markets in social care (and in health). This section also traces competing ideas of how social care should be organized and delivered. This identifies the central place of *trust* in the world of social care, the tensions around the movement from trust-based social processes to the more formal mechanism of the contract, and the reaction of influential professionals to redefining the nature of the contract-setting as a 'soft-contracting' process which reaffirms and even extends their codes of conduct. This is of particular importance in the context of the new markets in social care where the configuration of the market-place realigns social care workers from different settings which have process-based trust relationships (local government and, to some extent, the voluntary sector) with those which do not (independent, particularly private providers of social care). This consequence has important implications for trust relationships, as discussed further below, notably the existence of social service 'mistrust' in these private-care providers who have not yet formed 'process-based' trust relationships with social work contractors.

Proponents of contracting adhere to ideas of the market-place—the forum for choice to be exercised by the consumer with rights and obligations which may entail contract-setting. Indeed, we can place *contract-setting* at the centre of a libertarian agenda, although, within that school of thought, there is also recognition of the existence of tacit (or 'soft' in our terms) contracts or conventions. In the words of de Jasay (1991: 81): 'a convention is best understood as an informally concluded tacit contract binding a large number of people'. But recognition of the potential and relevance of 'tacit' or softer forms of contracting does not imply acceptance. Critics (such as de Jasay) of the use of 'convention' to enforce rights can point to the lack of any explicit or implicit obligations in conventions to undertake tasks. There is limited reciprocity but the convention may 'deliver'. This deliverance may come from self-enforcing norms where 'precedent eases negotiation and agreement, or makes it altogether unnecessary, custom economises on contracts' (de Jasay 1991: 87). However, in the eyes of libertarians, this may prove to be a denial of the rights of individuals. Here is the central factor in this thinking: the exercise of choice. And here is the prime role for contracts as an *enforcement mechanism* for the detailing of obligations and, if need be, the pursuit of non-delivery of such obligations. As de Jasay puts it:

contract is (an) obvious, self-evident source (of rights and choice), because only contracts provide proof that the correlative obligation has been *agreed* to by the obliger, hence its existence does not depend on controversial claims . . . contracts are negotiated and concluded deliberately and they are Pareto-optimal. Being voluntary, willed and non-imposed, and improving the lot of the parties, contracts are a quintessentially liberal institution. (de Jasay 1991: 91)

In our view the preceding viewpoint is stark, not only in its description, but also in its awareness of the potential for the impact of professional codes of behaviour (as in de Jasay's terms, 'self-enforcement norms') in absorbing and redefining the contract agenda.

The codification of best practice in social care—as in the legalistic enforcement (by formal contract) of what constitutes 'quality'—limits the role and judgement of the professional worker, emphasizing collective rather than individual knowledge and intensifying such 'self-enforcement norms' (Wilding 1994). The issue here is the malleability of the contract as a construct. In particular, this is pertinent when contract-setting is moulded with particular (professional) conventions within social care. This means that expectations about the need for (and style of) contracts is influenced by expectations between professionals which are themselves shaped strongly by social processes. This is Zucker's (1986) concept of process-based trust in which exchanges between participants establish levels of trust. This relies on a continuing series of exchanges (as in the accumulation of experience over time between professionals in the design of, arrangement of, and location of social care for the elderly). In the presence of a pattern of exchanges or arrangements there exists a strong social expectation that 'trust' is merited. Within this schema, norms, procedures, recognition of reciprocity, an awareness of, and regard for, issues beyond the narrow confines of the specifics at hand (the so-called 'et cetera assumptions') are matters for consideration, debate, and resolution. As Granovetter (1985: 490) puts it, 'continuing economic exchanges become overlaid with social content that carries strong expectations of trust and absorption from opportunism'.

Here the code of behaviour in social care affords a vehicle by which concepts used continually—such as client choice, dignity, independent living (SSI/SWSG 1991*a*, 1991*b*)—are taken for granted as having primacy within the planning of care of clients of social work departments. In this sense there is an a priori argument that, save for structural realignment of social services departments into the purchaser/provider split, there is a high level of trust and, therefore, little need for formal contracting mechanisms. This is described by Neu (1991) as the 'irony of contracting':

contracting requires the presence of trust. However, where high levels of trust are present, the introduction of a contract may result in a breakdown of trust. Conversely when low levels of trust are present, contractual devices are needed to align expectations, yet these devices are not likely to be effective given the lack of a common starting expectation upon which to base such contracts. (Neu 1991: 247)

This latter observation depicts the dilemma of the contract managers in social care—while a priori there would appear to be common expectations about what constitutes a good quality of social care, the market has produced a dual system in which purchasers within social work departments identify more readily with providers of such care *within* the local government sector (i.e. high trust exists and contracts may not be seen as necessary), but are mistrustful of the new providers (the private sector), with whom previous exchanges were limited (as explained in some detail, below), and for whom process-based trust has not (yet) emerged. Our findings demonstrate a dual structure: where there is a high level of trust which the manner of introducing contracting has not broken down; and where there are low levels of trust, or even mistrust, and contracting has been used to align expectations of the dominant cadre. Thus where there is already high trust, we have observed process-based trust which does not eschew the contract, but redefines, reinforces, and restyles it (as 'soft contracting') which is embedded in the values of the dominant professional code—in this case, social workers. And, furthermore, these values are being extended beyond 'high trust' areas, as contract managers work at building up process-based trust across the spectrum of institutions with which they negotiate.

The next section explains the research methods employed. The fundamental contracting structures and processes in the market for social care are then explored in more detail, to establish how the purposes of contracting are negotiated within this setting.

RESEARCH METHODS

This project examined decisions made by contract managers in social work departments in local authorities in Scotland. The particular focus of this study was on contracting for residential care for elderly people. The method of investigation entailed in-depth interviews with contract managers in all nine regional councils in Scotland, and interviews with members of staff involved in determining a given local authority's policy (usually senior social work staff, also finance staff). These interviews were conducted over two periods to capture the initial, and the developing, processes of contracting by social work departments. During semi-structured interviews, research instruments on referrals and the use of resources were discussed with social work department teams. A fuller explanation of the approach adopted is in Lapsley and Llewellyn (1995).

In this chapter we report on the perspective of the contract managers in these social work departments. In practice, different authorities have evolved different designations for such local authority officers, but all of those interviewed have a prime responsibility for social work contracts. To preserve anonymity, we have numbered the individual contract managers as CM1 (contract manager, region 1) and so on. This part of our research revealed a number of significant aspects of contract-setting in social work departments: the restructuring in social services for contracting; relational contracts in social care; the use of contracts to switch rationing from providers to purchasers; and fixing prices and using contracts to enhance quality. These issues are considered in turn.

RESTRUCTURING SOCIAL SERVICES AND THE NATURE OF THE 'MARKET' IN SOCIAL CARE

Before contracting can begin, the contracting partners must be identified. The identities of the providers of social care are well established (although contracting may change these identities), but the identities of purchasers are not. The purchasing function in the public sector generally has not been well developed and it has received little attention from policy-makers (Hunter 1993). To enable the identification of purchasers, previously unified social service departments have been reconstructed around the purchaser/provider split—although, significantly, this study found that these terms are not used, purchasers being dubbed 'planning and coordination' and providers labelled as 'operations'. The language of 'planning and coordination' suggests that purchasers within the social services are likely to be less concerned with purchasing *per se* and more 'responsible for maintaining a strategic overview within which the guidelines on which purchasing takes place are developed' (Cochrane 1994: 153). This observation again emphasizes the significance of the context within which action (such as purchasing) takes place—as it is this context (or strategic overview) which shapes the nature and impact of purchasing.

Departmental structures in the social services incorporate the purchaser/provider split at either the first or second level below the director of social work. Figure 5.1 shows a region where the split occurs below the senior depute director but in some regions the position 'senior depute' is omitted and, therefore, the split between operations (or providers) and planning and coordination (or purchasers) is incorporated immediately below director level. It is also usual in the regions for the assistant directors of finance and/or human resources to be located outside the purchaser-provider domains in organizational hierarchies but at the same level as that at which the purchaser/provider split occurs.

There are three structural elements to the purchaser/provider split: the starting-point, that is, the point at the top of the Social Services Department (SSD) at which the split starts; the end point, that is, the level in the department down to which the split extends; and the component responsibilities, that is, the range of activities (training, personnel, financial management, legal advice, and so on) which are allocated to the purchaser and provider arms (Wistow *et al.* 1992). In these terms, the split starts high in the regional social service departments and extends all the way down to front-line staff but the financial management and personnel functions are excluded from the responsibilities encompassed within the purchaser and provider domains.

This reconstitution of social service departments identifies a set of purchasers but the question of who these purchasers will contract with remains to be decided. Potentially, purchasers within the social services may contract with their own 'in-house' providers but, as yet, this has not occurred. This reflects, as argued earlier, the high level of trust and shared values within the social services as an organization and the low level of support held by social services staff for the principle of contracting (Deakin and Walsh 1994; Walsh 1995*a*). One contracts manager commented on the differences between contracting for care in the independent sector and the more direct links with the local authorities' own homes—links which, arguably, make contracting redundant:

We know what we are getting [in our own homes]. The lines of communication are there and so is the level of trust. Also, of course, we can influence it which is much more difficult for those we don't manage. For instance, you can get an inspection report for an independent home which brings something up—say for 1993 and the same thing is still a problem in 1994. Our own homes would never get away with that. (CM7)

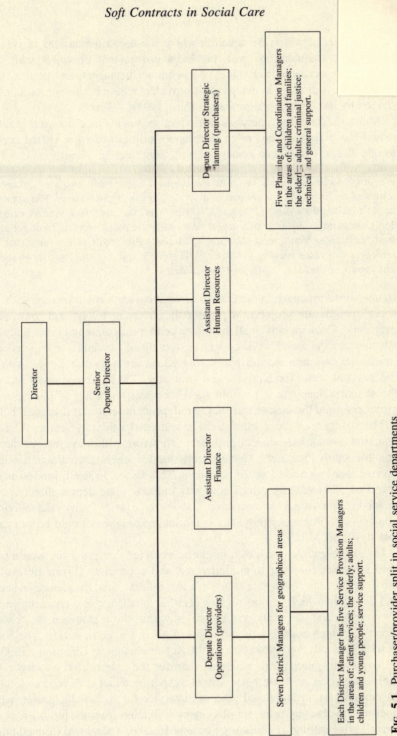

Fig. 5.1. Purchaser/provider split in social service departments

This comment typifies the situation where the broad dimensions of process-based trust are identified with the local government providers who share common expectations and values with contract managers, and the low trust, or mistrust, is directed at independent providers whose behaviour has not been shaped by the same social processes (Neu 1991).

Although, formally, a purchaser/provider split is in place, concrete practices reveal less clearly defined roles and responsibilities and some shared concern to alleviate any problems associated with 'too much of a split':

> We've got to be careful not to create too much of a split really, we are working as a team and we have both got our part to play. A split can create tensions. For example, I detect a feeling from some of the social work officers that they think the care managers don't use them as much as they might. But really the social workers have got to sell their services—*I don't mean literally of course*—they can't just assume that care managers will come running to them . . . There is a split but we don't shout about it and there's no rhetoric. (CM8, emphasis added)

Hence, unsurprisingly, although three regions are experimenting with 'in-house' purchasing projects, at present they remain 'pilots' and 'only paper exercises'. Consequently in all the regions either the community care budget or the mainstream social work budget is 'top-sliced' to fund the regions' own residential care homes, and purchasing teams are only contracting with the independent sector (both private and voluntary). These arrangements underpin the shared values ('trust') within social services—whether as purchasers or providers—and the lack of trust in the independent sector, as discussed below.

The structure of the market in the private and voluntary sectors is one of numerous, small independent providers. Therefore within the regions there is one monopoly purchaser (for publicly funded clients) contracting with a diverse and fragmented set of providers. This factor, in itself, renders highly specified, differentially priced contracts unlikely. One depute director commented: 'You've got to remember that we've over 500 and odd individual homes—with that many providers individual negotiations would be an incredible hassle' (CM6).

Under these circumstances it might be expected that providers would press hard for block contracts to minimize risk and uncertainty (Flynn 1992). That providers have not been able to achieve this reflects, first, the picture on supply and demand—which in most regions is either in balance or is characterized by oversupply, and, secondly, the emphasis within the regions on the 'choice' directive, which enshrines the principle of client choice in statute (The Social Work (Scotland) Act 1968; (Choice of Accommodation) Directions, 1993).

At present, purchasing residential care for the elderly is conducted on an individual client or 'spot' basis, where a 'spot' contract is defined as follows: 'A contract for an individual placement/service for an individual user, which does not involve any prior pre-placement obligation from the provider, or any overall price setting' (Purchasing Strategy 1995–6, *X* Regional Council Social

Work). The Accounts Commission (1994) has criticized the regions for relying on 'spot' agreements and has advocated greater use of block contracts—commenting that 'spot' purchasing fails to allow for effective and efficient service delivery from the *service providers'* point of view. One region has responded to this criticism by suggesting that from the *service users'* perspective, block contracts inhibit choice and flexibility. This region quoted the Joseph Rowntree Foundation (1994) as advocating, 'The adoption of "spot" purchasing as the norm by social service purchasers to promote flexibility and to meet individual needs more precisely' (*Y* Regional Council, Purchasing Strategy 1995–6: 9). This same region defines block contracts as follows: 'A contract which purchases a defined volume of service, rather than a service for an individual'. Purchasing staff within the regions described block contracts as incompatible with meeting the statutory client choice directive as block contracts would imply either reducing client choice to those homes which were in receipt of block contracts or committing monies for places which may not be used. One contracts manager commented: 'We're a big privately funded market which makes it more necessary to "spot" purchase. Also with the directive on choice we'd be falling flat on our faces if we bought block' (CM5).

Finally, before exploring some of the aspects of the contracting process 'in action', formal aims of purchasing in the regions are considered. These aims are characterized by Region *Y*'s statement, as follows:

- to ensure that needs can be met appropriately;
- to ensure that needs can be met cost-effectively;
- to enable service users to exercise preference;
- to develop and maintain the supply of a range of relevant services;
- to promote a mixed economy of care.

Whilst acknowledging that purchasing strategies 'in action' are linked with these objectives, the chapter now examines the a priori issues (or actual practices) which distance these aims (distilled from the official rhetoric on contracts) from pragmatic purchasing realities. The following sections explore these realities to find out why and how contracting has been redefined in a social service setting.

RELATIONAL CONTRACTS

Prior to the changes stemming from the 1990 NHS and Community Care Act, funding for residential care for the elderly flowed directly to provider units in the independent sector from the Department of Social Security. One facet of these arrangements was that SSDs had limited contact (essentially confined to preregistration and periodic inspection, by designated sections of SSDs) with private and voluntary sector providers. In consequence, the transfer of funds from the sphere of social security to the local authorities, and the latter's new concomitant responsibilities for funding and monitoring care in the independent sector, has entailed closer working relationships between the SSDs and the independent sector. Paradoxically, therefore, the new contracting regime has called for closer relationships with providers to supplant the more 'arm's-length' relationships which previously held. The following three quotes from contracts managers in different regions illustrate this perception.

Well, in many cases we didn't have a relationship before 1993 with providers. The new contract has clarified expectations and it's also meant that we focus more on the service. Both parties can challenge the contract—it's a two-way dialogue. Before there wasn't necessarily much contact—where there were maintenance rates providers just carried on—got on with it. Now there's a much closer relationship. (CM5)

A lot of bridge-building has been done in taking contracting forward. We're in a partnership with them now. (CM4)

We've got to learn how to work more closely with the independent sector—not to be just fighting each other and keeping each other at a distance. (CM7)

These closer working relationships have, through a greater 'focus on the service', produced clearer expectations or some formalization (Lewis 1993) of what is being purchased—although this formalization remains broadly stated rather than prescribed in detail. Therefore, contracting has involved 'getting to know each other' and these processes of familiarization come before the processes of formalization which, in turn, must precede judgements about the 'appropriateness' and 'cost-effectiveness' of services. Before contracts can become relational in the sense of forging long-term alliances and interlocking functions (Larson 1992; Powell 1991; Ring and Van de Ven 1992), they have to be established as relational in a much more basic sense—the contracting partners must engage in a process of finding out about each other.

Then there's the broad issues—we are clearer about what we're buying. For some organizations this has been a problem. For example, some voluntaries were doing the right things but they never put it into words—they've had to become much more professional. (CM4)

This analysis suggests that purchasers in the social services are working towards establishing high-trust 'obligational contract relationships' rather than low-trust 'arm's-length contract relationships' (Dunleavy and Hood 1994).

USING CONTRACTS TO SWITCH RATIONING FROM PROVIDERS TO PURCHASERS

Previous research has already indicated that contract negotiations can be most prolonged when issues over client access or 'who to contract for' are involved.

Lewis (1994) outlines a case where an SSD was engaged in a 'contract battle' with a voluntary provider of day care. The SSD concerned wished to ensure that the more dependent elderly were given priority for this service. The contract specified that all clients must be assessed by the SSD, with 60 per cent of clients being required to meet criteria for admission which gave priority to the more dependent. Arguing against this specification the voluntary provider was keen to maintain its previous policy of taking elderly people 'capable of "walking in" but experiencing "social isolation"' (Lewis 1994: 212).

This study indicated that where a similar policy is held by an independent organization, it can be interpreted by the SSD as the provider 'taking the easier people'. One contracts manager commented favourably on switching the processes of prioritization from the provider side to the purchaser side.

But one thing that has changed is, I think, that it has switched from provider-side rationing to purchaser-side rationing. Pre-1993 if there were no more places left at the day centre—well, it just didn't happen and I've always felt that providers had incentives to take the easier people. Now it's purchaser-side rationing—prioritization—it's being rationalized in purchasing. (CM1)

The rationalization of who is to receive the service concerned is happening through contracting. As to whether purchasers or providers make decisions on access—the balance of power lies with purchasers in the social services as they have the responsibility for needs assessment and, in addition, they hold the purchasing budget. The following comments exemplify the present thinking within the SSDs on prioritization (or rationing). First, the existence of waiting lists effectively prioritizes through queuing: 'It's too early to say much on rationing but there are waiting lists for nursing homes but we're not leaving anyone at risk' (CM1). Next, contracts managers consider how to 'lift thresholds of eligibility'.

Before anyone receives a package of care the budget must be available. What this means is that if this month's budget is committed then there might be a delay in, say, entry to residential care—they might not go in until the following month—but we have to make sure that it doesn't involve risk. The next stage is lifting thresholds of eligibility but we don't know how we are going to do that yet. (CM6)

We are starting targeting—two strategies—first, to reduce the numbers of people eligible for certain services, second, to define service costs and the client group more closely. (CM9)

There is prioritization going on, practitioners are looking at it with line managers—every Friday they go through the assessments and look at them in context. (CM4)

Moreover some regions are thinking of making distinctions between contracting for quality of care and contracting for quality of life. Where the care provided impacts only on quality of life, contracts managers think carefully before committing money.

We may have to distinguish between quality of life issues and care needs. We may have to accept that we may not be able to commit money to meet certain quality of life things—although this mustn't work to the detriment of someone with complex care needs. (CM2)

Given the difficulties of operationalizing concepts such as 'quality of life' (see e.g. Kind 1990) and consequently, of making fine distinctions between quality of care or quality of life, these observations present an opportunity for purchasers (SSDs) to impose their definition of what constitutes a quality service on provider organizations. Clearly the contracting process, as presently structured, places the 'obligation' on the providers to deliver the service specified to those clients which the SSDs judge to be of higher priority. Therefore the alignment of expectations can involve considerably reduced autonomy on the part of service providers to deliver the service they see fit, through the processes they choose, to those clients who they think most benefit from the service they offer. From the perspective of the SSDs this can equate to providers, particularly the voluntary sector, becoming more 'professional'.

Voluntary providers can be difficult because so much of it is given freely. They can have a very inefficient way of working—too much time spent travelling and admin costs too high. Basically they are not commercial enough—*they are not using sharp enough pencils.* (CM3, emphasis added)

The next section explores how the issues of the financial dimension (or 'sharper pencils') and quality are currently negotiated through contracts.

FIXING PRICES AND USING CONTRACTS TO ENHANCE QUALITY

Flynn (1994) outlines three strategic options for purchasers when making decisions about how to address price/quality issues through contracting within the public sector.

- purchasers may decide to buy the cheapest possible service subject to a minimum quality standard;
- purchasers may fix the price in advance and buy what they judge to be the highest quality service at that price;
- purchasers may make trade-offs between price and quality.

We would suggest that this represents an incomplete mapping of the set of strategies adopted by purchasers. In particular, it depicts a rationalistic approach to prioritization of contracts, which may not mesh with social work values, and which assumes explicit, measurable cost/quality relationships where these may not be known (see Bland *et al.* 1992; Llewellyn 1994; Lapsley 1995). Nevertheless, it provides a useful framework for the investigation of purchasing strategies. The evidence from this study is that current purchasing strategies on price/quality in the social services are closest to the second of these options, that is, fixing the price and attempting to buy a quality service.

However, this does not imply that purchasers are buying the highest quality service available at this fixed price—lack of knowledge about the services provided in the independent sector, the inevitable subjectivity inherent in quality of care assessments, and the difficulties in monitoring the delivery of quality services implies indeterminacy in judgements about the highest quality services available. Paucity of information about the nature of services delivered, along with the ultimate indeterminacy in judgements about quality, has mitigated the possibility of making price/quality trade-offs in the purchasing transactions of the social services, and on the basis of the research studies cited, there was no evidence of such 'trade-offs' occurring (for an analysis of the difficulties of making such trade-offs, see Llewellyn 1993). The multi-dimensional nature of quality of care in human services (Wilding 1994)—embracing not only procedures, guidelines, and legalistic forms of control, but also the culture of quality, the organizational structure, and user involvement—demonstrates the complexity of this aspect of the cost/quality trade-off. Also, there was no evidence from this study, of purchasers attempting to drive down prices in the independent sector. The observation of one contract manager crystallizes this perspective: 'People have got to make a profit and a return on capital, otherwise it's a brief flare here and a brief flare there and they're gone—rates are as close to the bone as they can be' (CM6).

On these grounds, purchasers may fear pressure to increase the prices paid to the independent sector. Also purchasers in this study were aware that the costs of care in the local authority sector are generally higher than those in the independent sector. Bland *et al.* (1992) reported average costs of residential care per resident week at £145 in private homes, £164 in voluntary-run homes, and £216 in local authority homes. Contract managers were sensitive to these kinds of discrepancies in their own contract-setting, as the following comment by a contract manager illustrates: 'We never keep the costs of our own homes from the independent sector—it's a case of here are the costs of our own homes and then we duck' (CM2). Rather than purchasers being in a position to negotiate on prices many found that their providers still expected 'purchasers' to fund their deficits.

We are under a lot of pressure from organizations over deficit funding. In the past if providers had 5–10 per cent voids [unfilled places] we would pay. Now they can have 20 per cent voids but there is just no way that we can make this up. (CM2)

Moreover, as discussed earlier, the generally balanced position between supply and demand mitigated against downward pressure on prices.

There's not the excess provision that would allow for negotiation. If at all, the pressures are likely to come from the opposite direction—homes offering a £5 discount or social workers being given backhanders. God forbid, I must say I've never heard of it. (CM3)

If contracting is not about 'getting prices down' it may be about 'getting quality up'. But contracting to 'get quality up' implies some working notions about the nature of quality in the social services. As noted above, definitions of what constitutes *quality* in the public sector are difficult to formulate and social services are no exception. Nevertheless, there is some general agreement in the approaches adopted by SSDs that a quality service satisfies need. This equates with the British standard (BS4778 1987) which defines quality as, 'the totality of features and characteristics of a product or service that bear on its ability to satisfy stated or implied needs'. Further clarity in thinking about a quality service has been achieved by SSDs considering the different dimensions of service packages. The development of the purchasing function in the SSDs has involved a much greater emphasis on service packages in their needs assessments (see SSI/SWSG 1991*a*, 1991*b*). As these assessments are agreed with the clients concerned, they provide some basis for establishing whether the proffered services meet stated needs. Staff in the social services were reasonably confident about using contracts to define and enhance quality in the areas of the *physical environment* and the *standards of service*.

We use contracting to get higher standards, to encourage conformity with standards— over physical conditions like regular reviews and choice of meals and we negotiated these with representatives of the independent sector and everyone accepted them. It's not about driving down prices—they know that doesn't work in the private sector and they've rejected all that—it's about getting quality up. (CM6)

Contracting can be used to enhance quality but price plays a big part too. We can specify the physical layout—that's an easy thing to monitor and measure. But the happiness factor—that's different—that's a very difficult thing to define and measure. (CM4)

However, these statements represent an incomplete statement of the quality of service offered. Sketcher (1992) pinpoints *four* elements of service quality: service characteristics (e.g. availability, standards of service, and performance); personal relationships (e.g. responsiveness, courtesy, and communication); physical environment (e.g. appearance, access, and functioning); and client power (e.g. rights, choice, voice, and redress).

Once the assessment of quality moved beyond the *physical* environment and the more tangible aspects of standards of service, contracts managers emphasized the innate subjectivity of measures and they expressed some reluctance to pay for 'intangibles': 'A report was done on quality by one of the inspectorate—it had 26 different variables but the problem is the subjectivity—it's not scientific and, anyway, we couldn't afford a quality banding' (CM4).

Over issues of client power, contracts managers expressed generally positive statements on using contracts to enhance clients' rights: 'Care managers do come to us [contracts managers]. If they're unhappy about some aspect of the client's care, they say, "Is there anything in the contract about this?"' (CM9).

Some regions were considering paying 'informal' providers or clients themselves to enhance client power over care.

People would be in control of their own money. I think it would reduce the number of complaints. We could use the review process to include questions around where the money had been spent. (CM4)

Contracting has freed up opportunities. There was a tendency to say—what you need is the day centre—now it could be what you need is for us to pay the neighbour to take you to the bingo. It has given people more power and control over how their needs are met. (CM1)

Where purchasers do not control providers through specifying inputs nor use contracts to specify outcomes, they must rely on some form of monitoring and inspection of the processes of service delivery (Flynn 1994). Staff in the regions did, indeed, rely on monitoring processes but this was not without problems.

We're not that confident about monitoring quality—at the moment there are three strands—registrations, the inspectorate, and care manager reviews. But we've got to bring the strands together—it's too ad hoc and diverse. We've got to develop a more coherent way. (CM6)

Previously a common fault was that social workers weren't precise about what they were buying nor did they monitor services to make sure that what was delivered was what they had bought. The reality was that after the initial review a social worker wouldn't know if a client had died in care. (CM3)

Underpinning the objective of enhancing quality is the expectation of predetermined minimum quality standards as purchasers in the social services will only contract with providers who meet their registration and inspection requirements. Hence, although strategies conform most closely to the second of the options outlined by Flynn (1994), the search for quality starts from an assumed minimum base line—secured by the local authorities' registration and inspection procedures.

An additional factor which confounds any neat pigeon-holing of purchasing strategies is that *one* region does negotiate on price—albeit that negotiations do *not* take place on the basis of the quality of the service provided but on assessments of clients' needs. An illustration of the operation of this form of pricing is shown in Table 5.1.

This distinguishes between components of needs (mobility/disability; intellectual impairment and personal care) over a three-point scale ('higher', 'medium', 'lower') and is varied according to specific residential requirements. In this region, price variability has been introduced but, significantly, differential prices have been linked to needs assessments, a core valued activity in social work practice.

TABLE 5.1. Pricing policy for elderly people based upon assessments of clients' dependency

Basic residential			197
Single room supplement			30
Mobility/disability	Higher	20	
	Medium	10	
	Lower	5	
Intellectual impairment	Higher	35	
	Medium	20	
	Lower	10	
Personal care	Higher	25	
	Medium	15	
	Lower	5	
'Higher' assessments in all three areas + supplement			307
'Medium' assessments in all three areas + supplement			272
'Lower' assessments in all three areas + supplement			247

Note: All prices quoted are in £ per resident/week.

CONCLUSION

This study has concluded that the contracting for social care in Scotland can be characterized as 'soft' contracting, in which the formality of contracts for exchange relationships is mediated by social work professional values and considerations of trust, including working towards trust relationships where these do not exist at present. These processes assume that providers will respond to incentives for 'working together'—as soft contracts eschew legalistic or adversarial forms. This contrasts with the libertarian vision of contracts as devices for ensuring choice because of their merits as enforcement mechanisms (see e.g. de Jasay 1991). Such soft contracting also contrasts with the more litigious environment of the USA. One depute director in the social services interviewed as part of this study compared the British and US contracting cultures,

In the States they say our contracts are statements of *mutual faith*—they test their personal integrity to fight contracts to the last cent. They [Americans] think our contracts are a joke but when they see the services we provide then they acknowledge that the services are good. If you nail providers to the floor—if you act like they are sharks—then they will behave like sharks.

This distinction is further supported by evidence on the USA which shows effectiveness of care delivery is unrelated to successful contracting by funding agencies, but is more a function of care providers' ability to market themselves, present a well-defined identity and a strong reputation, and an ability to activate networks on their behalf (Gronbjerg 1991). This behaviour and the above quotation exemplifies the 'irony of contracting' (Neu 1991). Contracting involves a certain level of trust or mutual faith, but where levels of trust have been *low* (as between the social services and private sector providers—who may behave like 'sharks') contracts must work so as to *align expectations*. Yet these processes of alignment are difficult given a lack of prior mutual understanding on which to build. Paradoxically, where *high* levels of trust are present, contracting appears redundant—even destructive. Within the social services in-house contracting has yet to get off the ground—reflecting the paradox of contracting *within* an organization where a high level of shared values has existed. Moreover we have argued that contracts with independent providers of social care are presently statements of 'mutual faith' rather than 'mutual trust', in particular, because of the lack of a prior relationship between the social services, as purchasers, and the providers in the independent sector.

These findings are of wider relevance to a general theory of contracts. At present, the theory of contracts is not fully developed. There are unresolved issues (of moral hazard, adverse selection, incomplete contracts, absence of long-term contracts) which make the prediction of the effects of contract-setting difficult (Hart and Holmström 1987). In this context, we argue that the alignment of expectations is an important consideration—an 'a priori' which must be engaged and worked at through contracting. This alignment encompasses processes of *familiarization* and *formalization* (Lewis 1993) as the contracting partners (particularly the purchasers) seek to clarify expectations about the nature of the services provided—including their price and quality. This is essential for process-based trust to take hold (Zucker 1986). Also of fundamental significance in shaping contracting is the structural form of the market within which contracting takes place. This structural form encompasses both sides of the contracting interface: on the one side, the restructuring of social service departments to identify purchasers and accommodate contracting, and on the other, the structural aspects of the supply (or provider) network which, although already established, may have to undergo change. Moreover decisions on access to services involving priorization (or rationing) take place through contract negotiations—as purchasers decide who to contract for. These prime tasks equate to establishing 'what to contract about', 'how to contract', and 'who to contract for'. Only after these a priori undecided issues are settled will any price/quality negotiations proceed. Therefore it is argued here that these a priori concerns are *pivotal* in shaping how contracting will develop; to label them as 'implementation tasks' misses the point that these are fundamental issues which help shape the purposes and impact of contracting in a given context.

The authors would like to acknowledge the support of the Economic and Social Research Council for funding this research (grant no. R000221128).

6

CONTRACTING IN THE NATIONAL HEALTH SERVICE: LEGAL AND ECONOMIC ISSUES

KIT BARKER, MARTIN CHALKLEY, JAMES M. MALCOMSON, AND
JONATHAN MONTGOMERY

INTRODUCTION: KEY ISSUES AND QUESTIONS

The National Health Service (NHS) quasi-market established a conceptual and operational separation between purchasers of health services (district health authorities, health commissions, general practice (GP) fundholders in their role as purchasers of services) and the providers of those services (NHS Trust and private sector hospitals, community health service providers, GPs in their role as providers of services). It requires provision of health services to be governed by contracts between purchasers and providers. The research reported in this chapter considers what forms of contract between health authorities and providers are appropriate within the context of this quasi-market.

A key issue in contracting for health services is how to ensure that providers deliver appropriate standards of treatment while keeping costs down. This issue cannot typically be resolved by specifying everything in a contract because, realistically, contracts are rarely going to be able to specify in detail all the different elements that comprise a 'standard of service' in a way that is enforceable. Our analysis of the issue is based on the economic theory of contracts and our main findings are outlined later in this chapter.

This first key issue arises with any contracts for health services, private or public. This chapter focuses on NHS contracts, those between NHS purchasers and NHS providers. These NHS bodies have a statutory status that requires two key legal issues to be resolved prior to an economic analysis of NHS contracts. The first concerns the constraints on contracts that arise because NHS purchasers and providers are public bodies, with constitutions and powers established by law, and are parts of the same overarching organization. The second concerns the enforceability of NHS contracts in view of the provisions of the National Health Service and Community Care Act (NHSCCA) 1990.

Before discussing the main findings, we provide a brief review of the concepts and methods used in the economic theory of contracts that underpins the research. Finally, we discuss some of the implications of our findings for policy and practice.

CONCEPTS, THEORIES, AND METHODS

The economic theory of contracts starts from a recognition of the limitations on what can be enforced by contract. Given those limitations, it then considers how the parties to a contract will respond to the different forms the contract may take, that is, how the outcome depends on the contract used. The final step is to consider the appropriateness of different forms of contract on the basis of the outcomes to which each form gives rise.

Obviously, what is appropriate depends on the criteria used. A widely used criterion is economic efficiency. As used here, *economic efficiency* is concerned with the purchaser getting as far down its list of priorities as possible for a given level of reward to the providing organization (and the people who work for it). *Reward* here is to be interpreted broadly to include non-monetary, as well as monetary, elements. It would not be economically efficient if, for example, a health authority was prepared to pay more for some service than the minimum a hospital would accept to provide it but the service was not in fact purchased. Economic efficiency is not synonymous with employees working longer hours for less pay or with many of the other senses in which the term efficiency has been used in debates on the NHS.

It is important to be clear about the limitations of this approach. It is concerned with what form of contract is appropriate given the use of a contracting system. There are clearly costs to running a contracting system. There are also benefits. The approach used here is not appropriate for analysing whether those costs are likely to outweigh the benefits, and so whether a contracting system is in some sense better than what went before. Nor is it an appropriate framework for discussing how the budgets of health purchasers are, or should be, determined. Here we simply start from the undoubted fact that these budgets are not (and are never likely to be) enough to purchase all the health services purchasers would like. Nor do we discuss how health authorities should, or do, decide on what services are to have priority given their limited budgets. The issues of concern here are the implications of different types of contracts for the cost and quality of the services provided given the priorities that have been set by purchasers with a limited budget.

In discussing efficient forms of contract, it is important to distinguish between providers with different objectives. One provider objective analysed extensively in the literature is profit maximization. But it is important to remember that, even in the USA where many hospitals operate for profit, there are substantial numbers of non-profit hospitals. For understanding contracting issues, it is instructive to consider three different types of objectives providers may have. The first is narrow (or short-term) *self-interest*. This is not synonymous with maximizing profit. Non-profit institutions can be equally self-interested (about, for example, the perks and the power of those who run them). But some providers are no doubt *benevolent* in the sense that they will do what is best for their patients for reasons other than the consequences that arise directly from a contract. Given a budget to spend freely, a benevolent provider will spend it on patients in exactly the way a purchaser that has patients' interests at heart would want the provider to spend it. A provider cannot, though, be guaranteed to know the purchaser's priorities for health care purchased from other providers and so even a benevolent provider may choose to spend all its budget on its *own* patients. (Since our brief here is not concerned with how the priorities of purchasers reflect those of patients, in what follows we discuss benevolence solely with respect to the purchaser's priorities.) Between the extremes of narrowly self-interested and benevolent providers lie what we term *partially benevolent* providers that give some, but not all, weight to the goals of the purchaser. Even with the best will in the world, it is only natural that provider employees have their own particular concerns. Benevolence in the sense used here may reflect genuine concern, professional standards, or managers' concern for their wider (or long-term) self-interest in, and the pressures of, the NHS. Its importance in the provision of health services has been recognized in the literature. See, for example, Newhouse (1970) and Ellis and McGuire (1986).

This chapter is concerned with the efficient design of contracts. For this purpose, we have identified selected elements of the legal structure that relate to the direct and indirect enforceability of contract terms, and to those elements of the constitutions of providers that may influence how far they act benevolently in the sense outlined above. In the next section, our main findings on these issues are set out. A more comprehensive range of legal issues arising from the research is reported in Montgomery and Barker (1996).

MAIN FINDINGS: LEGAL FRAMEWORK

The Context of Contracting

Health authority purchasers carry out the delegated powers of the Secretary of State under the National Health Service Act 1977. These powers are broadly defined (Montgomery 1997). While they may influence decisions about what should be purchased, they do not provide any significant limitations on the form that contracts take except that there is a statutory prohibition on charging NHS patients. In principle, health authorities can be made accountable for their purchasing decisions through the courts, primarily by actions for judicial review. However, the courts have been wary of becoming involved in this way. They have emphasized that it is inappropriate for them to consider political issues concerning the overall level of resources allocated to purchasers. They have also shied away from examining managerial decisions concerning prioritization within the purchasing process. Finally, they regard themselves as unqualified to examine clinical issues concerning professional judgements on both the urgency of treatment and the appropriateness of particular types of care (Montgomery 1997). The effect of this judicial restraint is that there is little accountability for purchasing outside the NHS management structures. Such legal action does not, therefore, have any impact on the form of contracts.

On the provider side, the bulk of NHS services are provided through NHS Trusts. From 1 April 1996, 98 per cent of services are offered by these organizations, so we concentrate on the position of these Trusts. A number of factors reduce the flexibility of Trusts in contracting. They are obliged to ensure that revenue covers outgoings (including a fixed return, currently 6 per cent on assets) taking one financial year with another (NHSCCA 1990: s. 10(1)). Should a Trust breach these provisions and create a reserve, the money can be clawed back by the Secretary of State (NHSCCA 1990: schedule 3, para. 6). These financial constraints are policed on an administrative basis by the regional outposts of the NHS Executive, which also control the amounts of money that Trusts may borrow. More formally the Audit Commission ensures that the rules are not breached. The implications for contracting are that, at least over all their contracts taken as a whole, Trust revenue must cover, but not exceed, costs.

A further aspect of the legal context is the bewildering array of bodies charged with overseeing the NHS. They include the Health Select Committee of the House of Commons, Community Health Councils, the Audit Commission, the Clinical Standards Advisory Group, the Health Advisory Service, and the Mental Health Act Commission. The influence of these quality control mechanisms is political rather than legal. The need to avoid adverse comment from official bodies is a significant practical constraint, and the quality control mechanisms provide an important feature of the contracting system.

Another powerful constraint on standards may be the governing bodies of the health professions. These groups have practical power and statutory responsibilities which may sometimes prevent NHS contractors doing what they wish. This may constitute anticompetitive behaviour (Miller 1992). However, it can also be seen as a mechanism for ensuring that clinical quality is not sacrificed. For example, the NHS relies heavily on staff in training, and it follows that many hospitals need to be accredited for training purposes if they are to be viable. For doctors, this accreditation is in the hands of the Royal Colleges, and it has been known for hospitals to be forced to close if accreditation has been withdrawn. Again, this operates to ensure that standards are maintained without the need for specific contractual terms.

The way that the bodies discussed in the last three paragraphs operate emphasizes that NHS contracts operate *within* the Health Service. This has implications for the behaviour of providers which in turn has implications for the design of contracts. Trusts are ultimately responsible to the same senior personnel as purchasers. The regional outposts of the NHS Executive can exercise control over behaviour by providers that is perceived to be contrary to the wider needs of the service, such as abuse of monopoly power or collusive behaviour amongst providers that reduces purchaser choice in defining the services to be provided (NHS Executive 1994). These, together with political and other pressures push NHS Trust managers in the direction of benevolence as defined above.

The framework for control of NHS Trust boards also indicates a concern with the conduct of Trusts. Such boards must have medical and nursing executive directors. Non-executive directors are appointed (and may be removed) by the Secretary of State, who carries overall responsibility for the NHS. This provides an incentive for them to establish a direction for their Trust which is in accordance with the needs of the NHS as a whole. This will usually, although not necessarily, mean accepting the responsibilities of purchasers for setting priorities. Finally, the Secretary of State may issue directions to NHS Trusts, and also retains the power to take over the management of NHS Trusts that are not acting in accordance with those directions (NHS Act 1977: s. 85). None of these factors guarantees that NHS Trusts will pursue the objectives of the purchasers, but they help to orientate them towards a recognition that they are part of the wider NHS.

Enforcement Issues

The National Health Service and Community Care Act 1990 is quite explicit in its rejection of the enforcement of NHS contracts as legal contracts: they 'shall not be regarded for any purpose as giving rise to contractual rights or liabilities' (NHSCCA 1990: s. 4(3)). While contracts between NHS purchasers and independent providers can be enforced by the courts, the intention is that disputes between NHS parties will be dealt with by a system of arbitration. This is expected to occur at two levels. The statute itself provides for a national arbitration scheme (NHSCCA 1990: s. 4(5); NHS Contracts (Dispute Resolution) Regulations 1996, Statutory Instrument 1996: no. 623). Internal NHS guidance advises that provision should also be made for informal arbitration (NHS Management Executive 1991).

It is not clear whether the primary function of arbitration is the enforcement of agreements, or whether it is the resolution of problems in the wider interests of the NHS. The statutory instrument that governs the official arbitrators is ambiguous. In addition to notifying the parties to the contract of the appointment of an arbitrator, the Secretary of State is to be told of the dispute, and invited to make representations (SI 1996: no. 623, reg. 3(1)). This suggests that the arbitration scheme assumes that the wider interests of the service need to be put before the arbitrator, and by implication that the views of the Secretary of State should be taken into account as well as the bargain struck by the parties.

It is impossible to be certain how the arbitrators would interpret their role, as the statutory level of arbitration has hardly been used (see Chapter 7). However, there are a number of reasons for thinking that they will focus on the enforcement of contracts. This is made explicit in relation to informal arbitration, where the guidance clearly indicates that the expectation is that agreements will be enforced: 'the presumption in determining a dispute is likely to be that the outcome will give effect to the agreement which was originally reached, rather than a new agreement which the parties should have reached' (NHS Management Executive 1991. para. 9).

In the one known example of statutory arbitration, from Wales, the terms of the contract were the focus of the process (Hughes *et al.* 1995). It should also be noted that the Regional Health Authorities, who are to represent the wider interests of the NHS, have been abolished with effect from 1 April 1996, and it is unclear whether their role in arbitration is to be continued.

It is probable that the reason for the ambiguity over the purpose of the statutory arbitration lies in the fact that it plays a dual role. One of the unusual features of the NHS quasi-market is that arbitration can be used in disputes during contractual negotiations, and can impose contracts even where the parties cannot reach an agreement (Harden and Longley 1995). In such circumstances, the role of the arbitrator cannot be to enforce a non-existent contract, but instead must be to determine what contract should be imposed. The need for consideration of the wider service issues in such disputes may be compelling. It is likely that the involvement of non-parties envisaged in the regulations is intended to apply to such pre-contractual disputes, not to the enforcement of concluded agreements. However, this has not been formally established. These ambiguities reduce the extent to which parties can be sure that the details of agreements they reach are enforceable through arbitration, and provide a reason for purchasers to use contracts that *induce* provision of what they want instead of explicitly requiring it.

One early commentator on the 1990 Act argued that it might be possible to evade the ban on legal enforcement through a number of strategies (Jacob 1991). Most importantly, he suggested that it might be possible to use the law to force a contracting partner to pay for services provided, without relying on the legal enforceability of the contract itself. Instead, the claim would be based on the idea that a party receiving the benefit of contractual services without payment would be 'unjustly enriched' at the expense of the provider. Technically speaking, such claims are 'restitutionary' not contractual, and are therefore not expressly excluded by the Act.

Whilst the conditions for a prima-facie claim for restitution will often be made out, on closer examination it seems likely that the courts would refuse to allow claims in this context (Barker 1993). This is primarily because courts are reluctant to allow restitutionary claims where the effect would be to undermine the policy (if not the letter) of a statute. In relation to NHS contracts, it seems clear that the intention of Parliament was to divert disputes away from the costly processes of litigation into a quicker and less expensive arbitration scheme. Further, the procedural complexities that would flow from allowing restitutionary claims to be brought alongside arbitration claims makes it highly unlikely that the former would be allowed. Whilst the arguments have not been tested in court, the difficulties confronting litigants are probably sufficient to deter attempts to invoke the law of restitution. There are, therefore, strong reasons for regarding NHS contracts as essentially unenforceable through the courts. Enforcement is expected to take place through the arbitration process. Although there is scope for dispute, it seems probable that this will usually result in parties being held to the bargain they have struck.

There may be some scope for contractual terms being indirectly 'enforced' by patients. They are not parties to the agreements, although they are intended to benefit from them. Providers can be sued for poor services that injure a patient (see Montgomery 1997). It is possible that breach of the terms of the NHS contract under which services have been commissioned could be a basis for such an action. If so, the negligence action can be used by patients to enforce contracts indirectly, and the risk of such litigation needs to be taken into account. Where contract terms provide precise specifications of the types of service to be provided, they may determine the standard of care required by the law, for two reasons. First, providers represent themselves as being able to attain those standards (Barker 1995). Secondly, because the standards of care required by law are fixed primarily by comparison with general levels of services, contract standards may serve to define which institutions should be used as comparators. This may thus drive the standard of care either up or down from what would have been the case in the absence of the contract (Montgomery 1997). These arguments could not be used to depress the standard of care below the minimum acceptable to health professionals (Newdick 1993), but they could affect the standards required.

The possibility of indirect contractual enforcement by patients provides an incentive for providers to resist the inclusion of precise quality standards in contracts. They will not wish to risk increased litigation, which would increase uncertainty over costs (particularly as NHS Trusts are not permitted to insure against litigation costs: see Montgomery 1997). Higher quality specifications would also increase transactions costs in relation to negotiation and monitoring. Thus, contract forms which do not primarily rely on enforceable specifications of service standards may be preferred.

MAIN FINDINGS: IMPLICATIONS FOR CONTRACT DESIGN

There are three main issues arising from the discussion above that are important for the design of contracts between NHS bodies. First, once a contract has been agreed, it seems likely that arbitrators will enforce it as long as they have the information to do so and it is not grossly unreasonable. Secondly, the structure of the NHS may induce behaviour of the type we have termed benevolent. And thirdly, in practice contracts are likely to be very imperfect in their specification of the quality standards of the services provided. A key contracting issue is thus to choose a contract form that provides an appropriate balance between maintaining those quality standards that, for whatever reason, are neither specified explicitly in the contract nor enforced by external bodies, and keeping the cost of those services at a reasonable level. We discuss below three mechanisms for maintaining such quality standards: cost reimbursement, patient demand, and provider benevolence.

Cost Reimbursement

One way of encouraging high quality is to reimburse providers for the full cost of supplying services. Cost reimbursement of this type has been used in traditional private health insurance in the USA and also in the provision of Medicare for the elderly until the reforms introduced around 1983. Such cost reimbursement, however, gives the provider no incentive to keep costs down and when, as is typically the case, it also allows a mark-up over costs to cover overheads, there is a strong incentive to increase quality in order to increase mark-up revenue. When not paying directly, patients have every reason to go along with this as long as the higher standards provide some benefit—they get a higher standard of treatment at no extra cost. It was the high cost of the high standard of care perceived to follow from this system that provided the impetus behind the Medicare reforms in the USA and the drive to provision of services by health maintenance organizations (HMOs) (see Weisbrod 1991).

The Medicare reforms of 1983 introduced the prospective payment system under which patients are classified according to a diagnosis-related group (DRG) and payment to providers is a fixed amount for each patient treated in each DRG. Crucially, that fixed amount is independent of the actual cost of treatment, except in a few cases with exceptionally high costs for that DRG. Thus, for most cases within a DRG, the payment system was changed from full cost reimbursement to no cost reimbursement. Absence of cost reimbursement has also been a feature of contracts used in the NHS. Cost-per-case contracts are fixed-price contracts like the Medicare prospective payment system. But even with simple block contracts and cost-and-volume contracts (with the amount paid per case explicitly related to the volume of work), the amount to be paid depends at most on the anticipated or actual volume of work and on the anticipated or average cost of treatment but not on the cost actually incurred by the provider in supplying treatment. Thus they also have no element of cost reimbursement.

Contracts with no cost reimbursement give providers a powerful incentive to keep costs down because any cost savings can be used for other patients, for purchasing new equipment (though with NHS Trusts it may need to be purchased in the current financial year to satisfy financial requirements), for rewarding owners in the case of private sector providers, or for providing a better working environment for employees. There is certainly evidence that the Medicare reforms in the USA altered the behaviour of providers. Studies of hospital costs reviewed in Ellis and McGuire (1993) indicate that, before the change, the average cost per hospital discharge increased at about 2 per cent per year. In the years immediately following the change, the cost per discharge declined by roughly 2 per cent per year. The change in incentive system may not have been the only reason for the change in costs but the evidence is at least suggestive that it had an impact in the direction theory predicts. The change seems to have altered other aspects of behaviour too (see Cutler 1995).

The concern with payment systems that have no cost reimbursement is that, just as they give providers an incentive to keep costs down, they also give providers an incentive to reduce standards of service in the interest of cutting costs. Thus, if standards are not enforced by full monitoring or some other mechanism, providers may cut standards of service below what the purchaser would like.

In between full cost reimbursement and pure prospective payment contracts are *cost-sharing* contracts that have a prospective-payment element and also partial reimbursement (at a rate of less than 100 per cent) of the actual costs incurred in treatment. Cost sharing has a valuable role in keeping costs down when the purchaser has only limited information about what costs will be (provided, of course, it is not too costly to monitor what costs in fact were, after the event). That may be because of genuine uncertainty about costs when, for example, the precise mix of patients who are expensive to treat and patients who are cheaper to treat (the *case-mix*) to be covered by a contract is not known in advance, though there are many other reasons why there may be uncertainty about costs. It may also be because the purchaser simply does not know how efficient a particular provider is. Cost sharing can be valuable in such situations for a number of reasons.

First, it allows the purchaser and the provider to share the risk that costs will turn out to be unexpectedly high. This can be especially important in contracts with NHS Trusts which are required to cover their costs and are not in a position to build up reserves or to borrow in order to meet such eventualities. Thus, if costs turn out to be higher than expected, an NHS Trust with a prospective payment contract may simply not have the financial resources to treat all the patients the purchaser would like. Secondly, a provider that turns out to have lower costs than the purchaser expects will make a financial surplus from that contract and this surplus may not be used in the way the purchaser would like. A contract with cost sharing ensures that the surplus to the provider will be smaller if costs are lower than the purchaser expects. It also, of course, reduces the incentive for the provider to keep costs down but, at the margin, it is worth relaxing that incentive a little in order to ensure, on average, less surplus to the provider (Laffont and Tirole (1993) have a detailed technical discussion of the precise form the contract should take under these circumstances).

Finally, if the costs of treating each patient individually can be audited without too great expense, cost reimbursement can be used to reduce the incentive for providers to lower quality for unusually expensive patients, to try to pass them on to another provider, or even (if they can) to refuse to treat them at all. This role for cost sharing is recognized in the Medicare prospective payment system, where hospitals can claim more than the fixed rate for exceptionally expensive patients and where some DRGs are related to the treatment the hospital actually uses for a given initial diagnosis (McClellan 1995). It is also recognized in the current system for setting the budgets for GP fundholders in the NHS where there is a limit (currently £6,000) on the amount fundholders are expected to meet from their own budget for any one patient in any year.

These examples indicate that cost sharing is, at least in some cases, a realistic possibility. It does not, however, overcome the basic dilemma that incentives to keep costs down are also incentives to reduce quality. In the case of a self-interested provider, the dilemma is particularly stark. If cost sharing is less than 100 per cent, a narrowly self-interested provider will always reduce quality to cut costs unless there is some mechanism to prevent that. On the other hand, if cost sharing is 100 per cent or more, the provider has no incentive at all to keep costs down. If quality standards are not fully specified in the contract (and there is no other mechanism to maintain them), a purchaser is thus faced with a stark choice. It can provide incentives for quality above the enforceable level with cost reimbursement of at least 100 per cent and abandon incentives to keep costs down. Or it can provide incentives to keep costs down with cost sharing of less than 100 per cent and abandon any attempt to achieve quality above the enforceable level. If it chooses the latter, the degree of cost sharing is optimally chosen to reflect the purchaser's limited information about what costs will be. Only in the extreme cases in which the purchaser has full information about costs or it is simply too expensive to monitor the actual costs incurred in treatment, is it optimal to have no cost sharing at all so that payment under the contract is purely prospective.

There may, however, be an incentive for even a self-interested provider to maintain quality standards above those specified in the contract if the number of patients coming to it for treatment (patient demand) is affected by the quality of service offered. This is one mechanism that can maintain quality. Another is the benevolence of providers. We discuss each of these in turn.

Patient Demand

If patients (or the GPs who refer them for treatment) are aware of the quality of service offered by a particular provider, the quality on offer may affect the number of patients referred to that provider. This is most apparent when there is a choice between providers, which is where the other main element of the recent NHS reforms, competition between providers, comes in. If providers have to compete with each other for patients who are not themselves paying, they have to do so by offering what the patients (or their GPs) regard as a better or a more convenient service. But, even without competition between providers, quality may affect patient demand. With some elective treatments, for example, some patients may choose not to undergo treatment if the quality on offer is not sufficiently high: the quality offered by a provider will then still affect demand.

When demand responds to quality, a fixed price (cost-per-case) contract can give even a self-interested provider an incentive to maintain quality because higher quality attracts more patients and more patients bring more revenue. Indeed, Ma (1994) shows that, under certain circumstances, the purchaser can achieve with a fixed price contract precisely the level of quality it would like to achieve, while retaining economically efficient incentives to keep costs under control. The more important of these circumstances for the present discussion are that there is only a single dimension to quality, that the cost of delivering any given quality is known to the purchaser, and that the purchaser does not mind paying more than necessary to the provider. The essential intuition for this result is as follows. Providers can attract more patients only by offering better services. The higher the fixed price per patient, the more valuable it is for a provider to attract patients and the more, therefore, it is worth the provider spending on quality in order to attract them. By adjusting the fixed price appropriately, the purchaser can thus induce providers to offer whatever standard of service it wants. With a fixed price contract, providers also have strong incentives to cut costs but only in so far as this does not adversely affect the quality of service.

But this setting is too simple to draw policy conclusions. One of the aims of our research has been to assess the extent to which such a mechanism will work in more realistic settings. In practice, purchasers do not want to spend more than they need on services, they may have limited information about the costs of providing a given quality of service, and there are many important dimensions to quality: quality of medical services, quality of nursing services, quality of hotel services, and so on. Chalkley and Malcomson (1995a) have shown that the first of these creates no essential problem for using the patient-demand mechanism to maintain quality. If the fixed price per patient required to maintain the desired quality yields too much reward to the provider, the purchaser can avoid that by simply deducting a lump sum (independent of the number of patients treated) from what it pays the provider (a two-part tariff in the technical terminology). Alternatively, the purchaser can use an equivalent cost and volume contract in which the price per patient depends on the number of patients treated. If the purchaser has limited information about costs, it will (for reasons discussed above) typically be optimal to add some cost sharing to the contract even at the expense of incentives to reduce costs. Neither of these affects the fundamental insight that, by manipulation of the price per patient, the purchaser can induce the provider to offer whatever quality of service it wants.

The many dimensions to quality may be more problematic. In Chalkley and Malcomson (1995a), it is shown that the patient-demand mechanism for maintaining quality standards will continue to work efficiently only if patients (with the advice of their GPs) perceive *every* aspect of the quality of service correctly and respond to all those aspects. Patient demand then keeps all aspects of quality in line even when patients do not themselves pay for the services they receive. This result emphasizes the importance of providing information about quality to patients, or at least to the GPs who guide their choices as to where to be treated. It also indicates the limitation of using this mechanism to ensure quality. As has been emphasized, certainly since the seminal article by Arrow (1963), health care is a service for which there are particular problems in ensuring that patients know as much as providers about the outcomes of the services they receive, problems that may not be entirely overcome by having a GP as an intermediary.

There are also other problems with relying on the patient-demand mechanism. First, it gives little incentive for hospitals that have long waiting lists for treatment to provide quality in order to attract yet more patients. Secondly, with payment based on numbers actually treated, a provider has an incentive to treat all those referred even where, on further examination, it turns out that the benefit is too small to warrant the cost. Thirdly, patient demand may not in practice respond to perceptions of quality. This is particularly true for non-elective treatments paid for by a purchaser that has a contract for that treatment with only one provider. Fourthly, some aspects of quality (experience, as opposed to search, aspects of quality in the technical terminology) can be assessed only while being treated. For many health services, an individual patient does not receive frequent treatment, so a patient's own demand is not affected by the quality received. The demand for services is then affected by quality only through the effects of reputation and only in the future, which may temper a provider's incentive to deliver those aspects of quality.

The first of these problems can be overcome by making part of the payment for each patient payable at the time a patient is added to the waiting list. By appropriate choice of payment, the purchaser can then provide exactly the same incentives for a hospital to provide quality as when there is no waiting list. (The rest of the payment is made only when the patient is actually treated and so still provides incentives for the hospital to reduce the waiting list by treating patients.) The second can be overcome by making the payment depend on the number of patients referred, as well as on the number actually treated. Then the provider still has an incentive to raise quality to attract patients even if they are not treated beyond the first consultation. Details of how to overcome both these problems are in Chalkley and Malcomson (1995a).

The third problem is most important where a health authority has a contract for treatment with only one provider. The fourth seems fundamental to any system of providing health services. It may be mitigated by GPs seeing patients after treatment and using the information gathered from this consultation to influence their decisions on where to refer other patients needing that treatment. But this mechanism may well not be perfect, especially if the purchaser is a health authority and not a GP fundholder. It can work only if the GP has a choice about where to refer patients or if the information is fed back to health authority purchasers who use it in making subsequent purchasing decisions. It is thus important to consider ways in which contracts can ensure high quality services when patient demand will not do so. Chalkley and Malcomson (1995*b*) explore what can be achieved with benevolent providers.

Provider Benevolence

At first sight, it might seem that there would be no contracting problems with fully benevolent providers even if the demand for their services does not respond to quality—given a budget to spend freely, they would choose to do what the purchaser would want them to do, so why not just give them the money and let them get on with it? But there is an important question of how much to give them. If they are given a fixed amount to treat patients with a particular diagnosis (a simple block contract) but the number of patients to be treated turns out to be larger (or the costs of treating them higher) than expected, the provider will not have enough money to treat them all. A hospital provider may then end up closing wards towards the end of the financial year (a familiar characteristic in UK hospitals in recent years) because it has run out of money to treat non-emergency patients as the result of treating a lot of patients earlier in the year. If, on the other hand, the provider is given enough money to treat the maximum number of patients to be treated under any circumstances at the maximum cost that might occur and the number of patients turns out to be fewer, or the cost lower, than the maximum, the purchaser will have used up funds that it might have preferred to use elsewhere. With a benevolent provider, a simple block contract will work well where the number of patients to be treated and the cost of treatment is known in advance—for example, routine non-emergency procedures for which capacity for treatments is limited and always fully utilized, and for which the costs are well known.

Where (as is obviously the case with emergency procedures) the number to be treated is not known in advance, ensuring that the provider has just enough money to treat the appropriate number of patients can be achieved only if the amount it receives depends on the number to be treated. It might seem that an appropriate form of contract would then be to pay the provider for each patient treated. However, even with a benevolent provider, such a contract can distort the provider's treatment decisions. The reason is rather subtle. Because a benevolent provider has the same objectives for its own patients as the purchaser, it will make the decisions that the health authority would want it to make about how to spend a *fixed* budget on them. But, if it receives a payment for *each* patient treated, it can increase its budget by treating more patients. If for any reason it would like to have more funds (to, for example, treat more non-emergency patients so as to reduce its waiting lists), it has an incentive to treat too many patients with a somewhat cheaper service in order that it can treat more patients in total. The detailed argument is given in Chalkley and Malcomson (1995*b*). One way to avoid this is to use a cost and volume contract that puts a limit on the number of patients for which payment will be made (a limit that may depend on the length of the waiting list). This discussion emphasizes the importance of putting a limit on the number of patients to be treated in non-emergency categories, even with a benevolent provider whose goals do not conflict with those of the purchaser.

We turn now to partially benevolent providers. Partial benevolence enables a purchaser to get better quality services without full monitoring than from a narrowly self-interested provider, even when demand does not respond to the quality provided. However, as explained in Chalkley and Malcomson (1995*b*), it will typically make sense for the purchaser to include some degree of cost sharing in the contract as long as the monitoring of actual costs is not itself too costly. The intuition is that having no cost sharing would provide the correct incentives to keep costs down but result in too low quality. At the margin, it is worth relaxing the incentive to keep costs down in order to achieve somewhat higher quality.

IMPLICATIONS FOR POLICY AND PRACTICE

The purpose of this research has been to investigate what forms of contract it is appropriate to use in contracting for health services in the NHS quasi-market. The basic principles that need to be borne in mind in choosing a form of contract have been explained briefly above and are discussed in more detail in papers that have come out of the research. There is also preliminary evidence in the pilot study of early NHS contracts reported in Chalkley *et al.* (1995) of significant correlations between the form of contract actually used and factors that the principles outlined above indicate should affect that form. Moreover, this is the case for the early contracts, which many commentators regard as reflecting little more than a continuation of arrangements that existed before contracting was introduced.

The most obvious message that comes across from the principles outlined above is that forms of contract need to be tailored to circumstances, how much patients (and the GPs who advise them) know about the quality of services provided, what type of condition is to be treated, what the objectives of the provider are, and how much is known about the costs of provision. It is simply not the case that, for example, fixed price (cost-per-case) contracts are to be preferred to other forms of contract in all circumstances. Unless the quasi-market has perfectly competitive providers, with free entry of additional providers with identical costs, the same quality of care can typically be obtained at lower cost with a cost-and-volume contract in which the price per patient depends on the number of patients treated.

Cost-and-volume contracts can work well when patient demand responds to quality, so that a provider has an incentive to maintain quality in order to attract patients. But even then, our research has identified a number of situations in which such contracts are problematic. The first is in contracting for a service that is used to capacity because the provider may then have no wish to attract more patients and so no reason to maintain high quality in order to do so. The second is when there are patients referred to a provider for whom treatment turns out, on further examination, to be inappropriate. In both these cases, the problems can be overcome if the contract can specify payments to providers for the number of patients *referred* to them, as well as for the number actually *treated* by them. Obviously, to do that, the number of referrals needs to be measured reasonably accurately and there may be problems with that. A third situation that is problematic is when patients (and the GPs who refer them) do not perceive correctly *all* the different dimensions of the quality of service offered by a provider. If they do not, providers may bias provision towards those aspects of quality that are most readily observable. This points to the rather natural conclusion that effort in monitoring quality is best focused on those dimensions that it is less easy for patients and GPs to observe. It provides an example of where theory can indicate that a contract is no substitute for collecting the relevant information.

It is not, however, enough for patients and GPs to observe the quality of service unless they can do something about it. Fundholding GPs may be in a position to switch referrals to another provider. Non-fundholders can only do so easily if the health authority for their area has negotiated contracts for treatment of each condition with more than one provider. In either case, there may be a problem for treatments provided only in main centres because patients may not be willing to travel the distance to the next centre. But it is important to remember that it is not necessary for *every* patient to be willing to switch providers for demand to be responsive to quality. As long as *some* (e.g. those living midway between centres) are willing to switch in response to quality differences, the demand faced by any one provider will respond to quality. Moreover, many large hospitals have more than one consultant in some specialties and referrals to the individual consultants may depend on the quality of service they individually provide. Hospitals can make use of this to ensure that the quality of consultant services is maintained.

It is important also to remember that the structure of the NHS may encourage what we have termed benevolence on the part of NHS Trust providers and that this can alleviate the problems of maintaining those aspects of quality of service that are not maintained by other means. In some circumstances, simple block contracts may be all that is required.

A robust conclusion is that, if a purchaser has only limited information about costs or case-mix, a cost-and-volume contract can be improved by the addition of some cost sharing, at least as long as the actual costs incurred in treatment are not too expensive to monitor. There are obvious reasons why purchasers with fixed budgets (and the Department of Health) may be concerned about using contracts with cost sharing because they cannot predict in advance what the payments will be. Moreover, they may be concerned that the actual costs incurred in treatment may be difficult to identify, so providers may be in a position to attribute to this treatment costs incurred elsewhere. However, even where costs themselves are difficult to monitor, there may be other indicators of cost (e.g. length of hospital stay) that can be used to achieve effective cost sharing. As long as cost reimbursement is less than 100 per cent, there is still an incentive for providers to keep costs down and, over all contracts and in the long run, the overall cost to purchasers of a given standard of service should be lower if contracts include cost sharing than if they do not.

Theoretical research of the type reported here obviously cannot prescribe exactly what contracts practitioners should use because details depend on specific circumstances, the particular treatments being contracted for, the costs of local providers, the extent to which demand responds to quality in their local area, and so on. Theory can, however, identify what general *forms* of contract are appropriate under what circumstances, thus giving practitioners a better starting-point for working out details than if they had to consider many possible forms that may turn out to be quite inappropriate. It can also identify what information might be worth collecting because it could be used to improve contracting, and what information is unlikely to do so.

The support of the Economic and Social Research Council (ESRC) is gratefully acknowledged. The work was part of the ESRC Contracts and Competition Research Programme and was funded by ESRC award no. L114251005.

7

SETTLING CONTRACT DISPUTES IN THE NATIONAL HEALTH SERVICE: FORMAL AND INFORMAL PATHWAYS

DAVID HUGHES, JEAN V. MCHALE, AND LESLEY GRIFFITHS

INTRODUCTION

The way social collectivities handle disputes can provide a revealing insight into the nature of the wider regulatory systems through which they achieve coordination and control. Collectivities of different types, standing in different relationships, characteristically favour different dispute resolution mechanisms. Disputes between enterprises in private markets are typically settled by negotiation between the parties themselves or, at the extreme, through litigation or arbitration. Disputes within administrative hierarchies may again be resolved by informal bargaining, but are also commonly dealt with through bureaucratic regulation—the top–down enforcement of rules via administrative processes and internal disciplinary procedures.

In the managed market of the NHS, the empirical importance of market, as opposed to administrative, processes remains uncertain. Dispute settlement may provide a revealing 'window' for examining the type of governance that is operating. On paper, the arrangements for resolving NHS contract disputes combine elements of both market and administrative approaches. There are limited parallels with commercial arbitration, but also potential for the exercise of power by the central departments. Much depends on how the arrangements set out in statutory instrument and guidance are applied. In this paper we review the legal framework governing NHS contracts and dispute-resolution procedures. We describe how in practice use of the formal procedures has been eschewed in favour of informal dispute-resolution processes, and discuss the role played by the centre in overseeing these processes.

The analysis reported here is based on a three-year study of contracts in the NHS in Wales. Three main data sources are used. First, unstructured interviews, focusing on dispute resolution, were carried out with respondents with special knowledge in this area, including Department of Health (DoH) and Welsh Office (WO) officials, and managers in purchaser and provider organizations.[1] Secondly, semi-structured interviews, relating to the 1994/5 contracting round, were completed with finance officers/contracts managers in all Welsh district health authorities (DHAs) and NHS Trusts then existing. Finally we draw on findings from an observational case study of relations between a Welsh health authority and its providers in the 1993–5 period.

CONCEPTUALIZING NHS CONTRACTS

The basic characteristics of the NHS reforms introduced as a result of the National Health Service and Community Care Act 1990 have been sketched out elsewhere in this volume. In essence the 1990 Act established a split between the purchasers and providers of health care, and created an 'internal market' in which DHAs and GP fundholders purchase health-care services from a range of competing providers, including NHS Trusts, the remaining 'directly-managed units' (DMUs), and private hospitals.

The bridge between providers and purchasers in the internal market was to be contract. However, it was immediately apparent that a number of contract forms would be involved, reflecting the different relationships existing between different categories of purchasers and providers. First, there were contracts between NHS purchasers and private providers which, just as before the reforms, were essentially conventional contracts enforceable in the courts of law. Secondly, there were service agreements between NHS parties standing in a direct management relationship such as a DHA and its DMUs. These were to be 'structured as contracts', but were essentially management tools enforced through ordinary management processes. Finally, section 4 of the 1990 Act made provision for a third contract form, the 'NHS contract'. This is an arrangement for the provision of goods or services between NHS purchasers and providers who are not in a direct management relationship, such as a DHA and an NHS Trust. As DMUs move to Trust status, these NHS contracts have become the predominant contract form.

The contract concept has considerable substantive importance as the key mechanism for structuring transactions in the internal market, but it also carries great symbolic significance. The NHS reforms represented the attempt to apply the 'contract culture' to the heart of the welfare state, with all the fundamental change that a shift in culture entails. The characteristics of NHS contracts have been discussed elsewhere (Hughes and Dingwall 1990; Hughes 1991: Miller 1992; Barker 1993; Allen 1995; Harden and Longley 1995), and we will not duplicate that discussion here. This paper considers how the original conceptualization of NHS contracts is reflected in the dispute-settlement procedures chosen, and how the subsequent use or non-use of these procedures sheds further light on the nature of these contracts.

The nature of the dispute resolution arrangements that were to apply was one of the most difficult issues in the policy debate that preceded legislation. In part, the problem could be traced back to a basic ambiguity in policy on contracting in the NHS. An official put the matter as follows:

In many ways the NHS contracts, so-called, bore as much resemblance to the cost centres in a very large organization, where one part of the organization having require- ments of another part of the organization agrees to pay money to it in return for its expertise and the money is passed across. And the whole thing is reconciled at the top of the organization once a year or intermediately during the year . . . At the same time they did have some of the features of real contracts, in so far as you would expect cost-centre approaches in big organizations not to need that detailed negotiation of specific terms of what was to be done for what money in the way of services. They were therefore hybrid between the two. But the important thing was that the bodies contracting were all part of one statutory organization surrounded in an envelope which is effectively the Secretary of State's statutory responsibilities to Parliament. Consequently they were not inde- pendent bodies. That I think as a statement is a particularly important thread that runs through a great deal of the analysis of how these contracts would work and the way in which dispute resolution was handled. . . . There's always a tension between the commercial idea of contracting and the cost-centre idea, to use my phrase. There was also a commitment that ministers needed to get a radical new idea hammered into the NHS as being a radical new idea. . . . There was a presentation need to signal very powerfully that this was going to be a new and much more competitive, much more challenging environment in which managers, both on the purchasing and providing side, have to demonstrate much more forcibly that there was going to be a good service and value for money to patients. And in some sense the use of words like trust and contract has a presentational force.

The tension set out here is important. On the one hand NHS contracts might be seen as a financial control and accounting mechanism for internal organiza- tional transactions: a way of arriving at more explicit, formalized agreements within what remained an integrated NHS, but there was also a thread of policy that looked towards the model of private business and, by implication, required contracts that were binding and formally enforceable. Comparisons with com- mercial contracts had presentational force in signalling the fundamental struc- tural and cultural changes required of managers and professionals.

Part of the difficulty lay in reconciling the market language with the prac- tical reform of a major public institution, whose form and functions were established in statute. A fundamental consideration was whether these con- tracts could be enforced in the courts in the same way as common law contracts. Our respondent recalls some of the arguments that entered the policy debate:

On the one hand judicial enforcement would give you a degree of certainty and it would give you an outside decision-maker—a judge—and that would by and large sharpen the minds of those drawing up contracts, and it would allow an independent decision as to what the meaning of those contracts was: the very reasons that one has a judicial system to enforce normal contracts between independent autonomous bodies. On the other hand it would have been in some sense artificial because these were movements of money within one statutory organization. It would have led to intense legal interpreta- tion—such as judges give—which would have generated heavy overheads in terms of barristers, heavy overheads in terms of legal bills within every new NHS Trust and health authority, for what could not be seen to be much practical result in terms of better management or better health care.

Apart from the costs issue, it was immediately apparent that judicial involvement would raise major constitutional and practical difficulties. Judicial intervention in NHS resource allocation might break the chain of accountability from Secretary of State to Parliament. An additional complication with the NHS internal market, arising from its 'imposed nature', was that many disputes were likely to arise from parties' inability to agree terms rather than from breach of contract. The resolution of such pre-contract disputes would be crucial to the effective working of the new system, but fell outside the ambit of traditional English contract law.[2] Policy-makers were clear from an early stage that a special NHS dispute-resolution procedure would be needed. Section 4(3) of the 1990 Act provided that NHS contracts should 'not be regarded for any purpose as giving rise to contractual rights or liabilities', and allows parties to refer disputes to the Secretary of State for determination.

NHS DISPUTE-RESOLUTION ARRANGEMENTS

The arbitration and conciliation regime created for the NHS had three elements: the 1990 Act makes provision for a statutory arbitration procedure, while arrangements for non-statutory, 'agreed arbitration' and for conciliation are set out in guidance. A system that encompassed both arbitration and conciliation allowed for the potential use of a wide spectrum of alternative dispute resolution (ADR) strategies, but also carried the risk of conceptual confusion at the implementation stage. Arbitration is applied widely in commercial contract disputes, particularly in the construction industry, shipping, and commodity markets. It is a form of third-party determination, that differs from conventional adjudication in that it depends for its force on the parties' agreement to be bound by the decision of the arbitrator. It cannot be imposed without consent, and generally derives from a contract between the parties, usually in the form of arbitration clauses that specify the procedures that will apply in the event of a dispute. Conciliation is located further away from the adjudication end of the spectrum, with the third party's role including advice-giving, help with communication, and involvement in joint decision-making.

The Statutory Arbitration Procedure

The 1990 Act provides for references of disputes to the Secretary of State at both the contract and pre-contract stages. Section 4(3) provides that *any* dispute arising from an NHS contract may be referred to the Secretary of State for determination. Section 4(4) extends the right of referral to disputes 'in the course of negotiations intending to lead to an . . . NHS contract', subject, however, to the requirement that the dispute arises out of the provider's position as the 'only practical provider' of services, or the unequal bargaining position of the parties. References under these sections may be determined by the Secretary of State alone or by nominees appointed by the Secretary in accordance with regulations (section 4(5)).

The powers vested in the Secretary of State are very extensive. Since the Secretary can specify terms to be included in a proposed contract and direct that it is proceeded with (section 4(6)), he or she can effectively impose a contract. With regard to concluded contracts, the Secretary of State may vary the terms of an arrangement to bring it to an end (section 4(7)). He or she has the power to impose directions (including directions regarding payments) needed to resolve the dispute (section 4(7)). This may involve directions to give effect to variation or termination, and these are to be treated as though they were the result of agreement between the parties themselves (section 4(8)). In contrast to the position in commercial arbitration, the determination is binding even in the absence of the prior agreement of the parties to be bound.

These arrangements for statutory arbitration are set out more fully in a statutory instrument laid down in April 1991.[3] A procedure is specified for the appointment of an adjudicator selected from a central panel,[4] and time limits are set for notifying parties that a reference has been made and for preparing written submissions. There is a requirement for the adjudicator to request written representations from the parties and the regional health authority (RHA) and Secretary of State, but no right to oral representations (e.g. a conventional hearing), though the adjudicator may 'invite' parties 'to appear before him'(*sic*), either together or (subject to mutual agreement) separately.[5]

Another important consideration is the statement in *Operational Principles* (DoH, 1989*b*) that determinations should take a pendulum form:

> The Secretary of State is minded to stipulate that the arbiter should be free to find for one party or another and not be able to compromise. This is known as pendulum arbitration and would impose the maximum pressure on both the parties to make sensible final offers to each other. (DoH 1989*b*: para. 5.6).

We explore below how far the pendulum principle may have affected attitudes towards use of statutory arbitration.

Agreed Arbitration

While statutory arbitration is binding on both parties even if it is initiated by only one of them, DoH guidance also describes a second category of arbitration that depends on prior agreement. The April 1991 guidance (still operative in England) states that NHS contracts

> should include clauses for agreed 'arbitration' if a party believes a contract has been broken. The parties to the contract may choose the arbitrator . . . and name them in the contract. They may also agree terms on which arbitration would take place.[6]

Although a similar statement appeared in the original WO guidance, revised guidance on disputes released in 1995[7] contains no reference to agreed arbitration.

When *Operational Principles* (DoH 1989*b*) was drafted, it was intended that arbitration clauses should feature in all NHS contracts, and that the decisions of the named 'arbiter' would be binding. Formal referrals to the Secretary of State would apply only to pre-contract disputes, where no arbitration clauses were in place. The position was subsequently modified so that parties who had agreed arbitration clauses, or entered contractually authorised arbitration, nevertheless retained the right of recourse to the formal dispute-resolution procedure.[8] An official offers some insight into the policy considerations behind this change.

There is only one NHS, and there are reasons of public policy why an independent arbitrator chosen by both parties to an NHS contract may not necessarily have the final say. And the Secretary of State, accountable to Parliament, may need to have the final say. In exactly the same way that the Secretary of State needs to have reserve powers to direct a Trust to do something if he feels that his duty to Parliament requires that the Trust do something.

Binding judgement by independent arbitrators might have fostered a system of decentralized, private arbitration that was in some ways analogous to arbitration in the commercial world. This path was blocked by the decision to allow a dissatisfied party what was effectively an appeal to the Secretary of State, and—as we shall see—agreed arbitration now plays a much less central role in dispute settlement than was originally envisaged.

Conciliation

Alongside statutory arbitration and agreed arbitration, guidance[9] sets out arrangements for conciliation. Where no contract is in force and thus no 'agreed arbitration system in place',[10] parties are expected to seek the assistance of their regional general manager as conciliator (or in Wales, the Director of NHS Wales who will nominate a conciliator) 'to obtain an impartial view of reasonable terms for a proposed contract'.[11] Participation in the conciliation process is mandatory, and both parties are required to agree to interim arrangements while the outcome is determined, so as to safeguard residents' access to services and the flow of resources. Where parties are still unable to agree—and as 'a last resort'—a reference may be made to the Secretary of State under section 4(4) of the 1990 Act, although for this to happen it must be argued that one party is taking advantage of an unfair bargaining position.

Within the spectrum of dispute-resolution processes, arbitration is most like adjudication. Both result in an imposed decision, binding on the parties, and both are commonly contrasted with conciliation and mediation, which are directed towards negotiation and compromise. The difference has sometimes been portrayed as one between authoritative interpretation and pragmatic settlement.[12] It seems clear that NHS statutory arbitration and agreed arbitration are both at the adjudication end of the spectrum. NHS conciliation is further towards the centre. It encourages compromise solutions, but differs from mediation in that the conciliator will give an opinion on the dispute (an 'impartial view' which is not binding).

THE SHIFT TO INFORMALITY: ENGLAND

By April 1991 a judgement appears to have been taken that the statutory arbitration procedure would function as a remedy of last resort. The statement in guidance that: 'The aim of all NHS bodies involved in the contractual process must be to reach agreement without recourse to the formal system for resolving disputes',[13] hardened into the message in informal communications within the NHS hierarchy that use of the formal procedure would be seen as a sign of bad management.

In England, informal dispute settlement at regional level has become the accepted pattern, and the centre appears to have had little direct involvement with individual disputes. Responsibility for contracting policy lies with the NHSE Purchasing Unit, but overseeing dispute resolution is only one of many tasks undertaken by the small number of officials working on contract issues. A source in the DoH Solicitors Department described NHS contracts as 'a dead letter legally speaking'. Requests for specialist legal advice have been restricted to a few enquiries regarding the possible applicability of EC directives on public service contracts (compare Harden 1992).

A recent survey by Harden and Longley (1995) on dispute settlement in fourteen RHAs reveals considerable diversity in local practice and terminology. The researchers anticipated that RHAs would use procedures that reflected the distinctions drawn in official guidance between the formal dispute-resolution procedure, agreed arbitration, and conciliation, and that regional arbitration would apply to concluded contracts, while conciliation would centre on pre-contractual disputes. Actually this was not the case, and all the procedures examined focused mainly or exclusively on pre-contract disputes. Four RHA referred to their own procedures as 'conciliation' and four as 'arbitration' (in two cases, 'compulsory' arbitration). Others used a two-part procedure of conciliation followed by arbitration. Those who regarded their own procedures as conciliation referred to the statutory procedure as arbitration.

Harden and Longley (1995) found that most RHAs sought to discourage use of both statutory and regional procedures. In the latter case, discouragement took a variety of forms, including specifying financial thresholds and requiring evidence of past attempts at grievance settlement. Where informal 'arbitration' was used, one RHA had adopted pendulum arbitration as a means of resolving disputes on the lines of the formal procedure. There was no consistent pattern as to who filled the role of conciliator/arbitrator, although representatives from the NHSME outposts were usually included.

Little firm information is available on how much use is made of regional arbitration as opposed to conciliation (as defined in guidance). Appleby (1994) states that 30 per cent of English DHAs and 20 per cent of providers surveyed were involved in arbitration in 1992/3, while Raftery *et al.* (1994) put the figure for DHAs at 36 per cent in 1993/4.[14] Our interviews with DoH sources indicate that, at the time of writing, no references to the Secretary of State under the formal dispute-resolution regulations had been made in England. It remains unclear whether the survey data refer to regional arbitration, agreed arbitration, or (given the different terms used by different regions) a mix of regional arbitration and conciliation.

CONTRACT DISPUTES IN WALES

Our data relate primarily to Wales. The Welsh Office (WO) position is complicated in that, for certain purposes, it functions as both a region and a department of state. In practice, however, the Welsh Office Health Department (WOHD) personnel dealing with conciliation or other informal dispute settlement would also arrange statutory arbitration.

Until 1994/5 WO followed a similar path to the English one. WOHD officials make a distinction between 'formal arbitration' (the statutory procedure) and conciliation via an appointed third party, but also themselves liaise informally between parties to encourage negotiated solutions and sometimes refer to this as informal 'conciliation'. Many potential disputes have been headed off simply by opening channels of communication between the parties, but it is also clear that pressure may be applied to encourage resolution of more intractable disputes. WO keep no statistics on numbers of disputes, but a senior source suggested that WOHD advise or instruct on 'three or four cases a month'. In our interviews with Welsh DHAs and Trusts, we were told of thirty-four contract disputes where WO had been involved in 1994/5.[15] Apart from contract disputes proper, WOHD also deals with disputes concerning extra-contractual referrals: informants report that over 300 of the latter were notified to WO in early 1994.

As far as we can determine, agreed arbitration has not been used in Wales in relation to NHS contracts. Our interviews with DHAs and trusts brought to light only one contract (for ambulance services) with a clause naming an arbitrator.[16] Almost all Welsh NHS contracts contain clauses, said to be based on a model contract circulated by WO in 1990/1, which state only that the parties will be entitled to have recourse to the agreed NHS processes of arbitration.[17]

By the end of the fieldwork in September 1995, we had located only five cases that had gone to conciliation and one to formal arbitration (none before 1994). The arbitration case—at the time of writing still the only example of use of the formal procedure in England and Wales—was decided in October 1994 and centred on a contract between a DHA and Trust signed under pressure against a time deadline imposed by WO. Full information on transfers of revenue from DHAs to new-wave GP fundholders is generally not available until well into the financial year. To circumvent this problem it was agreed that the final amount to be paid by the DHA to the Trust would be the sum specified in the contract less the value of the GPFH allocation. The Trust provided the DHA with data that it assumed would be used for this purpose. The DHA, however, agreed revised figures with the GPFH allocation. This change increased the GPFH's allocation and reduced the value of the DHA's contract with the Trust. The DHA, which was a 'capitation loser' under the recently revised NHS resource allocation system, was unwilling to inject additional revenue to correct a shortfall that now appeared in the Trust's budget, and claimed that it had followed the correct procedure for determining the GPFH allocation. Conciliation failed to get either side to move and the case went to arbitration. Interestingly WO (with the agreement of the parties) looked outside its preselected panel of senior NHS managers to nominate as adjudicator an academic with expert knowledge of the GP fundholder resource allocation mechanism. The adjudicator deemed that it was implicit that the contract between the DHA and Trust would be based on the data supplied by the Trust to be used in deriving the fundholder's allocation, unless the Trust was told otherwise by the DHA. The Trust claimed that the DHA did not inform the Trust of the change in the value of the allocation, and the DHA was able to present no evidence that it had informed the Trust. The adjudicator found for the Trust and (in accordance with the pendulum principle) required the HA to pay the contract sum claimed by the Trust.

The similarities to, and differences from, arbitration in the private sector are instructive. As with most private arbitration there were issues of principle, centring here on the interpretation of rules for GP fundholder adjustments and whether too much revenue had been transferred from the DHA's budget (and contract) to GP fundholders. However, the attention given to this internal NHS guidance may have moved the arbitration determination further from the terms of the contract than would have been likely in private arbitration. Arbitration was used to address both administrative concerns (clarifying WO guidance to smooth a major service transition) and quasi-legal principles (the contractual rights and obligations of the parties). The dispute was precipitated by the need to sign a contract to meet the centrally imposed NHS timetable, before essential financial information (provided by WO) was available, and this again highlights the difference from private sector contracting. The case is really only one step removed from the pre-contract dispute where parties who cannot agree price or activity, nevertheless find themselves constrained to enter a contract and seek third party assistance to find a way forward. In both cases the principle of contract as a freely entered bargain is violated.

The calculation of GP fundholder adjustments was a major issue in three of the conciliation cases mentioned above (one of which constituted the first stage of the arbitration case). The fourth case arose from a secondary provider's attempts to restructure costs and raise contract prices within the contract period, while the fifth related to a dispute over whether historical, base funding levels for ambulance services understated provider costs. This last case almost proceeded to statutory arbitration, with the dispute only finally settled in eleventh hour negotiations on the day before the scheduled hearing. In all cases the conciliators were senior NHS managers from other areas.

Before 1994, WO appears to have been reluctant to use the procedures laid out in official guidance, even though it intervened to deal with a small number of more intractable disputes. For example, one case that attracted national publicity and led to a major service review, involved a dispute between a DHA and one of Wales's flagship Trusts:

The nearest we've had to formal arbitration was a situation where the difference between the DHA and the Trust was pretty fundamental and the financial difference between them was very wide. . . . The Trust was and is in danger of a major shortfall. In the real world it would have gone bankrupt and the DHA claimed it simply did not have . . . the resources to pay these additional costs. There were endless complications to this, like the Trust argued that the HA was deliberately moving services out and it was having access to a lower proportion of the HA's expenditure as a whole. There were complaints coming in on a daily basis from both sides. . . .

Senior WO representatives met the parties and thrashed out an action plan, which, among other things, involved bringing in a neutral DGM to investigate the background to the dispute and injecting additional revenue. Here WO appears to have adopted a strategic management and financial control role, rather than the role of facilitation and neutral advice usually associated with conciliation.

The above events suggest that officials were willing to go to considerable lengths to avoid using the arbitration procedure described in guidance. Several respondents reported that messages had been passed down the line that recourse to arbitration would be perceived as poor management, and this picture is confirmed by contemporaneous research in England (Loveridge *et al.* 1994). Clearly such messages have a significant influence on senior managers subject to short-term contracts and annual performance review. Informants in the DoH and WO told us that disputes would not be allowed to get to the stage of a formal referral without approval from high-level officials. To date, only one dispute has progressed to statutory arbitration in England and Wales, and there are no indications that the flow of cases is set to increase. In the next section we explore some of the factors that may account for reluctance to use the formal procedure.

THE NON-USE OF STATUTORY ARBITRATION

One straightforward explanation is that the same considerations apply that lead to the emergence of alternative dispute resolution arrangements in many other contexts. When we interviewed senior civil servants in WO and the DoH, they recalled worries that a proliferation of arbitration cases would be a costly exercise, and suggested that informal compromises would generally bring more flexible and enduring solutions. Certainly, statutory arbitration is a relatively high-cost option for individual purchasers and providers.

One of the things I think, certainly just from a personal perspective on it, that would prevent me allowing a degeneration . . . follow up to arbitration is that the consequences of it must be much worse in practical terms than . . . It's not the threat of chastisement or whatever, it really is the practical problem . . . of how you then investigate an external body and present your case and argue your case and substantiate it and give evidence on it. It is not, it seems to me, something that an organization, already with a large agenda, wants to take on board, it creates a tremendous amount of work, I suspect. . . . And that's the last thing that heavily laden backs want is another bale of straw thrown on it. I think to some extent that is one of the fears. (DHA source)

The costs argument is less relevant to the central departments, since informal liaison may consume as many resources as would the referral of a dispute to an external arbitrator. For the centre, the chief advantages of informality are probably lower visibility and greater control. While informal negotiations can remain private, arbitration is likely to excite local media interest, and the arbitrator's determination is a public document.[18] The outcomes of arbitration may also be less predictable than those of negotiations in which senior managers are directly involved.

This last point brings us to another set of issues linked to the nature of NHS disputes and the action required to resolve them. Many of the more intractable disputes concern fundamental questions of resources and strategy that have wider implications than the terms of a single contract:

Where the disputes are more intense, they tend to be coming from outside the contracting process. But because the contracting process is at the end of the cascade if you like any deep tensions or issues that aren't resolved as you come through from your strategic plan and down—if they are not resolved before that will ultimately appear in the contracting process. So if you have an issue, for example, like contraction of psychiatric services that really needs to be resolved at a strategic plan level, if you haven't resolved it there, ultimately you come to contract. The provider will have huge fixed costs out of all proportion to level of service. The rules are you must hand on your costs in the present contracts, and the purchasers are saying: 'Oh come, come'. It's essentially not a contracting issue. It's essentially a strategic planning issue, that finds itself washed up in the contracting process. And you have similar problems across the board. So for example, you have one trust which was financially not necessarily on a very sound footing to start off with. It didn't get its act together and because it didn't, ultimately it was trying to pass on costs or recover income in contracts, which put its contract prices out of all comparison with everyone else. But the issue as I say washed up on the shore of contracting but was essentially about the sound management of the Trust. So what we find is because we're at the end of the line anything that's not resolved can find its way to us.

We have a similar situation in another part of Wales where another unit is [substantially] overspent. It's a DMU. Now that is being addressed jointly between the unit and the HA, not within the contracting round. And very properly so because the problems are not about reaching agreement. I think they've got a shared view about what they'd like to provide and what would be a sensible price to pay. It's just how do we manage the situation to make that possible. So there's a working together there. Welsh Office are involved in the same way. But they are much more central problems than the contracts.

Our WOHD informants state that most disputes are pre-contract disputes rather than disputes regarding concluded contracts. Failure to agree contract terms often arises because of long-term funding or strategy issues and, although pre-contract disputes are technically within the remit of statutory arbitration, it may not provide effective solutions. If a dispute is not about nuances of a decided contract, but arriving at an agreement against the background of deep-seated financial problems, arbitration has limited utility. The issue is not the authoritative interpretation of contract principles but the pragmatic settlement of complex problems.

The statutory arbitration procedure, incorporating a pendulum determination, is based on an adjudication rather than a settlement model. Our interviews suggest that the pendulum principle is itself a major disincentive to use of the statutory procedure, both for the central departments and parties to disputes. This issue was highlighted when a WO informant described the special arrangements made to resolve the dispute between the flagship trust and DHA mentioned earlier.

The politics of it were you could go to pendulum arbitration, but you couldn't live with a decision that would force a Trust out of business if it was almost a monopoly provider in part of Wales.

Respondents in both WO and the DoH suggested that the pendulum principle was a major factor in discouraging disputing parties from pushing for statutory arbitration. An English source presented the structure of incentives in the following terms:

as I say the clear line we have taken consistently in the last two years has been that if a dispute was to come to the centre . . . then we've always advised that we would work on the basis of a pendulum decision. . . . We're not suggesting that regions need to exercise a pendulum decision—but what it does mean is that both purchaser and provider have to think through very carefully before continuing an appeal to us because obviously we work on the basis there will be both a winner and a loser. We do not see ourselves as conciliation. And I think to a certain extent there has been a discipline in the service.

In our interviews with the parties to the ambulance contract dispute mentioned earlier, the risk of an all or nothing decision was cited as an important factor that encouraged a negotiated settlement on the eve of arbitration.

MATCHING DECISION PROCESSES WITH PROBLEMS

It can be seen that a number of the above factors interact to constitute a powerful disincentive to formal referral. The complex nature of disputes and the pendulum nature of the decision, when taken together, suggest that there may be a mismatch between dispute forms and dispute resolution mechanisms.

We can develop this line of thought by examining some parallels with the arguments developed by Lon Fuller (1978) on the limits of adjudication. According to Fuller, adjudication is a form of 'social ordering' characterized by the mode of participation that it gives to the affected parties: it allows the parties to participate by 'the presentation of proofs and reasoned arguments'. In Britain and the USA it is an adversarial procedure, and a 'process of conversion' operates whereby the parties' arguments and proofs are reduced to competing claims about rights or fault, on which the adjudicator must reach a principled judgement.

Fuller argues that one limitation of this decision-making procedure is that it does not cope well with 'polycentric problems'. The concept, borrowed from Michael Polanyi (1951), points to the complex nature of many real world problems which have multiple aspects, affect multiple parties, and involve 'interacting points of influence'. Fuller (1978: 395) uses the metaphor of the spider's web:

A pull on one strand will distribute tensions after a complicated pattern throughout the web as a whole. Doubling the original pull will in all likelihood, not simply double each of the resulting tensions but will rather create a different complicated pattern of tensions. This would certainly occur, for example, if the doubled pull, caused one or more of the weaker strands to snap. This is a 'polycentric' situation because it is many centred—each crossing of strands is a distinct centre for distributing tensions.

Among the examples of polycentric situations given by Fuller are problems of economic management and resource-allocation decisions. The difficulty that adjudicators face in these cases is that a dispute is rarely put to them in terms that allow them to deal with, or even comprehend, its multiple aspects and repercussions, and they are anyway limited as to the solutions they can impose. Generally, adjudicators are not able to exercise what Fuller calls 'affirmative direction'—the summoning and reordering of human and financial resources to solve problems—but must use conventional remedies such as damages.

Fuller argues that, instead of adjudication, the appropriate decision procedures to resolve polycentric disputes are management direction and contract, by which last term he means 'reciprocal adjustments' between parties such as those that occur when bargains are negotiated in markets.[19] Interestingly, one variant of contract is the 'political deal', where those concerned are called together in a hearing or conference and 'an accommodation of interests' is worked out. The Welsh flagship Trust case described earlier could be subsumed under this category.

Many of these arguments seem to us to have relevance to dispute resolution in the NHS. Pendulum arbitration is an adversarial procedure that fits Fuller's model of adjudication, and it is also true that many NHS contract disputes are, at base, disputes about resource allocation. There is the risk that, as in Fuller's examples, decisions might have unanticipated consequences. For example, to require that a service must be bought at the providers' specified price, is likely to affect the allocation of resources in other areas—perhaps the contingency fund for extra-contractual referrals. Fuller has been criticized for neglecting the potential of judicial expertise and investigation to get to grips with complex problems (Allison 1994). It might be argued that NHS adjudicators could take on an 'expert-investigation' role. They do have powers to invite evidence from a range of sources. However, irrespective of the information available, a decision that looks beyond the cases put by the two parties appears to be at odds with the pendulum rule—the adjudicator can only find for one side or the other. In any event, the adjudicator probably lacks the power to organize the affirmative direction necessary to deal with polycentric problems. In practice, as we have seen, the NHS tends to address complex problems through management processes or bilateral negotiation (Fuller's version of contract)—the two decision procedures that deal best with polycentric situations.

OVERVIEW

The preference for informal solutions can be regarded as a rational attempt to find dispute-resolution processes that will adequately manage the types of disputes emerging in the NHS. What needs to be emphasized, however, is that informal solutions in this context rarely equate with the bilateral negotiations characteristic of contract relations between private firms. Crucially, such negotiations are facilitated and enforced by an overseeing third party, which in the extreme can use hierarchical authority to ensure that matters are brought to a satisfactory conclusion.

What was said was about us being conciliators . . . but there is always the veiled threat: if you don't get your act together chaps we cannot afford to see a situation where either a Trust or a commissioning authority goes bankrupt. You know that we can't afford to see that happen and you know that ultimately action will be taken. Nothing was ever said formally in that meeting but the threat was conveyed. (WO source)

I think we always assumed that there would have to be an arbitration arrangement, on the principle that in some rare cases people would find themselves at loggerheads and that they would feel they had no option but to call upon this mechanism. At the same time, as well as that, managing by a form of regulation, there was also in the NHS a lot of managing needing to be done by managing. (DoH source)

Dispute settlement cannot be disentangled from ongoing administrative processes, bound up with the management of organizational change. Further evidence for this interpretation comes from the new Welsh guidance, which allows the Director of NHS Wales to arbitrate on behalf of the Secretary of State where the value of the dispute is £20,000 or less.[20]

The shift to informal processes leaves the statutory dispute-settlement procedure as something of an empty shell. Its existence may help to lend legitimacy to the NHS contract concept, since contracts are perceived to need an enforcement mechanism, but this symbolic force is likely to diminish over time with non-use. Of course, we may be looking at a transitional phase in an NHS internal market that is already evolving in other directions. A move towards privatization, whether through full-blown ownership transfer or a more gradual drift towards pluralism, would result in a change in the nature of contracts and the associated dispute-resolution arrangements. At the extreme, this would mean a move to legally binding contracts enforced in the courts. In a 'managed competition' environment with significant private sector involvement, there might still be a place for a special regime of regulation, possibly incorporating elements of the present system.

The gap between the formal language of dispute resolution through arbitration and conciliation, and the informal reality of negotiations conditioned by administrative processes, reflects tensions in the original conceptualization of contracts in the NHS. One of the costs of the 'presentational' appeal-to-the-market metaphor is that policy-makers are constrained to develop some analogue of the legal regulatory framework associated with private sector practice. The appearance of a market becomes more difficult to sustain as one moves away from core transactions to functions that are carried out in private markets by supporting institutions like the courts of law. The virtual non-use of quasi-legal remedies in the NHS internal market can therefore be seen as a revealing indication of the present limits of the market metaphor.

The authors would like to acknowledge support from the Economic and Social Research Council's Contracts and Competition programme, grant no. L114251102/101, for supporting this research.

NOTES

1. Nine respondents in senior positions were interviewed specifically in relation to dispute settlement, three on two occasions. We have not revealed identities and locations because of the sensitive nature of the data involved. In three cases telephone interviews were substituted for face-to-face interviews. These were recorded in note form; face-to-face interviews were tape recorded and fully transcribed.

2. There are circumstances where events that occurred before a formal contract is entered into are relevant to the adjudication of contract disputes (e.g. where a contract is voidable because of duress, misrepresentation, or mistake), but the law does not generally concern itself with the parties' inability to agree a bargain.

3. Statutory Instruments 1991, no. 725, National Health Service England and Wales, The National Health Service Contracts (Dispute Resolution) Regulations 1991.

4. English guidance (EL(91)56) indicates that the panel of adjudicators should be composed of NHS managers nominated by RHAs. Welsh guidance (D362E218: para. 7) specifies that it should comprise NHS managers nominated by district health authorities and family health services authorities.

5. The use above of the words 'arbitration' and 'adjudicators' reflects a shift in terminology that occurred after 1990. This leads Harden and Longley (1995) to refer to the statutory procedure as 'adjudication'. We prefer 'arbitration' since this is the term in current use in the NHS.

6. The passage is common to the English EL(91)11 and the Welsh equivalent DGM(91)39.

7. DAP40A under cover of DGM(95)7, published 20 January 1995.

8. Operating Contracts (DoH 1990: para. 4.33) states that 'the Secretary of State has decided that appeal to him should be permitted potentially in any case of dispute over the interpretation or performance of a concluded contract'.

9. In England, HO302: para. 7, under cover of EL(91)11; in Wales, D362E218: para. 8, under cover of DGM(91)39.

10. HO302, para. 7.

11. HO302: para. 7; D362E218: para. 7.

12. One of the concerns of critics of informal justice, such as Fiss (1984), is that an emphasis on compromise may undermine traditional judicial functions.

13. HO302: para. 2; D362E218: para. 2.

14. Both studies are surprisingly imprecise about the processes to which the figures refer, but it appears that they relate to informal regional arbitration (with the possibility, given the mixed pattern found by Harden and Longley (1995), that some conciliation cases were also counted). Our own information from senior NHSE sources is clear that, by September 1995, the formal NHS dispute-resolution procedure had not been used in England and all 'arbitration' to date had been carried out at regional level.

15. This may be an understatement since several of the contracts managers/finance officers involved said they would not necessarily be aware of all such communications, particularly at chief executive level.

16. In this instance, the Director of NHS Wales.

17. The contradiction here is that guidance in effect from 1991–5 (and which describes this procedure) states that contracts should name an arbitrator.

18. HO302: para. 15 and D362E208: para.15. The recent Welsh guidance DAP40A released under cover of DGM(95)7 contains no similar statement, and it is unclear whether this affects access to Welsh arbitration findings. In fact, the DHA and the Trust involved in the single case to date refused to provide us with a copy of the adjudicator's determination. In the interests of good fieldwork relations we have not taken this matter any further.

19. The use of the term 'contract' may cause some confusion in this context. In Fuller's framework, 'adjudication' includes the adjudication of contract disputes, and contract (as reciprocal bargaining) is an alternative decision procedure. There is no suggestion that contract adjudication is inherently flawed because of polycentricity, but certain risks do arise. 'The court gets into difficulty', says Fuller (1978: 404), 'not when it lays down rules about contracting, but when it attempts to write contracts'.

20. DGM(95)7: para. 16.

8

RHETORIC AND REALITY IN CONTRACTING: RESEARCH IN AND ON THE NATIONAL HEALTH SERVICE

PETER CHECKLAND

INTRODUCTION

The rhetoric of 'contracting' between 'purchasers' and 'providers' was strong when it was introduced into the NHS as part of government reforms. It was to be a feature of an 'internal market' that would lead to 'competition' which would drive up standards. From the start, the rhetoric was stronger than the reality. In view of the fact that the 'contracts' were not legally binding, the force of the notion of a 'contract' was considerably diminished. In fact the reality of contracting has been that the word is shorthand for a complex social process which has been evolving steadily since the reforms were introduced. Assuming the purchaser/provider split will remain, which is now rarely questioned in political debate, the contracting process seemed an attractive research topic for multidisciplinary investigation.[1]

At the start of this work, therefore, the research team consisted of experienced members from a number of disciplines. There was also a readiness to give coherence to the research by the use of a systems framework (soft systems methodology), and a belief that in order to get to the heart of the new contracting process it was necessary to carry out 'action research' in NHS locations as well as university-based research. How the systems framework was used and how the action research was carried out is described in the sections on research methods and activities below.

RESEARCH OBJECTIVES

The objectives of the research stemmed from how we pictured its context, namely the current situation in the NHS. Here we had a very large and complex organization (Europe's largest employer) undergoing a massive amount of change which was externally imposed rather than internally generated. This was far from being a static situation, and we needed objectives which both accepted the changing nature of the situation researched, as the NHS reforms unfolded, and matched the experience and expertise of the team.

Our focus was on the managing of the contractual relationship. Our prime objective was therefore to understand the nature of the relationship as it developed in the early experiences of contracting, with a view to defining how it could be improved. The second and third objectives followed from this: first, to examine the required information support to the contracting process between purchasers and providers, and secondly, to derive insight into the organizational learning which occurred as the NHS reforms were absorbed.

This work needed a well-defined methodological framework, which was to be provided by soft systems methodology (SSM). This led to a fourth objective, which was methodological: to capture learning by continually reflecting on the research and its methodological frameworks as it unfolded.

The first three objectives were tackled together in a research design which included in its central phase a number of research projects carried out on NHS sites. These each focused on a nationally-relevant local concern at the site in question (such as links with GPs at an acute hospital, or the evolving relationship between a purchasing authority and its main provider). They yielded findings which fed a rich account of the complex interactions between purchasers and providers. This relationship emerges in this research as one *marked by* the required annual agreements which are the 'contracts', but not *driven by* that requirement.

Ham (1992) refers to the 'gulf' between detailed work in health-care organizations and work on the role of the state in a national health service. Our aim was to cover more than one level of analysis by doing specific research projects at particular NHS sites and trying to make sense of them at a higher level relevant to the NHS as a whole. This point will be returned to in the final section. This research thus contains a number of pieces of research carried out *in* the NHS, all related to the first three objectives. Taken together, however, they constitute research *on* the NHS and its management, a claim which the later sections will seek to justify.

RESEARCH METHODS

The work followed a three-part design. Phase 1 consisted of extensive interviewing at twelve NHS locations in order to gather a wide range of perceptions of the contracting process as it was being initiated in the NHS. This work took place in 1992–3. Phase 2, carried out in the period 1993–5, consisted of a number of action research projects carried out with collaborating sites. Phase 3 consisted of gathering all the results together to draw general conclusions. This included the valuable addition (not originally intended) of repeating the phase 1 interview programme in order to capture the learning about the 'contracting' process which had taken place in the NHS. This phase also included starting dissemination of the research findings, which will continue throughout 1996.

The detailed activities will be described in the next section, but first it is necessary to introduce the methods by which the design was executed. The core of the methodology of this research, aimed at making the work a coherent whole, can be described as action research based upon an explicit framework of systems thinking. Both elements need brief explanation.

The most common model of research is still that it consists of hypothesis testing, within a methodological framework inherited from the natural or physical sciences. However, whereas natural scientists can assume that natural phenomena remain what they are independently of whether or not anyone is theorizing about them, human and social phenomena are more complex because of the human ability to perceive and interpret the social world autonomously. To try to cope with this, and to complement the kind of social research which produces broad statistical generalizations, 'action research' has been developed. This stems from Kurt Lewin's view of the limitations of trying to study complex social events in a laboratory environment. It involves entering the action process, so that the object of study becomes the change process itself (Blum 1955; Foster 1972; Susman and Evered 1978; Hult and Lennung 1980; Checkland 1991). This involves researchers giving up the pure 'observer' role and entering the problem situation to research *with* participants rather than simply *on* them. The aim is to find the changing structures of meaning which lead individuals and organizations to act in the ways they do in turbulent environments.

However, this poses a considerable problem for the researcher seeking objectivity. How can action research in (changing) human situations lead to findings which are more than anecdotal? How can action research be rigorous? To bring rigour to the work, to make it more than anecdotal, the position which has to be adopted is that in starting action research it is necessary (a) to declare in advance the framework of ideas (the epistemology) in terms of which what counts as knowledge will be expressed, and (b) to record carefully the process of sense-making (Checkland 1991). This makes the process recoverable. It enables an interested outsider to follow what has been done and to see how the conclusions arise. It makes possible coherent debate if there are differences of interpretation. This does not give the knowledge derived from action research the same status as that derived from the repeatable happenings in experiments in scientific laboratories. But that is the inevitable consequence of the fact that it is not based on natural science's assumption of an external reality unaffected by our thinking about it; it is part of the tradition which sees social reality as the product of a continually changing process of social construction (Berger and Luckmann 1971; Giddens 1979; Checkland 1981).

Here the declared methodological framework is that of soft systems thinking as embodied in soft systems methodology (SSM) (Checkland 1981; Checkland and Scholes 1990; Checkland and Poulter 1996, which describes uses of SSM in the NHS). SSM, used flexibly in this work, is a process of inquiry based on acceptance that human situations will continually change, and will be subject to multiple interpretations which ultimately drive action. It focuses on the fact that problematical situations will always contain people trying to act purposefully. It explores such situations by questioning them in an organized way. It uses, as a source of questions, models containing linked activities which constitute purposeful 'human activity systems'. These have to be built on the basis of relevant, declared world-views, since purposeful action will always be capable of multiple interpretations. This means that the models called 'human activity systems' are never thought of, axiomatically, as would-be descriptions of real-world purposeful action, which is always much more complex than such models. They are simply devices for enabling well-structured debate about a problem situation to take place.

Thus, in phase 1 of this research, interviews were semi-structured by a set of questions derived from a simple model of 'contracting' which reflected the researchers' interests. Then from the interview material was teased out the model of the contracting process implicit in what interviewees said. The difference between the models defined learning from phase 1. Phase 2 included twelve pieces of research, all but two of them carried out in the 'action research' mode. Ten of the twelve researches were based in NHS sites, the remainder drawing on a number of sites. Learning in phase 2 consisted both of study-specific findings and also of a model of the contracting process which reflected perceptions in the NHS after several years of experience of the developing purchaser-provider relationship. This was debated with NHS professionals and also 'tested' in further interviews with many of the phase 1 interviewees.

This approach to the research as a whole enabled twelve specific pieces of research, involving purchasers, providers, and GPs to contribute their insights to our overall understanding of the emergent pattern of purchasing/providing in the NHS. This pattern developed experientially over the first few years of contracting in a form much more complex than that implied in the language used about it when it was introduced.

RESEARCH ACTIVITIES AND RESULTS

Since we were researching a situation which was itself changing continuously as the NHS absorbed the consequences of the introduction of both contracting between purchasers and providers and the formation of Trusts, it is not possible to separate sharply the research activities from the research results. In using the methods described above, the learning emerged continuously, and itself helped to direct the next appropriate detailed research within the agreed broad structure. Activities and results are therefore taken together here, with the main results summarized in the next section.

The overall course of the research will be described throughout in relation to Figure 8.1, which is roughly chronological from [1]–[16]. Figures in square brackets refer to items in the diagram.

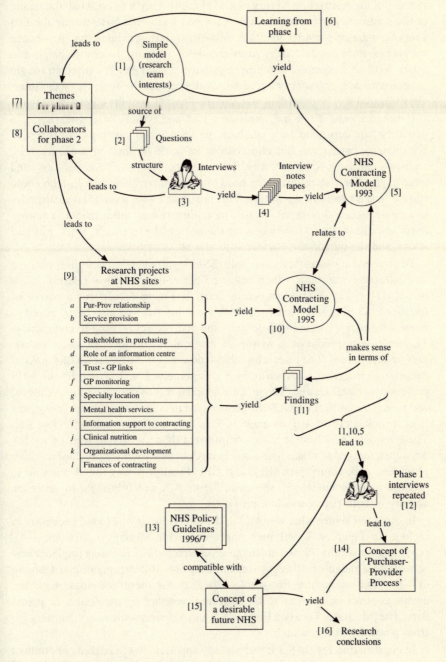

FIG. 8.1. The overall course of the research

Phase 1 Research

Phase 1 of the research, covering items [1] to [8], sought to establish the nature of the contracting process as it was perceived within the NHS during the first year of purchaser-provider contracts. More than sixty structured but open-ended interviews were conducted by team members, working usually in pairs, at a dozen NHS sites covering purchasers, providers, and GPs. The research sought general findings, not simply anecdotal evidence, and the analysis of the inter-view material will be described as a general illustration of the approach adopted.

It became clear from the interviews that perceptions of contracting at a particular site depended very much on the history and geography of that site. For example, managers and clinicians at an acute hospital in a conurbation, with two similar hospitals nearby, were very conscious of 'competitors', and were paying early attention to the need to attract referrals from GPs who could choose to refer patients elsewhere. This contrasted with more relaxed attitudes in a district general hospital situated more than twenty miles from the nearest hospitals. This was at a time when the rhetoric of 'the internal market' was still strong and the purchaser/provider split was still controversial.

To structure the interviews a simple (SSM-style) model of activities entailed in contracting was built which reflected the research team's interests. This model ([1] in Fig. 8.1), is shown in detail in Figure 8.2. It was a source of questions asked in interviews [3], with those interviewed also being asked to name what they expected to emerge as the main issues relating to contracting. The interviews produced a wealth of material in the form of interviewers' notes and tapes [4]. The research problem now was to extract from this mass of material an image of contracting as it was perceived at that time by the NHS professionals interviewed. The process adopted was to note the entities (nouns) and processes (verbs) which NHS people used in talking about contracting, and then to link these in activity models. One was built for each interview site. These models, which were more complicated than the simple starting model, were then merged to make four *generic* models: one each for purchasers, acute providers, community providers, and GPs. Finally, it was found possible to produce a single model [5], shown in Figure 8.3, which brought together the activity of both purchasers and providers.

In order to capture what was said in the interviews it was found necessary to include in Figure 8.3 activities concerned with: strategy (activities 1–4); providing capability (6, 7); developing contracts (8–13); managing relation-ships with a range of different stakeholders (14–16); organizational learning (17–19); and managing the whole (20–22). All these activities, together, enable contract obligations to be delivered, whether by purchasers or provi-ders. The difference between Figures 8.2 and 8.3 represents major learning [6] from phase 1 of the research.

In constructing Figure 8.3 it was already apparent that the details of contract type were not the main concern. The focus was on determining the local

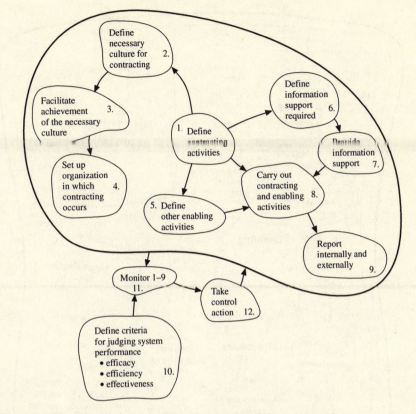

FIG. 8.2. The simple activity model used to structure phase 1 interviews

pattern of the provision of services, with different players (purchasers, provider trusts, GPs) placing emphasis on different activities in Figure 8.3 depending on their history and geography. The many questions and uncertainties which surfaced in interviews were often of a 'strategic' kind:

- coping with pressures from the centre;
- involving clinicians in resource-related decisions;
- shifting resources into community care;
- improving informational support at all levels;
- improving monitoring of performance;
- monitoring not only 'outputs' (e.g. the short-term result of an operation) but also 'outcomes' (e.g. the effect on quality of life);
- developing and managing relationships with a range of stakeholders.

Following this analysis, we sought and found NHS collaborators for action research in areas covering both strategy development and operational improvement (including such issues as information support, the marketing of services, and the impact of GP referral behaviour on contract management).

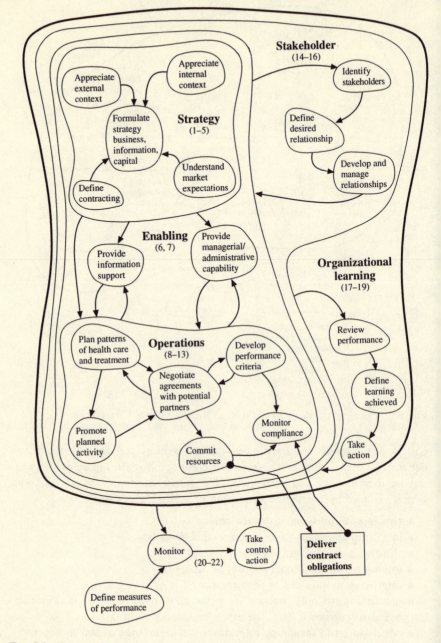

Fig. 8.3. The activity model of purchasing/providing extracted from the phase 1 interviews

In summary, the phase 1 work left us with a richer understanding of 'contracting' issues as they were perceived at the start of the separation of purchasing and providing, together with research collaborators ready to provide opportunities for specific research projects. Methodologically, the teasing out of activity models from discourse, as a means of condensing and structuring expressed perceptions, represented an innovative use of SSM which is potentially transferable to many situations in which qualitative research is conducted. At the start of phase 2 the team felt that the overarching framework of SSM had been successful in making the phase 1 work coherent, but the experience suggested that managing a set of projects based on a number of different intellectual perspectives in phase 2 would be a serious challenge.

Phase 2 Research

In phase 2, twelve pieces of research were carried out. Because of the potential difficulty of creating coherence out of several projects which overlapped in time or were carried out simultaneously (the problem alluded to above), one thrust of the research consisted of four action research projects conducted using SSM and following very directly from the phase 1 work. These are the projects [9a, b, c, d] in Figure 8.1.

This provided a useful anchor, and two of these pieces of work in particular [9a, b] were valuable in building directly upon the phase 1 insights. A purchasing authority and its main acute provider agreed that we should research their evolving relationship. This was done over two years, and entailed our attending a variety of meetings including those between purchasers and providers, receiving all relevant documents and conducting further interviews. This work illuminated the nature of the purchaser-provider relationship, revealing it to be far more complex than the simple rhetoric of 'contracts' implies, and it was illustrated in a detailed study of a contentious issue, the location within the purchaser's geographic boundary of a dermatology service [9b].

The nature of the developing purchaser-provider relationship was not well captured in the simple phrase 'negotiating contracts'. Rather, agreeing a contract was but one interaction among a set of purchaser-provider, purchaser-purchaser, and provider-provider interactions as the parties concerned wrestled with the problems of settling the pattern of the provision of care within the purchaser's geographical area. Contracts provided an annual snapshot of the outcome of agreements; they did not drive the process.

Our aim was to make sense of this and the other research experiences in the form of a model. To help in this, forty-seven previous models relevant to purchasers and providers from ten reports on SSM-based work in the NHS were analysed in order to establish what language had been found relevant to describing either purchasing or providing in earlier studies. This, and the specific teasing out of processes from the present experience, yielded a model

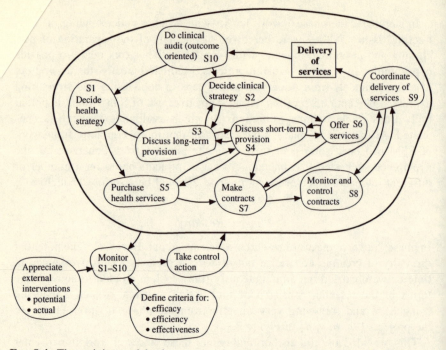

FIG. 8.4. The activity model relevant to real-world purchasing/providing in 1995

which is item [10] in Figure 8.1, the NHS contracting model 1995. This model is shown in Figure 8.4.

The status of this model is subtle: it is an activity model the operation of which in the real world *could* generate all the happenings which had been observed over the two-year period. It can be related to the phase 1 model of 1993 [5] but is more complex. It represents a set of processes which generate the pattern of service delivery. It can explain observable happenings in real NHS situations, such as the debate about possible relocation and reduction of a dermatology service in the area we were investigating [9*b*]. But to do this we have to note four features of the real-world manifestation of this model. First, the processes in the model are enacted not only between purchaser and provider but also between purchasers and purchasers and between providers and providers; furthermore, these dialogues are not all one-to-one; they may be one-to-many or many-to-many. Secondly, all interactions take place in the knowledge of other parallel dialogues, actual and potential. Thirdly, the overall set of processes, though affected by external interventions (such as NHS Executive directives) is not itself managed and controlled by anyone as a unitary whole. Finally, it is ongoing. Contracts mark specific outcomes of its processes but *they do not drive it*. It is driven by the ongoing momentum of providing health care under changing conditions of epidemiology, demography, resource availability, financing, medical knowledge, and medical practice.

TABLE **8.1.** The ten research projects carried out in the NHS

[9*c*]	Stakeholders in purchasing	[9*h*]	Mental health services
[9*d*]	Role of an information centre	[9*i*]	Information support to contracting
[9*e*]	Trust-GP links	[9*j*]	Clinical nutrition
[9*f*]	GP monitoring	[9*k*]	Organizational development
[9*g*]	Specialty location	[9*l*]	Finances of contracting

In parallel with the work just described, the ten other pieces of research referred to above were carried out, eight of them with collaborating NHS sites. The ten are listed in Table 8.1 and are described briefly in turn.

A purchasing authority formed from three DHAs requested a study of the problem of managing a complex network of multiple 'stakeholders' involved in contracting (such as GPs, local authorities, potential providers, other purchasers, and so on). Here, the multiplicity of relationships defeats an analytical approach, not least because an authority is represented by many different people on different occasions, depending on the circumstances of the interaction in question. Instead, a heuristic process was developed for the purchaser in which a perceived *issue* triggers an examination of the current and desired state of relationships with stakeholders relevant to that particular issue. This approach was tested using as an example the purchaser's need for an ongoing relationship with local GPs. People in the authority felt that they had worked hard on this; but the GPs felt they had 'no relationship' with the purchaser. This revealed that the GPs sought active involvement in the planning of services rather than simply information about what had been decided ([9*c*] in Fig. 8.1 and Table 8.1).

At an acute hospital in a large town the role of a just-completed 'integrated information centre', a project inherited from pre-reform days, was now problematical. Here the outcome was not a once-and-for-all answer to the question 'What should the role be?' but a defined *process* by which the management committee could continue to manage the new facility, as uses and the roles of users changed ([9*d*] in Fig. 8.1 and Table 8.1).

At a 'whole-district' Trust (acute and community) a study was made of the information links between the Trust and GPs who could refer patients to this or other nearby hospitals. Models of hospital-GP activity led to definition of required information support which could be compared with both existing provision and with GPs' aspirations. Following a presentation to the Trust Board of our findings, the chief executive himself visited each of the GP practices concerned, in order to cement and enrich the relationships with his Trust ([9*e*] in Fig. 8.1 and Table 8.1).

Links with GPs were also the focus of work in an acute hospital in a conurbation. The hospital felt it important to 'market' services to GPs, who could refer to three nearby hospitals. A personal-computer-based monitoring system was designed and implemented which incorporates data from the existing patient administration system for out-patients and in-patients in such a way that activity and cost can be linked to individual GPs. This system serves an embryonic marketing system being developed in the hospital (Hindle 1995; [9*f*] in Fig. 8.1 and Table 8.1).

In another piece of action research, a purchasing authority had made proposals to three relevant Trusts concerning the location of small specialties within their area. Our work was for one of the Trusts, which was anxious to examine the likely consequences of such 'service rationalization'. A patient-flow model was developed making use of information available to the Trust on existing patient flows, census data, and travel distances. This work questioned traditional definitions of 'specialty' in terms of medical expertise, trained staff, and facilities; the model stimulated discussion of what services other than out-patients could be provided away from the specialty centre. At a broader level this project illustrated how much of the information relevant to service planning by purchasers is generated and held by providers; it suggests that resource-efficient solutions will be achieved by purchasers and providers jointly analysing relevant data, enabling accommodations to be reached (if not necessarily agreements) on differing interpretations and judgements of relevance ([9*g*] in Fig. 8.1 and Table 8.1).

This message from project [9*g*] was also emphasized in research undertaken for a purchaser to assist their planning and purchasing of acute mental-health services. The work involved analysis and interpretation of available demographic and patient care data; it compared the relative needs of neighbourhoods and the provision of acute mental-health services to the same neighbourhoods using data collected by Trusts, and also investigated the implications of alternative ways of allocating intensive care beds using a queuing model. Again, this work suggested that the interpretive analysis of data needs to be done jointly by purchasers and providers if better use is to be made of the information needed for service planning and monitoring ([9*h*] in Fig. 8.1 and Table 8.1).

The purchaser-provider pair in projects [9*a*] and [9*b*] above were also the location of a study of the information support to contracting. It was hoped to deduce an implicit model of 'contracting' from examination of data exchanges over the first three years of contracting, but those exchanges were too incomplete for this to be possible. This was an area which both parties felt was 'improving', and there was evidence that this was so. Current data collection and processing was modelled, and a further model of the organizational processes involved was built. It was a significant finding that virtually all the attention given to information support had focused on contract monitoring, with little attention so far given to information support of the broader process of planning and delivering an agreed pattern of service provision ([9*i*] in Fig. 8.1 and Table 8.1).

The NHS has defined clinical nutrition as an area in which cost-effective practice can be achieved, and central funds are available for projects in this area. 'Business cases' have to be made to secure this funding; a project was carried out with an acute hospital provider and its main purchaser in order to help make such a case, taking into account service development and audit requirements. This work continues ([9*j*] in Fig. 8.1 and Table 8.1).

During the course of this research NHS organizations were turbulent: purchasing authorities forming themselves (often from several DHAs) and trying to define their detailed role, providers creating clinical directorate structures. Study of these changes revealed some commonality in internal arrangements. For example, many acute Trusts initially formed many directorates and later reduced these to a handful. External organizational relationships were more diverse, depending on both local history and geography. There was found to be some recognition of the need for explicit organizational development, if the new roles were to be enacted smoothly, but no clear picture of what form such projects might take. Initiatives taken in that area were ad hoc ones ([9*k*] in Fig. 8.1 and Table 8.1).

At the start of the work the form of contracts and their financial aspects were expected to be significant features of the contracting process. In fact they have not been found to occupy the central role imagined in the initial rhetoric of purchasing and providing. A study of contracts in the context of new patterns of governance in the NHS (Mumford 1996) examined how contracting parties were dealing with incomplete knowledge of key variables—service quality, quantity, costs, and prices. At the start, purchasers and providers with crude 'block' contracts expected to move fairly quickly to fuller specification of cost-and-volume and cost-per-case contracts. This expectation was found, typically, to have given way to modified block contracts extended informally on a rolling basis. Another study was initiated to examine alternative sources of capital for innovation, given NHS rules on borrowing, subsidies, and profits: can the Private Finance Initiative meet this need? Information is being gathered on successful PFI applications but very few have so far been agreed. This work will continue, as will a survey of whether access to six forms of innovative care/diagnosis is associated with competition or collaboration among acute providers ([9*l*] in Fig. 8.1).

This completes the brief account of the twelve specific researches carried out in phase 2 of this work, which constitute item [9] in Figure 8.1. As that figure indicates, phase 1 of the research gave us the 'Contracting Model 1993' (shown in Fig. 8.3); the research projects [9*a*] and [9*b*] yielded the initial version of the 'Contracting Model 1995' ([10] in Fig. 8.1). The other ten projects (eight of which involved action research in particular NHS sites) then served to confirm the relevance of the former model and to test the latter one. The question of whether a sense-making model like Figure 8.4 precedes or follows the research is a chicken-and-egg question. Such models are part of hermeneutic learning, in which an early version of the model helps structure research which then enriches (or changes) the model or our understanding of it. Thus as the end of phase 2 approached we had as research outcomes three

TABLE 8.2. Summarized findings from the repeated interviews

Health strategy	'Health of the Nation' gives targets but there is tension between a command structure and local action; outcome orientation is desirable but agreed definitions (e.g. of what is meant by 'day care', are lacking.
Clinical strategy	There are no easy mechanisms to change this; changes are reactive rather than proactive; difficulties are compounded by the needed reduction in junior doctors' hours.
Clinical audit	A strong national effort is needed, edging towards evidence-based medicine; could the purchaser role derive from this?
Provision of services, long term and short term	A zero-sum game; given uncertainties, a pattern of collaborations is emerging; innovation is very difficult; contracting is incremental not a mechanism for major change; of crucial importance (politically) is the notion 'my local hospital', also issues of access and equity; 'preserve what you've got' is a strong force.
Purchase services	The purchaser/provider split is sensible but information collection is made difficult—collaboration over more than a year is needed; purchasing is segmented, given FHGPs; again collaboration needed.
Offer services	There is acceptance of the need to 'make known services'; 'marketing' is a concept which has stuck, but it is hard for clinicians to think of respected colleagues elsewhere as 'competitors'.
Make contracts, monitor, and control them	Does not drive change; is not a source of change; it has not itself been a force for improving quality and performance, it concerns activity level and money; three-year agreements are emerging with annual contracts on 'one sheet of A4'; it can deflect from audit and an outcome orientation; data provision is improving.
Coordinate delivery of services	Smooth mechanisms are not worked out for coordination between providers, e.g. hospitals and local authorities; little evidence of concern for this; it is important, given need for links between purchasers and four groups: providers, local authorities, GPs, public.
Overall monitoring and control	Not manifest in coherent unitary overall processes, manifest in local arrangemetns with public issues important, e.g. waiting lists; purchasers, holding the funds, have to balance: 'Health of the Nation' targets/lean organization/avoidance of 'political' turmoil
Role of GPs in the above	A significant player with a complex role (increasingly both purchasers and providers) and far from settled; future of fundholding activity being worked out 'on the hoof'; GP activity can destabilize; patients are confused; there is more activity by groups of GPs; there is need for more focus on primary care.

TABLE 8.2. (continued)

Information systems	Quality and accuracy of data for contract monitoring is improving incrementally. But information support for the contracting process is still poor. Information required by GPs for purchasing is a new entity.
Organization development	A need to work on organization culture is recognized in some places but there is no shared concept of how to do it; some ad hoc projects have been mounted.

compatible things: the findings from the researches [9a–9l] and two models, one expressing the aspirations in the NHS in 1993, the other making sense of the reality in 1995.

As the shape of the research findings as a whole emerged—on a much broader canvas than the initial narrower concept of 'negotiating contracts' implied—the virtue of repeating some of the phase 1 interviewing became apparent. More than thirty interviews were repeated, at ten NHS locations, this time structured by both the 'Contracting Model 1995' ([10], Fig. 8.1), and our knowledge of the findings from the researches [9a]–[9l]. Several hundred points made in the interviews were recorded as annotations to a version of the model drawn on a (very large) piece of paper! The model served very well as a web to capture the concerns expressed, which could then be analysed to yield more general findings. (This annotated model is item [14] in Fig. 8.1.) Some of the more important of these findings are expressed here with great brevity in Table 8.2.

From the work as a whole we now had the findings from the twelve research projects (item [9] in Fig. 8.1), the enriched understanding of the purchaser-provider process ([14]) which came from both sets of interviews [3] and [12], and the two sense-making models, the NHS Contracting Models 1993 and 1995 ([5] and [10], respectively). These findings all suggested that NHS activity cannot be captured at all adequately in the words: 'a market driven by contract negotiation'; neither is the description 'a managed market characterized primarily by contract negotiation' adequate. On the other hand, the NHS certainly cannot be described as a command structure managed from the centre, even though pressure from the centre is felt, especially by Trust and authority chief executives. The reality is more complex than any of these simple nostrums.

DISCUSSION AND CONCLUSION

This final section summarizes all the results from this research and describes how the outcome of the work can be expressed in the form of a model which embodies aspirations for the NHS which are plausible in the light of present realities. This research set out to understand, in order to improve, the new process of contracting between purchasers and providers in the NHS. It sought to do that by working, mainly in an 'action-research' mode, on real problems in NHS organizations.

Flowing from the way the research was conducted, it has produced results of two kinds. From twelve specific pieces of research have come specific findings valuable in their own right. They were discovered at particular Trusts or purchasing authorities, but also have a broader relevance to the NHS as a whole. This broader relevance stems from two sources: from the guidance a good case history can provide (a frequent mechanism for the diffusion of good practice in the NHS) and from the fact that the projects were regarded not as isolated pieces of work but as tributaries to a single research effort which was held together by a framework of systems thinking. This strand of work (represented by [1]–[5], [10], and [12]–[15] in Fig. 8.1), has produced general findings relevant to the NHS as a whole but rooted in real-world experiences. Through it we have tried to work simultaneously at different levels, attempting in that way to bridge the 'gulf' which Ham (1992) noted between detailed and broad-level work in the NHS, and to which we refered in the first section above. This is why the research was not only *in* but *on* the NHS.

Specific findings from the twelve projects can be summarized in the following statements.

1. Given the context of ever-changing turbulence in the NHS, projects [9*a*] to [9*h*] all show the importance of seeking not simply here-and-now solutions to specific problems (which will rapidly become outdated) but solutions in the form of *processes* which will survive changing circumstances. Thus [9*d*] developed a process for managing the education centre in its new building at an acute hospital; [9*f*] demonstrated the process whereby PAS data can be analysed to monitor GP referrals as part of a 'marketing' process. Such processes are all relevant to different aspects of the processes encapsulated in the 'NHS contracting model 1995' shown in Figure 8.4.

2. The important but ambiguous role of GPs was a feature of much of the research, especially in projects [9*c*] to [9*f*]. Their role in the processes of Figure 8.4 is emerging fitfully. One generalization from this work is that attention needs to be paid to the communication and information links between GPs and both purchasers and providers. Projects [9*e*] and [9*f*] showed ways in which this could be done.

3. The NHS contains large amounts of data, especially on the uptake of services and on the relevant populations; but there are many problems in converting it into usable information. Whilst often possible, this conversion typically involves checking and further manipulation of the data, as projects [9*f*] to [9*j*] demonstrated. NHS organizations are often ill-equipped to carry out such work. Increased purchasing by GP fundholders and GP purchasing consortia will exacerbate this problem unless they receive specific support.

4. Information support for contract monitoring is improving (project [9*i*]) but there is much weaker support for the purchaser-provider interaction in general, as projects [9*a*] to [9*j*] indicated. Data held by providers needs joint interpretation by purchasers and providers.

5. There is some recognition that achieving the maximum possible value in services from a finite resource requires cultural change in NHS organizations, but little evidence that organization development projects as such are seen as meeting the requirement (project [9*k*]).

6. It was anticipated that contracts would become more detailed over time, with shifts to cost-per-case and cost-and-volume contracts, but this has been slow to happen as contracts *per se* have come to be perceived as having a more limited role than at first envisaged (project [9*l*]. (This has restricted work on contract finances.)

The more general findings are those which stem from viewing the research as a single project to understand and decide how to improve purchaser-provider interaction, not simply contracting. The experiences in this research make sense when seen as the outcome of a complex operation of the activity model in Figure 8.4. Looking only at the model itself, it is possible to imagine a smooth enactment of its activities. But the real world is not like that. Complexity in real situations stems from the fact that operation of the model has the following four characteristics. It is ongoing; conducted between multiple players (purchasers, providers, GPs, local authorities, users); at several levels; over different time scales. Not driven by negotiation of contracts, this iterative and imprecise process, looked at overall, generates somewhat erratic oscillations as attention settles on first one, then another current issue—such as waiting lists, junior doctor hours, the number of intensive care beds or particular local issues.

In the model it is easy to indicate an overall 'monitoring and control' function, as a concept. But in real life there is no such unitary function, even though some 'system regulator' is desirable in order to avoid chaos. In the NHS it would not be possible or desirable to introduce a command structure which did in fact 'monitor and control' the service in the sense of managing it from the centre. But it would be useful if a clearly articulated vision of a future desirable NHS, as a standard, norm, or yardstick, enabled any NHS organization or group to ascertain whether or not it was edging towards that vision in what it was doing.

In order to try to develop such a standard we brought together the enriched concept of the purchaser-provider process from this work and the NHS Executive's priorities as expressed in their document, *Priorities and Planning Guidance for the NHS: 1996/97*. From the latter document we extracted a model of the NHS which is implied within it. This model ([13] in Fig. 8.1) is shown in Figure 8.5.

In the model a purchaser works with providers, GPs, local authorities, and

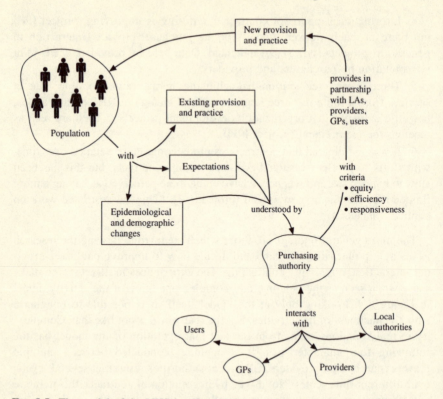

Fig. 8.5. The model of the NHS implied by the document, *Priorities and Planning Guidance for the NHS*: 1996/97

users of services to shift existing provision and practice to new provision which meets the criteria of equity, efficiency, and responsiveness. The future-NHS model from this research ([15] in Fig. 8.1) is more detailed than Figure 8.5 but is entirely compatible not only with it, but also with our enriched concept of purchaser-provider processes, and, indeed, with the language in which health professionals now commonly express aspirations for the service: such words and phrases as 'evidence-based health-care'; 'outcomes'; 'primary-care led'; 'health gain'; 'clinical audit'; 'user involvement', and so on. Our model is shown in Figure 8.6. It also shows a service which steadily edges existing provision and practice towards improved provision and practice through collaboration between purchasers, providers, GPs, local authorities, and users. In the current NHS, 'contracts' and 'contracting' play a part in the process depicted but are not its driver. What drives it is the motivated professionalism of those who work in health care.

The model in Figure 8.6 could be used to help those professionals to get the maximum 'health gain' from a finite set of resources. It could be used as an

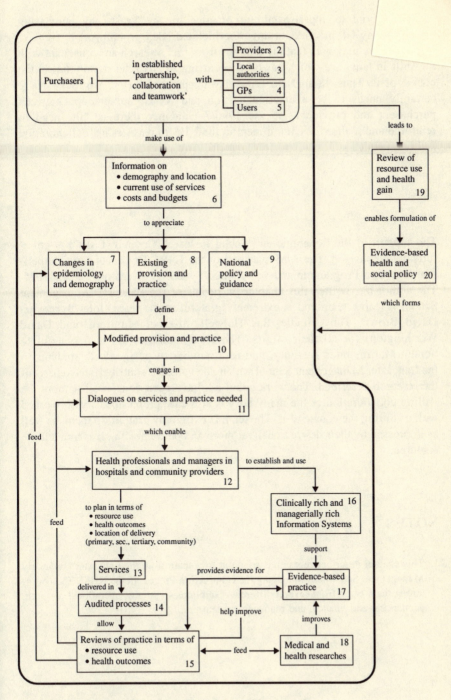

FIG. 8.6. A 'future NHS' model derived from this research

evaluative tool to appraise current practice in any Trust, any purchasing authority, any GP practice, or any other defined NHS grouping.

Finally, we may note that the findings from this research are consonant with the shift in language which has been occurring in NHS discussion during the course of it. Thus, in an NHS Executive document of 1993 we find: 'There certainly needs to be a creative tension and robust negotiations between purchasers and providers'; in the 1996/7 Guidance there is: 'the need to reinforce and realise the commitment in the NHS to partnership, collaboration and teamwork'.

The support of the Economic and Social Research Council (ESRC) is gratefully acknowledged. The work was part of the ESRC Contracts and Competition Research Programme and was funded by ESRC award no. L114251025. The author has written this chapter on behalf of the Lancaster Management School research team and is extremely grateful to the team (John Burgoyne, David Brown, Tony Hindle, Sue Holwell, Michael Mumford, and David Worthington) for all their efforts. The team members are also grateful to Sophia Martin, Janis Duxbury, and to a number of postgraduate students in the Lancaster Management School who made valuable contributions to parts of the research described. The work could not have been done at all without the willing collaboration of the many busy health-care professionals who worked with us during the course of it. The team is extremely grateful to them, as well as impressed by their desire to deliver more and better health care from a finite resource.

NOTES

1. This chapter describes research carried out by a team from the Lancaster University Management School on 'Managing the Contracting Process in the NHS'. The seven-strong team came from several different disciplines—systems, operational research, accounting and finance, and management learning.

9

THE EXPERIENCE OF CONTRACTING IN HEALTH CARE

PETER SPURGEON, PAULA SMITH, MARY STRAKER, NICHOLAS DEAKIN, NEIL THOMAS, AND KIERON WALSH

INTRODUCTION

This chapter is based on work undertaken by staff from three departments in the University of Birmingham—the Department of Social Policy and Social Work, the Institute of Local Government Studies, and the Health Services Management Centre. The project was a comparative study focusing on the impact of contracting on the management of services in three sectors: local government, health, and social care. This chapter will concentrate on the experiences of the health sector.

There were two main strands of work on the project. The first was the analysis of approximately 350 contracts including 118 first-round contracts for health care (i.e. those drawn up for 1991/2) and fifty-eight third-round contracts (i.e. those drawn up for 1993/4). The second involved case-study work in four sites per sector (i.e. twelve in total).

The first part of this chapter will present a framework for analysing contract documents—which has been used for analysis of health, social care, and, to a lesser extent, local government (CCT) contracts—supported by data on the health contracts to provide a flavour of the key characteristics of early contracts and, later in the paper, trends in contracts over time. The second part of the chapter will focus on the case studies and 'living with contracts', more broadly.

The Context of Contracting

The overall research strategy was based on a number of assumptions. First, contracts were seen as being not just a technical device or tool, but as needing to be set in the context of the ambitious political programme of reform in the public sector set in motion by successive Conservative administrations. Secondly, we hypothesized that the organizational changes we set out to study would have a number of features in common which could be explained in general terms through the application of what we described as the 'framing concepts'. The most significant of these, derived from principal-agent theory, are the pattern of interests and incentives created by contracts, the problems of risk and information, and, more generally, the relations of purchaser and provider.

The first assumption relates to the political context in which contracting takes place. There are different aspects of this, but one that has been particularly significant in shaping the contracts developed in the NHS is that contracts for health care cannot be enforced in the courts in the same way as common law contracts. This places a clear emphasis on the continued importance of internal and administrative processes in what has come to be known as the 'managed market'.

The notion of managed markets is not peculiar to health care and has also been used in relation to social care (Deakin 1994*a*). It is, therefore, a reflection of the belief that public services generally and health services specifically are different. For example Flynn, Pickard, and Williams (1995) argue that 'conventional assumptions about the economics of contracting and market relationships cannot be directly applied to community health services' (Flynn *et al.* 1995: 542).

The phrase was originally coined to reflect the tension between calls for the introduction of rigorous supply-side competition into the NHS, which, it was believed, would achieve the goal of efficiency; and the school of thought that excessive dependency on the market could threaten other goals, such as equity or quality (Appleby *et al.* 1994).

The concept reflects both contested organizational goals and directives and instructions to managers in the new environment as to how to achieve these goals. For example, competition was deliberately constrained by an initial emphasis on, in the jargon, 'steady state', or maintaining the status quo in the first year of the reforms, and also by restrictions on district health authority purchasers' ability to move contracts between providers and to alter the scope and content of existing contracts in subsequent years. More recently, there has been an emphasis on making purchasing more effective, developing more sophisticated contracts, and on the use of sanctions in contracts. At the same time, purchasers are being encouraged to develop 'health alliances' and collaborative relationships with providers (Walsh 1994), including moving to longer term contracts transcending the arbitrary year-on-year structure created by the vagaries of public sector financing.

Contractual Relationships

The second assumption applies more specifically to contract documents and contractual relationships and helps us identify which sorts of contract, and in which particular contexts, appear, on the face of it, to bring what sorts of benefits and problems, for which sorts of services.

Briefly, the role of contract in handling uncertainty is summarized by Gordon (1985: 565) who states that:

The purpose of contract is to make the future more tractable by developing both mechanisms for dealing with unforeseen events, and through establishing patterns of social relationships and communication that will be robust.

A key factor in the development of health-care contracts is that in the vast majority of cases they are purely internal documents. As one purchaser said:

They are not legal contracts because hospitals cannot sue each other. They have no legal force so the only real threat is that you can go to arbitration at the regional level. The region has made clear that they will see any need to refer to them for arbitration as evidence of failure to manage properly. We would have black marks against us if we did go. The purpose of contracts is really to act as statements of intent and to cut out any room for argy-bargy. (Purchasing officer—case-study site)

The lack of formality is apparent in the contract documents that have been produced. They are unlike those in local government and social care in two ways. First, they are not typically written in a strongly legalistic form. There is more use of everyday language than in other service areas, and contract conditions and service specifications tend to be different in form. Secondly, there tends to be less detail on key contract issues such as payment or variation, and issues of default are less likely to be dealt with.

The identities of purchasers and providers in health are reasonably clear, though, as in other cases, they can be identified at a number of levels. Specialist providers may provide to a large number of purchasers; alternatively there may be 'lead' purchasers for such services (Mullen 1994). Regions act as purchasers for certain specialties. The growth of general practitioner fund-holders is rapidly increasing the number of purchasers. Providers dealing with a large number of purchasers may face volatile funding. The NHS is also increasingly involved with social care in the process of purchasing and providing. Neither purchasers nor providers are totally free in the decisions that they make, given the strong governing control of the Department of Health.

Initially, contracts in health care operated on a block basis, that is, payment of a given charge for access to a range of services, with indicative volumes. The NHS Management Executive (NHSME) review of contracting for 1993/4 (NHSME 1993: para. 31) reports that: 'Almost all regions and outposts reported significant movement away from "simple block" contracts to more "sophisticated" contracts . . . Most contracts now have some form of trigger mechanisms or threshold with indicative activity levels'.

The various approaches that are possible involve different levels of uncertainty about the future, and, indeed, the past. As one purchasing manager said:

We started off with block contracts for most of the output because the output data for the preceding two years was sketchy and basically awful. You could have cost and volume for most of the output but the trouble would be getting the information, which would be difficult. (purchasing manager—case-study site)

Information is improving rapidly, though it is asymmetrically distributed, with providers having the detailed data necessary for monitoring.

Contract Outputs

Contracts are typically defined in terms of outputs, which partly reflects the difficulty of defining inputs and methods in highly specialist professional areas. It also reflects the purchasers' lack of knowledge. In this situation they must, necessarily, trust the providers, who are the ones with the detailed professional knowledge, to some degree. This is a clear example of the need for what Sako (1992: 10) calls 'competence trust'. There is concern to develop a closer knowledge of outputs:

We have always had the view that the way the contract is delivered is for the provider to decide, and you don't want a lot of detail. So, for example, you contract for a number of hip operations but do not say that the providers should have particular staff numbers or whatever. They are really output rather than outcome contracts. They are described in terms of FCEs [finished consultant episodes]. It's not the way it should be, but it's the best currency that's available. It's not really appropriate for purchasers to lay down how the work should be done. (purchasing manager—case-study site)

The output statements have mainly been workload specifications. Concern for more closely defined targets is increasing. As Stockford (1993: 7) says: 'Purchasers need to be more determined to target resources on clinically effective interventions'. The drive to evidence-based medicine continues and as information is more widely available so purchasing will develop more radical approaches to what and what is not. The influence of other targets, derived from, for example, the *Patient's Charter* and the *Health of the Nation* are being incorporated into contracts. These are likely to continue to be output based, but with outputs more clearly defined, with attempts to identify effective procedures, and some specification of method.

Risk-Bearing

The pattern of risk-bearing is strongly influenced by the form and content of the contract. Fundholding general practitioners are more likely to use cost-per-case contracts, which leave most of the risk with the provider. The distribution of risk in block contracts depends upon the accuracy of implicit assumptions about workload. In the various forms of cost-and-volume contract, threshold contracts, and so forth, risk varies with the way that triggers work and the way that payments vary with workload. In some cases, workloads may vary by up to 15 per cent before payment changes are made, in others small changes may trigger payment variations. These contracts involve risk-sharing, but the fact that reduction and increase are treated in the same way would suggest that they would be favoured more by the risk-neutral than the risk-averse, given psychological attitudes to risk. The distribution of risk is affected by the way that any deductions or additions are dealt with. This is normally done on the basis of marginal costs rather than full or average costs, which will generally tend to favour the provider, but there are examples of full cost of deduction.

The fact that most contracts are one year in duration makes the management of risk more difficult. Over- and under-performance in any period is more difficult to manage with short contracts, as the experience of hospitals completing their contract early in the year has shown. The Royal College of Surgeons found in a survey in 1993 that 44 per cent of surgical units had been told to reduce or stop some activity (Royal College of Surgeons 1994). This may well overstate the problem, but annual budget systems will tend to exacerbate it. The NHS Management Executive found that authorities were beginning to address this issue (NHSME 1993: para. 14).

The nature of financing makes such developments difficult, as Propper (1993*b*) has shown.

The way that these factors combine in the case of health makes it difficult to develop a stable form of contract that does not create disadvantage either for the purchaser or the provider. There is evidence that adjustments are made not so much by changing the formal nature of the relationship, as laid down in the contract, but rather in the actual process of management, through informal adjustment.

Variations

Variations in cost and activity may be dealt with jointly in contracts, or left to the provider. An example of the first approach is: 'Any additional costs to the provider resulting from major incidents will need to be the subject of joint discussion with the purchaser' (Contract document).

More commonly cost variations are seen as wholly the provider's problem:

The provider will be responsible for providing the agreed level of services at the agreed cost levels. The provider is expected to be responsible for any increase in costs or decrease in volume of service that occur as a result of but not restricted to:

   (i) pay awards not reflected in national agreements;
  (ii) changes in clinical practice not notified to the purchaser;
 (iii) failure to take action on cost improvements;
 (iv) local industrial relations and other disputes;
  (v) change in the cost of non-pay items of expenditure;
 (vi) change in the statutory obligations of the provider.

(Contract document)

New costs, more expensive equipment, errors and omissions cannot be compensated for by an increase in funds being made available. It is questionable whether such terms would be appropriate if the contracts were being made with private providers and were enforceable. Private providers would be likely strongly to resist such provisions.

Default

Default is not specifically addressed in the majority of NHS contracts. There are some instances of contracts referring to deduction of money for failure, and some purchasers, at least, are moving towards a more sanctions-based approach. The NHSME has encouraged the 'greater use of sanctions and incentives', though within the 'context of "shared risks"'. Sanctions operate most commonly for failure to produce full information or to produce information on time, and failure to meet relatively precise targets, such as waiting times. The emphasis on sanctions for providing inadequate information reflects the information weakness of the purchaser in the NHS.

The need to engender trust in health contracts is recognized by the NHSME (1993):

Concern has been expressed by some purchasers and providers that the use of sanctions may undermine the development of contracting relationships. A mature working relationship being based on collaboration rather than coercion. The NHSME has encouraged purchasers and providers to make greater use of sanctions and incentives—they need, however, to be agreed and undertook by both parties and explicit in contracts. Their use needs to be considered within the framework of 'shared risk'. (para. 75)

This implies the development of longer term contracts, but, as yet, contracts generally remain for one year. The sharing of risk is made more difficult by the large number of contracts with a range of providers. For example, in one hospital visited there were sixty-three contracts. As the Trust chief executive argued: 'Relations with purchasers vary. With some it's very collaborative. With others it is on a war footing, particularly with those who are likely to run out of money'. The nature of relationships depends, in large part, upon the relative power of purchasers and providers, and is likely to change as purchasers amalgamate.

Monitoring

Monitoring of contracts is difficult because of the information advantages of the provider. Even if they had the competence, the observation of any significant amount of work by purchasers would involve high costs. The vast majority of contracts, about 90 per cent, do make reference to quality and monitoring both through reports and inspection, and to checking against standards such as waiting times. Again, power distribution will influence monitoring, with large providers in a strong position:

There is an annual review by the purchaser that takes about three weeks. The purchaser team at this annual review will check on quality systems and look at each directorate's provision. They will look at levels of staffing and so forth. They will then come to see the chief executive and say what they would like to see improved. The hospital then says that will only be possible if there is more money because of the costs. Of course there is no money so nothing changes. Really it's the provider that does most of the measuring and monitoring of quality at the detailed level, with the purchaser doing very little. (provider manager—case-study site)

Over time, more informality of relationships is tending to develop, involving the resolution of differences and difficulties outside formal meetings. There is heavy reliance on self-monitoring by providers.

Views on health contracting vary. Research has found that managers in the NHS generally favour the introduction of the market (Appleby *et al.* 1992). Contracts are seen, though, as adding formality and complexity; one hospital manager felt 'generally extremely sceptical of the change in that all it had done was increase paperwork and complexity for very little gain'. In practice the actual written contracts used between 1991–4 have changed relatively little. The development of relationships tends to develop alongside the formal contracting system as much as through it.

A FRAMEWORK FOR ANALYSING CONTRACTS

The project team's original intention was to model the contracts formally (according to aspects such as the degree of specification and the emphasis on formality or informality), but it soon became apparent that our ambitions would have to be modified.

Contracting in health and social care was, on the whole, a new activity. In the case of health care there was very little guidance as to what the contracts should cover and what form they should take (certainly in comparison to local government (CCT) contracts). One fairly simple reflection of this is in the different organization of health and local government (CCT) contracts, with the latter comprising tender documents, conditions of contract, specifications, and bills of quantities and the former, at least in the early stages, neither using terms like contract conditions nor separating the different sections.

With the health contracts, our sample was selected from a database of contracts collected by the National Association of Health Authorities and Trusts (NAHAT) as part of a feasibility study into the setting up of a computerized contracts database. NAHAT wrote to all purchasers (including GP fundholders) in England and Wales requesting copies of all contracts. The response was varied: some purchasers did not return contracts; in other cases the contracts sent were incomplete (in the sense that quality specifications and other sections were missing). The contracts which constituted our sample were randomly selected only in the sense that they were scanned onto the computerized database in order of receipt by NAHAT from purchasers and according to the quality of the hard or disk copy. We also analysed all contracts sent by GP fundholders.

We therefore had to revise our original intentions. Instead of developing sophisticated quantitative data on the contracts, we produced tables using simple categories relating to key aspects of contracts (e.g. what they covered), supported by illustrations from the documents themselves (to show how these issues were dealt with). Broad judgements could be made about the extent to which, for example, risk was shared or borne more by the purchaser than the provider, or vice versa. These judgements were supported by qualitative data (a file of coded illustrations of the approach to risk and uncertainty; the emphasis on inputs and methods or outputs and outcomes) and were cross-checked by different members of the project team. The framework for analysing contracts (designed to facilitate comparison across the public sector) was based on three dimensions: focus, form, and content.

Contract Focus

The *contract-focus* dimension covers two issues: the extent to which contracts are narrowly or broadly focused in terms of the services to be delivered; and whether the primary emphasis in specification is on inputs and methods or outputs and outcomes.

The majority of contracts in our sample were broadly focused. That is to say, they covered most or all of the specialties offered by a provider unit, as the example below illustrates:

Services to be limited to the following specialties: anaesthetics; accident and emergency; burns; cardiology; children; dental; dermatology; ears, nose, and throat (ENT); general medicine; genito-urinary medicine; GP other; gynaecology; infectious diseases; maternity; neurology; neurosurgery; oncology; ophthalmology; orthopaedics; other medicine; other surgery; pathology; plastics; radiology; radiotherapy; rheumatology; urology.

Given this, one might expect these contracts to be enormous. In fact they vary in length from 1 to 119 sides, with an average length of 20 sides. This compares, for example, to a narrowly focused local government contract for refuse collection which could be three feet high!

Contracts for health care tend to specify the service very broadly, mainly focusing on activity (or outputs) and aims and objectives. For example where a single contract covers all the specialties offered by a provider unit, 'specification' of the service might simply constitute a list of these (as in the example) or, at the most, one or two pages for each specialty.

The extent to which the primary emphasis in specification is on inputs and methods or outputs suggests that the nature of the good is relevant to the contract focus (Smith and Thomas 1993). Distinctions may be made within public services between 'simple' services, like refuse collection and cleaning, which are relatively easy to specify, and 'complex' services such as health and social care (Walsh 1994). These distinctions may not be clear-cut as Flynn, Pickard, and Williams (1995) argue: 'The difficulties encountered in acute hospital services are exacerbated in contracting for community health services . . . Community health services may be more difficult to codify, enumerate and evaluate than clinical/medical treatments' (Flynn *et al.* 1995: 534).

Informational inequalities—the extent to which information is shared equally between parties to the contract—are also relevant. Weisbrod (1988) argued that under-informed consumers are not completely ignorant about a commodity, only about certain aspects or attributes which they find difficult to evaluate.

He identifies two kinds of attributes. Easily assessed or type-1 attributes, might include: waiting times; the information provided to patients (e.g. about visiting times and car parking); or qualifications to be held by staff. These tend to be specified precisely in the contracts. Type-2 attributes are those that are more costly to assess, such as: how appropriate an intervention is to a particular patient; how effective treatment will be; and the sensitivity of care. These are specified in much broader terms.

Contract Forms

The *contract-form* dimension reflects whether contracts are real or 'quasi'-contracts (i.e. health contracts cannot be enforced in the courts in the same way as common law contracts, but rather rely on internal administrative processes); their language and legal content, and the way that risk has been allocated, for example under a cost-based, volume-based or combined approach; and with a fixed or variable price. The majority of contracts for health care are block although in practice distinctions between block, cost per case, and cost and volume are somewhat blurred. Under block contracts, the provider carries the risk of unpredictable demand and uncertainty and the purchaser the risk, because of the lack of specificity in description of what is being bought, that existing patterns of provision will be retained.

However, within block contracts, levels of sophistication varied. The illustration below is of one extreme:

Block contracts . . . will cover all specialties offered by the individual units, except where there is a clear indication based on 1988/89 and 1989/90 activity information that certain services available within that unit have not been used in the past by residents [of the purchasing authority].

At the other end of the scale were more sophisticated, but rarer, forms of block contract which specified 'ceilings' and 'floors' on activity which, if reached, would act as triggers for the renegotiation of the contract.

In comparison to local government contracts, health contracts were relatively informal in terms of the language used, although there were examples of contracts where legalistic clauses had obviously been lifted from elsewhere and did not sit comfortably with the tone of the rest of the contract.

Contract Content

The contract-focus and contract-form dimensions relate to the contract function of regulating the exchange, of a given level of funding in return for a specified service. The contract-content dimension covers the function of contracts as regulating the relationship between purchasers and providers, through which the service is to be delivered. Key aspects of this relationship are: how the service is to be monitored; whether the specified service can be varied and if so how; how failure to achieve the required standards is to be dealt with; and how disputes are to be handled. Each of these will be considered in turn.

How is the Service to be Monitored?

It seems reasonable to assume that there will be a direct relationship between what is monitored and what is specified. The problem, as we have seen, is that health contracts specify very little. Within the early contracts, the intention was for standards to be agreed and developed during the contract term. The approach to ensuring a quality service, therefore, was to be incremental:

It is necessary that an incremental approach to quality of service is taken and it is expected that during 1990/91 the Authority will work with the Unit to determine and agree measures and indicators of quality in services which will be acceptable to the Authority and possible for the unit to achieve.

This may also have been a *pragmatic* approach given Kerrison's comments (1993) that the construction, production, and control of information about quality is dominated by clinicians. Obtaining information to define and monitor quality in contracts is dependent on: the extent to which yardsticks are available against which quality can be measured; the legitimacy of the standards or outcome measures chosen (i.e. are they acceptable to influential players); how easy it is to check that the standard has been achieved. All these issues must be negotiated with the medical profession.

In this example, although the specification of standards was to be developed during the contract term, the methods for monitoring the service had been sent out. The first thing to note was that the monitoring of quality was to be carried out by a provider unit's major or host purchaser, and often the quality standards applied would also be determined by this purchaser. To explain this, a health authority purchaser would normally purchase the bulk of health care for the residents living in the area for which it was responsible, from a provider unit (or units) situated within that defined area (or district). However, it might also supplement this by purchasing from provider units situated in other districts. GP fundholders constitute a further set of purchasers in the equation. Thus, contracts stipulated that:

Monitoring of quality aspects of care will be primarily undertaken by the DHA in whose district the unit is sited.

The quality of services provided to the practice and its patients will be to the standard of those provided to the unit's major purchaser.

The favoured mechanisms for collecting data on the service provided were inspection and formal monitoring reports. With the latter, there were potential issues of information asymmetry and opportunism, given that these were compiled by the provider. It is also necessary to be sceptical about how effective inspection would be, given the lack of development of standards.

Can the Specified Service be Varied and if so How?

Just as there was an emphasis on working together and pragmatism in the monitoring of the service, a similar approach was adopted for variation of contracts. On the whole, variations were to be mutually agreed, and this also applied to any cost implications arising from them.

During the period of the agreement, either party may propose a variation in the service, the contract price or workload. There will be no variations to the agreement except where discussed between purchaser and provider and mutually agreed and followed up in writing.

Flexibility in dealing with variation was built into health contracts, though this did not mean that the purchaser was willing to bear all the risk if the need for a variation arose:

An unforeseen cost increase . . . will have to be discussed between purchaser and provider, and options considered—these will include the possibility of increased efficiency and/or a reduction in service commitments. They may lead to a renegotiation of agreements. There should, however, be no automatic assumption that all increases in costs can be passed on directly. The purchaser will seek the opportunity to increase the workload or lower prices if inflation is below the anticipated figure.

The content of variation clauses, focused mainly on price and workload variations and far less commonly on the service specified (including quality).

How is Failure to Achieve the Required Standards to be Dealt With?

Contracts were less likely to contain provisions for dealing with failure than they were for varying or monitoring the contracts. Thus, 89 per cent referred explicitly to monitoring; 87 per cent referred to variation; and 58 per cent referred to failure conditions.

Also, although the term was used broadly, the detail tended to focus on failure to meet workload targets rather than failure to provide the actual service or to meet quality standards. For example, variance from planned activity levels was monitored on a monthly basis, but meetings to discuss failure to meet quality standards were held less frequently (e.g. on a quarterly or six-monthly basis). The nature of the good is again relevant here. For example, a missed bin, in a refuse collection contract, can be collected later in the day if the customer complains, whereas default cannot always be put right in health care and a potentially wide range of contributory factors mean it is not always easy to attribute blame.

Generally, the emphasis was on dealing with default on a case-by-case basis, with action to be taken negotiated:

The Provider shall give notice as soon as possible should it become apparent that it will not be possible to meet contract specifications in any significant respect . . . together the purchaser and provider will agree on a course of action, or if appropriate renegotiate that section of the contract.

Other contracts stated that the agreement was to be 'enforced through the ordinary management process'. Only a few set out specific procedures and these were mainly contracts where the purchaser was a GP fundholder, perhaps reflecting the greater physical and organizational distance between these pur-chasers and their providers.

Where one party considers that the other party has under-performed its contractual obligations, that party will instigate a meeting with the other within 2 weeks. Following the meeting, the party which has not performed adequately will be given 4 weeks to resolve the issue to the satisfaction of the other party. It is assumed that there will be joint discussion between both parties to reach a mutually acceptable outcome. Where non-performance has not been rectified within the agreed time-scale the other party will have the right of recourse of arbitration.

Failure incurred financial consequences in only 15 per cent of contracts but at this stage these mainly included the requirement for the provider to redo the work (assuming that this was possible) at no extra cost; or to meet the costs incurred by an alternative provider carrying out the work.

Termination was a further option for dealing with failure, although 19 per cent of contracts contained termination clauses (the majority of which were actually 'break' clauses where contracts could be terminated by either party, with notice). Thus for example:

The Agreement may be terminated: forthwith if either party should be formally dis-solved or cease operations; upon 6 months written notice by either party following a failure by the other to remedy a breach of the Agreement after rectification within one month has been required in writing; by a period of notice agreed mutually by the Purchaser and the Provider.

This contrasts with local government (CCT) contracts which usually contain lengthy sections on default in the contract conditions and operate a range of approaches dealing with failure including written warnings, fixed deductions per default, sliding-scale deductions, the use of default notices, and termination if a certain level of default notices is reached.

How are Disputes to be Dealt with?

This brief overview has stressed the considerable emphasis within the contracts—in terms of monitoring, variation, and failure—on mutual agreement, negotiation, and cooperation. Given this, the procedure for resolving disputes assumes vital importance, as Chapter 7 also shows.

Dispute resolution in the NHS is extremely complex with a number of procedures which can be followed. Under the formal procedure, disputes can be referred to the Secretary of State and determined by representatives from an appointed central panel. However, in practice, disputes are handled under an *informal* procedure, usually begun by regions. One possible explanation for this, suggested by our interview informants, is a perception that resorting to the formal arbitration procedure would be viewed as 'poor management'.

The adequacy of informal mechanisms is dependent on the ability of regions to determine disputes in an independent manner. Given the political visibility of the NHS, and the emphasis on managing the market, this is questionable.

Trends in Contracting

To ascertain any broad trends in contracting over time, a sample of fifty-eight contracts from the third round of contracting was subject to a less detailed analysis. The main findings, which are backed up by a recent survey on contracting (Appleby 1994), were as follows:

- Contracts were still extremely variable although generally more detailed and better organized.
- Contract forms were becoming more sophisticated and there was greater specificity about formats for and frequencies with which information was to be supplied. For example, rather than specifying total activity, volumes were increasingly given by *service* in a variety of contract currencies. There was also more extensive use of 'ceilings' and 'floors' on activity.
- More precision in pricing and costing facilitates greater specificity in contracting so contracts may be becoming more narrow in focus. However, the use of procedure-based costing and contracting for episodes of care, whether FCEs, HRGs, or whatever, represents a continuation of emphasis on outputs which is not, as Appleby (1994) points out, the same as contracting for health outcomes.
- Although there was not much overall change in content and specification was, on the whole, still limited, within contracts there was greater formality in terms of language and internal organization. For example, the

Patient's Charter initiative has provided a focus for the specification of quality and monitoring arrangements: targets relating to waiting times and information for patients were included. However, standards for clinical care were still very much the domain of clinicians.

- There was considerably greater use of sanctions but again, mainly in relation to things like waiting and the provision of management information, rather than clinical care. One purchaser was applying what was described as a 'quality bond', at a rate of £15,000 per month where management information was inadequate and at a rate of £45,000 per quarter in relation to performance on Charter standards and rights, especially cancellations and waiting times. Funds were to be 'available for redistribution to providers, who will be invited to put forward bids for quality improvements over and above the level specified through contracts'.

- There was greater use of guidelines on referral. In one example priority was to be given to emergencies, then clinically urgent cases, then long waiters, and then other elective admissions. Another contract specified 'purchaser exclusions from contract' or services that would not be funded (such as reversal of sterilization; fertility procedures; and complementary medicines).

- One other important aspect of greater formality (see above) related to the contract-letting process. Nearly 40 per cent of providers had already been involved in tendering and a further 20 per cent expected to be so in the next year.

So, to summarize, the changes introduced under the NHS and Community Care Act 1990—markets, contracts, new organizational forms such as NHS Trusts, purchasers, and providers—can be seen as part of a search for more efficient institutions for the delivery of socio-economic goals, in this case health care. However, the goals of the institution of the NHS are contested, as the paradox of the managed market illustrates, and its efficiency is constrained by informational inequalities.

Contracts—as the mechanisms for regulating the exchange of a specified service for a given level of funding, and the relationship between the parties to that exchange—are influenced by and in turn influence the environment in which they are produced. The confusion inherent in the mixed messages from the environment, and the conflicts between the extent to which there is a market and the extent to which the market is managed, is reproduced in the contracts.

On the one hand, NHS contracts are relatively complete in that they cover most of the key elements of the contractual relationship; they increasingly use formal, and in some cases, legalistic language; contract forms are gradually becoming more sophisticated in specifying cost and volume; and sanctions are increasingly penal in form. On the other hand, contract content emphasizes collaboration and mutual agreement; the service is specified in very broad terms; and disputes are resolved through internal administrative procedures rather than through any independent mechanisms.

The nature of contracts is also influenced by the nature of the good and the extent to which there are informational inequalities. We have argued that health care is a complex good. In coping with problems of information asymmetry, somewhat inevitably, the contracts focus on those aspects which are easier to specify; impose sanctions in relation to these areas; and ignore or postpone specification and monitoring of other aspects. The formal is increasingly driving out the informal, and consequently the interests served in contracting are those of managers and politicians who benefit from greater control of expenditure and activity and a more efficient service. However, if other organizational objectives, for example, quality or responsiveness to patients, are considered, the contracts are less explicit.

As we have seen, quality standards are on the whole broadly specified or not at all and although there are provisions for varying the contract and dealing with failure, the focus of these is on price and workload. Furthermore, over time there is more emphasis on access to health care or rationing—who is entitled to care and under what circumstances—and what we are now seeing is that people are explicitly being denied treatment on the NHS (e.g. because of their age or their lifestyle).

This has been a very brief attempt to summarize the main characteristics of contract documentation in the NHS, including developments over time, and to set these in a context, determinants of which include the political environment in which contracts are developed, the market context, and more general factors relating to the service, such as how easy it is to specify and the extent to which information about the service is equally available.

The next section of the chapter will consider the more dynamic aspects of contracting, based on observations from the case-study sites.

CASE-STUDY EXPERIENCE

Market Characteristics

One of the most consistent and remarkable impressions from all case-study sites was a sense of ambivalence about embracing market forces. This impression is not so much a reflection of ethical or value conflicts, nor is it seen in the rhetoric where there is great emphasis upon statements such as 'ensuring value for money' or 'planning contracts so as to maximize the utilization of public monies'. It is more to do with the practice of how to create and implement a market environment, and how to overcome the barriers of geography, local access, and the viability of provider organizations offering services with high levels of interdependence.

Some simple statistics about the nature of the contracts let by each purchaser illustrate the degree of effort and energy to move such a structure to a dynamic market situation. Site *A* places 90 per cent of its contracts with five main, local providers; site *B* spends 92 per cent of its budget on standard, routine secondary care in local hospitals; site *C* similarly spends half of its total budget with two local hospitals; and finally, site *D* allocates 95 per cent of its budget to four main providers. It is clear immediately that there is strong pressure towards inertia, as significant change to these buying patterns would result in major disruption and disturbance to local provision. Local 'political' forces, local opinion, and a desire on the part of purchasers to maintain a range of local provision make an attempt to engineer radical change extremely difficult.

Interestingly, in Site *A* (90 per cent local-provider contracts) the focus of what might be described as market-led change has been upon the remaining 10 per cent of the contracts. It is within these contracts that the conditions for market-oriented behaviour begin to come together. Each contract is relatively small, both in financial and activity terms, and therefore potential providers are both able to withstand the loss of such contracts and also have the capacity to encompass the additional work. Moreover the purchaser has no long-term loyalty to these less local providers. Thus one form of market that may have been said to have emerged is that of 'peripheral' markets. Although these may also be described as marginal in terms of finance, they offer an opportunity, especially where specialist or tertiary services are involved, for the purchaser to bargain forcefully for both practice and quality since alternative suppliers may well exist and they will not destabilize their own local providers.

It is possible to discern perhaps three other forms of market structure within the case-study sites. The first of these might be characterized as 'symbolic' markets and tends to be used by purchasers through mechanisms such as market testing, or tendering for services. Quite frequently, these mechanisms are used to prepare for major changes in the pattern of services. However, equally frequently they rarely produce dramatic movement of contracts. None the less, they do tend to serve notice of the purchasers' intention to examine services seriously and thereby encourage positive responses in provider organizations. Thus the action taken can produce useful change by symbolizing the process of market forces at work.

A further form of market force may be captured by the term rationalization. In a number of instances purchasers, particularly in large cities, recognize a need to reduce the total levels of over-provision. However, purchasers have largely felt unable to let market forces, unhampered, settle the problem. In part this is because the market process will not necessarily focus upon the specific issue required but may have other undesired consequences. Thus, the attempt has been to seek to rationalize services by either enjoining providers to sort it out between them or by moving, usually with intense resistance, contracts to a single provider.

Finally, the last form of market relates to the GP fundholder purchasing function, and might more accurately be described as 'deals'. Here either a single fundholder or multifund, perhaps dissatisfied with a specific service, simply agrees a deal, usually within year, for a fixed number of cases with an alternative provider. Although initially small-scale, such movements can lead to much broader levels of change, sometimes within the deserted provider who reacts by improving services or by other purchasers following the fundholder lead.

Market Relationships and Strategies

In all sites, virtually all provider units had attained self-governing Trust status. The timetable of this process obviously varied both across and within sites. The sooner Trust status became the norm, the sooner providers began to operate as independent units and the more 'hands off' the activities of purchasers. The evolutionary nature of the process of acquiring Trust status acted as an important inhibitor upon the establishment of the market. The existence of one or two main providers as directly managed units acted as a significant brake upon the purchasers' capacity to move contracts around. Manufacturing financial crises within units for which one is directly accountable is a strange, if not vaguely schizophrenic motivation. Thus, in many instances, historic patterns of service, and thus contracts, were preserved.

The advent of a largely Trust environment has enabled the purchasers to address the issue of rationalization of services. This process takes different forms in different locations but is driven by a number of common pressures. These include: changes in medical practice which dramatically reduce the length of stay and therefore the need for the existing number of hospital beds; the increasing influence of clinical-outcome studies suggesting the merits of concentrating resources on centres of excellence; and a requirement to alter the balance of service provision from the acute sector to primary care.

All case-study sites are committed to reviewing the pattern of services, and to the reconfiguration of services (and organizations) that will alter previously established patterns of patient referral and clinical activity. Despite this commitment, the process of implementation was rather less clear.

Even where purchaser-provider relationships were good the response of providers to proposals to rationalize services was on the whole defensive. On occasions this resistance was manifested through the mobilization of public displeasure at the projected closure of buildings or the loss of local service provision. The tension surrounding this process was exacerbated in those sites where purchasers were in a 'no-growth' situation and thus unable to release resources for alternative, compensatory activities. In such circumstances, there was pressure to reduce the capital estates and to release the money obtained to support developments.

It was apparent that in at least three out of the four case-study sites the issue of rationalization of capacity was subject to both national and regional influences. This highlights not only the high profile and sensitivity of the health service but also the degree to which the market, as far as it exists at all, is managed. For example, in order that proposals can be implemented to move towards centres of excellence for services such as trauma or paediatrics, there must be an overriding regional perspective on the appropriate size and location of such centres. In this setting individual purchasers lose some degree of control, or at best become agents of a regional plan or process of managed competition aimed at producing a predetermined outcome. It will be interesting to see how the new 'civil-service' regional offices operate in this context. Larger purchasing organizations may be able to make some radical decisions about the shape of provider units.

At a more specific level, purchasers are able to focus upon bringing down costs or improving standards of service in their immediate environment. One of the key strategies used to create immediate changes in the pattern of contracts is that of competitive tendering. The attraction of the approach is speed. Official Department of Health guidelines require that providers are given six-months notice of intention to shift services. This is not required for a service put out to tender.

CONCLUSION

Overall it is clear that there is limited development of a market in health. The rhetoric and intention is strong, but so too are the constraints. Perhaps the most powerful countervailing influence to market principles is the requirement, reinforced by local views, to maintain locally accessible services. This is in part a political issue with few purchasers willing to risk the political and public fall-out of threatening local providers. Similarly, the difficulty of market capacity and the limitations upon organizations moving in and out of the market has not been solved. The market in health appears then to be a source of marginal movement, with other national forces, both political and clinical, being responsible for rather more significant changes in the overall pattern of health-care provision.

The support of the Economic and Social Research Council (Contracts and Competition Programme: project no. L114251007) is gratefully acknowledged.

10

HEALTH-CARE CONTRACTING AND SOCIAL SCIENCE: ISSUES IN THEORY AND PRACTICE

GARETH WILLIAMS AND ROB FLYNN

In this book we have collected together work by a number of researchers from a range of disciplinary backgrounds who, with support from the ESRC Contracts and Competition Programme, have examined and explored different facets of the NHS internal market. Alongside this predominant focus on the health service, in the contributions from Lapsley and Llewellyn (Chapter 5) and Broadbent and Laughlin (Chapter 3), complementary topics are explored: contracting decisions in social work departments in Scotland, and the effects of local management of schools in England. Rather than diluting the health content of the book, these additions seem to us to provide contrapuntal evidence which highlights the *generic* character of some of the *issues* emerging in research on the development of managed markets in the public sector. We hope that this collection of research studies will be of interest beyond the world of academic research, and will help inform those working in policy and practice in the health service and other parts of the public sector.

One of the major themes emerging from a number of the contributions here is that contracting, in and of itself, is not the solution to problems of public sector organization and management, but rather the stimulus to new questions for both theorists and practitioners. At the start of the NHS reforms, contracts were regarded as the mechanism through which services were to be secured by purchasers from a range of potential providers lined up on the supply side of the internal market. Contracts, it was argued, would provide the leverage for purchasers to insist on more responsive and efficient services from both hospital and community providers.

The extent to which this has happened, and the variables which intervene between the *de facto* existence of a quasi-market and the outcomes of services in terms of price and quality is explored in some detail in the contribution from Propper and Bartlett (Chapter 2). In the context of the regulatory framework defined by the Trust financial regime, they develop an empirical analysis of the extent to which market forces have an observable impact on the pricing behaviour of Trusts. Their conclusion is that prices are not wholly regulated, and that market forces exert some influence, which will vary with the elasticity embedded in the demands of GP fundholders on the one hand and DHAs on the other. They indicate that the impact of competition varies between market segments and clinical specialties, and further case study analysis leads them to conclude that various dimensions of management structure and style—such as the mix of managerial and clinician control—intervene between competition and pricing.

This important examination of the operation of the health-care market-place raises questions about the nature of the agreement represented by health service contracts. What are these contracts which bind purchasers and providers, in the short term, within the quasi-market? This question is explored in different ways by Barker and Hughes and their colleagues in Chapters 6 and 7. Drawing on the disciplines of economic theory and law, Barker *et al*. point out in opening their analysis that the issue cannot be resolved by specifying the total contents of a contract, because it will never be possible to describe all those elements of a 'standard of service' in a way that is enforceable. In other words, forms of contract need to be tailored to circumstances: cost-per-case, cost and volume, and block contracts may all be appropriate in different situations; and this will partly depend on the degree to which 'provider benevolence' provides the foundation for a coalescence of purchaser-provider interests.

However, there will inevitably be circumstances of dispute in which conflicts between purchasers and providers require resolution through some formal mechanism. Hughes and his colleagues show how formal arbitration procedures for the resolution of disputes between purchasers and providers have been used only with the greatest reluctance in the NHS. There are many reasons for this, but one of the most important is the way in which disputes within the NHS internal market are bound up with other managerial, administrative, and resource issues. In other words, contracting within the internal market in the NHS can never be a pure economic or legal issue. It is one element in the political structures which shape the NHS. It is against this background that Hughes and his colleagues describe the more typical, informal reality of negotiation as the preferred strategy of dispute resolution (a point reiterated by Spurgeon and his colleagues), and one which indicates the present limits of the market metaphor in the NHS.

The limits of the market, and the tension between the language and politics of contracting and the quasi-market on the one hand, and, on the other, the nature of the activities in which those working in the health service see themselves as engaged, are themes which emerge particularly strongly in the chapter by Broadbent and Laughlin, comparing contractual changes in schools and GP practices, and in those by Flynn and his colleagues, and Lapsley and Llewellyn, in their examinations of contracting for community health services and social care. The introduction of the new managerial ethos into both general practice and school education has created enormous strains for general practitioners and headteachers. In their comparative study, Broadbent and Laughlin look at how the 'unwelcome intrusion' of contractual changes within organizations is dealt with over time by the key actors involved. In spite of numerous differences, they note how both GPs and headteachers attempted to develop an 'absorbing group'—based on practice managers and bursars—which can undertake the new requirements within the organization without interfering with the core activities of general practice, on the one hand, and education on the other.

The chapters on contracting for social care and community health services explore some of the difficulties involved in using contracts as the basis of the purchaser-provider relationship. In particular, both chapters address the issue of how contracting interacts with the social organization of trust between professionals working within health and social-care services. Drawing on detailed case study material Flynn and his colleagues demonstrate the reluctance of both health authorities and GP fundholders to contract in a 'hard' style with providers of services with whom collaborative relationships are a *sine qua non*. However, health authorities, in particular, are shown to oscillate between 'hard' and 'soft', or adversarial and relational, styles of contracting, a process which sometimes seems to undermine the mutual trust upon which collaborative working for the development of community health services was seen to depend.

Lapsley and Llewellyn describe their study of contracting for social care within social work departments in Scotland. They note that the 'hard', formal quality of contracting processes becomes mediated and thereby transmuted into 'soft' contracting by social work professional values and considerations of trust. As in the study by Hughes and his colleagues on the NHS in Wales, they note that social-care contracting in Scotland eschews legalistic or adversarial forms. While emphasizing the importance of mutual trust, they note that social service contracts with independent providers of social care are, at present, statements of 'mutual faith', owing to lack of prior experience. The development of future contracting relationships, they suggest, will depend to a large extent on the structural forms—the resources and the policies—of the market within which the relationships are formed.

The chapter by Spurgeon and his colleagues compares different public sector contracts that have been developed in health services, local government, and social care. Drawing on a wealth of empirical data they explore the focus, form, and content of contracts in these different sectors. As in many of the other chapters, they draw attention to the difficulty of reconciling a desire for contracts to be as complete as possible in terms of their information content, with the need for broad statements of agreement which allow space for the collaborative, mutual relationships.

Some other general observations can be made from these studies. One extremely important point is that contrary to initial expectations and official rhetoric, contracts *per se*, despite their potential importance, may not have had a direct, immediate, or overwhelming influence on the production of health care. Thus, for example, Checkland clearly indicates that in the context of enormous local diversity and a constant flux in NHS policy-making, contracts were not the sole, or even the major, driving force in providing health services. His research revealed that the form of contracts was not, as anticipated, a significant element in the overall conduct of the contracting process. Contracts had a much more limited role than imagined in government policy. Similarly, Spurgeon *et al.* argue that until 1994, relationships between purchasers and providers had continued to develop *alongside* the formal contracting system as much as through it. It can be argued therefore that the contracting process, while having a profound impact on inter- and intra-agency relationships, does not appear to have systematically determined the outcome of particular local decisions.

Another issue concerns the degree of formalization implied by contracts, and the common finding that information, monitoring, and regulation of standards is highly problematic. All the contributors have noted the fundamental problems of obtaining valid and reliable information in purchasing and evaluating health services. Barker *et al.*, from both economic and legal standpoints, emphasize the difficult choices faced in designing a contract framework which balances costs and quality. Spurgeon *et al.* note increasing signs of a move towards greater formalization in recent contracts, with increasingly explicit guidelines and sanctions. They also observe that there is evidence that the formal is 'driving out' the informal.

This leads back to the other overarching issue which is raised by all the contributors, directly or indirectly—the problem of trust, and the socially embedded nature of the contracting process. The chapters by Lapsley and Llewellyn, and Flynn *et al.* demonstrate that contracts for health and social care are socially constructed, and that the relationships between parties are conditioned by many factors. They also emphasize that because of the inherent indeterminacy of many aspects of effectiveness and quality in health and social services, there must be a necessary reliance on professional discretion and mutual trust between purchasers and providers. As Lapsley and Llewellyn argue, if there is low trust, contracts can be used to seek a closer alignment of expectations and values; where trust is already high, then contracts may either be redundant or possibly damage relationships. Following Giddens (1991), Flynn and his colleagues argue that trust is a 'project' which requires work, and that even where relational contracting is desired by both purchaser and provider, trust remains a precarious and volatile quality.

This then leads back to the structure of the internal market itself, as well as the culture or ideology of competition which it has sought to institutionalize. Propper and Bartlett show that regulation has blunted the incentive properties of the NHS quasi-market. Nevertheless, they also indicate that more devolution to Trusts where managerial influence is strong is associated with the pursuit of predominantly financial objectives, whereas in Trusts where clinician influence is strong, other objectives are paramount. Broadbent and Laughlin, however, point out the controversial and contested nature of quasi-market reforms, and report the variety of strategies of negotiation and incorporation used by education and health professionals. Lapsley and Lle-wellyn and Flynn *et al.* separately identify the salience of professional values in the implementation of contracts, and other chapters too provide evidence of the varied ways in which health workers cope with the contradictory demands of the NHS-managed market. There is, as many of the chapters show, a constant tension between official declarations about the need for collaboration and cooperation, and a simultaneous preoccupation with competition and surveillance. These ambiguities are then inevitably reflected in the contracting process and contract documents, and impinge on the wider sets of relationships between NHS agencies and personnel.

Clearly, these contracting relationships represent a major challenge for social scientists from many disciplines, and all the chapters collected here reflect the thinking about method which research on contracting and the reform of the health and welfare services requires. Many of the authors have found that qualitative methods of one sort or another are necessary for studying the multidimensional, dynamic processes encapsulated in the changes under way in the NHS. Taken as a whole, the collection demonstrates the need for different disciplinary perspectives, and the growing recognition, within dis-ciplines, of the need for a combination of theoretical and empirical, and quantitative and qualitative, approaches to the research task. The chapter by Checkland explicitly addresses the need for new methods. Like many of the chapters here, his work was concerned with the *process* of contracting, and how to develop innovative methods for capturing that process without freezing it into something different. Checkland brings together findings from twelve pieces of research which have utilized 'soft systems methodology', a research approach which seeks to bridge the gulf between theoretical and practical discourses. In this way the research process itself is seen to provide a means whereby purchaser-provider interaction can be enhanced, both within the contracting process and outside it.

The NHS internal market is still in a state of considerable turbulence, and the move towards a primary-care-led NHS is bringing further changes in commissioning and contracting for services. Against this background, the chapters collected here provide a thorough examination of some of the key changes affecting the contracting culture within the health and related services. They illuminate the dark complexity which is unfolding in the project of bringing markets and management into public sector organizations, which have long histories of operating outside markets and with non-linear manage-ment structures. They show some of the complex economic issues to do with price and quality which contracting in a quasi-market involves. They illustrate the psychological ramifications of introducing contracts into public sector organizations at a time of severe constraint in the overall funding of public sector organizations.

The NHS is experiencing contradictory developments. On the one hand, there is increasing fragmentation of both purchaser and provider functions within health and social care, breaking up traditional forms of organizational relationships and creating the need for more formal mechanisms of surveillance and regulation. On the other hand, GPs, teachers, social workers, purchasers, and providers of district nursing and health visiting are, *de facto*, involved in social contexts which make it impossible to regard contracts simply as formal documents between a 'principal' and an 'agent'. These contracts are, as we argued in the introduction, better regarded as 'treaties' embedded in complex organizational, professional, and political relationships.

If the chapters in this book say anything about the future development of contracting for health and social services, it is that it cannot be understood without an examination of the culture and political economy of the NHS in general. At the time of writing a general election is not far away, and although it would be foolish to assume that a Labour government is a forgone conclusion, it is a distinct possibility. The Labour Party have already indicated, in relation to the NHS as in many other areas of public policy, that they now share many of the Conservative Party's broad assumptions. In relation to the NHS, they are vague about Trusts and GP fundholders, but they are clear about their intention to keep the purchaser-provider separation in some form. This will probably be somewhat attenuated, with annual contracts being replaced by longer term—three- or five-year—service level agreements (Labour Party 1995).

While there may be a cosmetic element in the elimination of the term 'contract', much of the work reported here, with its emphasis on the need for long-term collaboration with limited contestability, would support the strategic and organizational sense of the move towards some kind of service-level agreement with a longer time-scale. Some may see this as contracting in another guise, but the work reported here indicates that much of the important negotiation between purchasers and providers takes place outside the contracting process, as part of the long-term relationships developed by the clinical and managerial professions in the health service. What has been described in this book in terms of contracting is actually a complex legal, economic, and social process in which personal and professional values mediate and interpret the financial and legal terms of contracts.

To put the argument in a broader context, the processes involved in contracting for health services, or education and social services, cannot be understood entirely from within the disciplines and discourses of economics or law. There is much to be learned from those disciplines in understanding aspects of the contracting process within the NHS. However, what a number of the chapters and the collection as a whole demonstrate is that while traditional contract theories may illuminate certain aspects of the current developments in the NHS, contracting takes on a different meaning within the culture and politics of the health service.

Disciplines have their particular histories and philosophies, and it would be simplistic to expect an easy meeting of minds between the proponents and practitioners of them; and calls to interdisciplinarity are sometimes premature. However, examination of the contracting process in health and social care provides a useful opportunity for interdisciplinarity to become more than a rhetorical flourish. It requires innovative use of methods, and because methods emerge from disciplines with different perspectives, movement across the high walls between social science disciplines is a necessary consequence. Moreover, in view of the development of a 'research and development' strategy for the NHS with evidence-based health care as its goal, social scientists may find themselves increasingly drawn into the process of translating their own research findings into practice. Just as no single social-science discipline is sufficient to explain the current predicament of British society (Hutton 1995), so a multidisciplinary methodological pluralism is required if we are to understand the political and social processes and outcomes of the NHS reforms, with multiple stakeholders involved. We hope that this collection will stand as a contribution to that understanding.

BIBLIOGRAPHY

Accounts Commission (1994), *Squaring the Circle: Managing Community Care Resources*, Sept.

Allen, P. (1995), 'Contracts in the National Health Service Internal Market', *Modern Law Review*, 583: 321–42.

Allison, J. W. F. (1994), 'Fuller's Analysis of Polycentric Disputes', *The Cambridge Law Journal*, 53: 367–83.

Appleby, J. (1994*a*), 'The Reformed National Health Service', *Social Policy and Administration*, 284: 345–58.

—— (1994*b*), *Developing Contracting: A National Survey of DHAs, Boards and NHS Trusts* (Birmingham: National Association of Health Authorities and Trusts).

—— and Little, V. (1993), 'Health and Efficiency', *Health Services Journal*, 6 (May).

—— —— Ranade, W., Robinson, R., and Smith, P. (1992), *Implementing the Reforms: A Second National Survey of District General Managers* (Birmingham: National Association of Health Authorities and Trusts).

—— Smith, P., Ranade, W., Little, V., and Robinson, R. (1994), 'Monitoring Managed Competition', in Robinson, R., and Le Grand, J. (eds.), *Evaluating the NHS Reforms* (Hermitage: Policy Journals).

Arrow, K. J. (1963), 'Uncertainty and the Welfare Economics of Medical Care', *American Economic Review*, 53: 941–73.

Atkin, K., and Lunt, N. (1993), 'A Census of Direction', *Nursing Times* (23 Oct.), 38–41.

Audit Commission (1996), *What the Doctor Ordered* (London: HMSO).

Ball, S. (1994), 'Schools in the Market-Place: An Analysis of Local Market Relations', in Bartlett, W., Propper, C., Wilson, D., and Le Grand, J. (eds.), *Quasi-Markets in the Welfare State* (Bristol: SAUS Publications).

Barker, K. (1993), 'NHS Contracts, Restitution and the Internal Market', *Modern Law Review*, 56: 832–43.

—— (1995), 'NHS Contracting: Shadows in the Law of Tort?' *Medical Law Review*, 3: 161–76.

Bartlett, W. (1991), 'Quasi-Markets and Contracts: A Markets and Hierarchies Perspective on NHS Reform', *Public Money and Management*, 113: 53–61.

—— and Le Grand, J. (1994), 'The Performance of Trusts', in Robinson, R., and Le Grand, J. (eds.), *Evaluating the NHS Reforms* (Hermitage: Policy Journals).

Bartunek, J. M. (1984), 'Changing Interpretive Schemes and Organizational Restructuring: The Example of a Religious Order', *Administrative Science Quarterly*, 20: 355–72.

Berger, P. L., and Luckmann, T. (1971), *The Social Construction of Reality* (Harmondsworth: Penguin).

Bion, W. R. (1968), *Experiences in Groups* (London: Tavistock).

Bland, R., Bland, R., Cheetham, J., Lapsley, I., and Llewellyn, S. (1992), *Residential Homes for Elderly People: Their Costs and Quality* (Edinburgh: HMSO).

Blum, F. H. (1955), 'Action Research—A Scientific Approach?' *Philosophy of Science*, 22: 1–7.

Bradach, J., and Eccles, R. (1991), 'Price, Authority and Trust', in Thompson, G.,

Frances, J., Levacic R., and Mitchell, J. (eds.), *Markets, Hierarchies and Networks*, (London: Sage).

Broadbent, J. (1992), 'Change in Organisations: A Case Study of the Use of Accounting Information in the NHS', *British Accounting Review*, 24: 343–67.

—— (1994), 'Practice Managers and Nurses: Gatekeepers and Handmaidens? A Consideration of the New General Medical Practitioner Contract', Discussion Paper 94.19, Sheffield University Management School.

—— (1995), 'The Values of Accounting and Education: Some Implications of the Creation of Visibilities and Invisibilities', *Advances in Public Interest Accounting*, 6: 69–98.

—— Dietrich, M., and Laughlin, R. (1993*a*), 'The Development of Principal-Agent Contracting and Accountability Relationships in the Public Sector', Discussion Paper 93.34, Sheffield University Management School.

—— Laughlin, R., Shearn, D., and Dandy, N. (1992), ' "It's a Long Way from Teaching Susan to Read": Some Preliminary Observations from a Project Studying the Introduction of Local Management of Schools', in Wallace, G. (ed.), *BERA DIALOGUES* 6: *Local Management of Schools: Research and Experience* (Clevedon, Avon: Multilingual Matters).

—— —— —— —— (1993*b*), ' "Doing LMS": The role of the Headteacher and the "Absorbing Group" ', in Wallace, G. (ed.), *Local Management, Central Control: Schools in the Market Place* (Bournemouth: Hyde).

—— —— —— —— (1993*c*), 'Implementing Local Management of Schools: A Theoretical and Empirical Analysis', *Research Papers in Education*, 8: 149–76.

—— —— and Willig-Atherton, H. (1994), 'Financial Controls in Schools: Accounting in "Public" and "Private" Spheres', *The British Accounting Review*, 26: 255–79.

Burgoyne, J. G., Brown, D. H., Hindle, A., and Mumford, M. J. (forthcoming), 'A Multidisciplinary Identification of Issues Associated with Contracting in Market-Oriented Health Service Reforms', *British Journal of Management*.

Chalkley, M., and Malcomson, J. (1994), 'Contracts and Competition in the NHS', paper presented to the ESRC Contracts and Competition Programme Conference, Sept., Robinson College, Cambridge; forthcoming in Culyer, A. J., and Wagstaff, A. (eds.), *Reforming Health Care* (Aldershot: Edward Elgar).

—— —— (1995*a*), 'Contracting for Health Services with Unmonitored Quality', Discussion Papers in Economics and Econometrics 9510, University of Southampton.

—— —— (1995*b*) 'Contracts and Competition in the NHS', Discussion Papers in Economics and Econometrics 9513, University of Southampton.

—— —— (1995*c*), 'Contracting for Health Services when Patient Demand does not Reflect Quality', Discussion Papers in Economics and Econometrics 9514, University of Southampton.

—— —— and McVicar, D. (1995), 'Forms of Contract in the National Health Service: An Empirical Study', University of Southampton, Department of Economics.

Challis, L., Day, P., Klein, R., and Scrivens, E. (1994), 'Managing Quasi-Markets: Institutions of Regulation', in Bartlett, W., Propper, C., Wilson, D., and Le Grand, J. (eds.), *Quasi-Markets in the Welfare State* (Bristol: SAUS).

Checkland, P. (1981), *Systems Thinking, Systems Practice* (Chichester: Wiley).

—— (1991), 'From Framework through Experience to Learning: The Essential Nature of Action Research', in Nissen, H.-E., Klein, H. K., and Hirschheim, R. (eds.),

Information Systems Research: Contemporary Approaches and Emergent Traditions (Amsterdam: North-Holland).

—— and Poulter, J. (1996), *Guidelines for the Use of Soft Systems Methodology*, NHS Executive, Hospital Information and Support System Central Team, Winchester.

—— and Scholes, J. (1990), *Soft Systems Methodology in Action* (Chichester: Wiley).

Cochrane, A. (1994), 'Managing Change in Local Government', in Clarke, J., Cochrane, A., and McLaughlin, E. (eds.), *Managing Social Policy* (London: Sage).

Culyer, A. J., and Posnett, J. (1990), 'Hospital Behaviour and Competition', in Culyer, A. J., Maynard, A., and Posnett, J. (eds.), *Competition in Health Care: Reforming the NHS* (Houndmills: Macmillan Press).

Cutler, D. M. (1995), 'The incidence of adverse medical outcomes under prospective payment', *Econometrica*, 63, 29–50.

Deakin, N. (1994a), 'Evolving Relations Between Government and Third Sector in Britain: The Case of Community Care', Paper prepared for a Conference of the International Society for Third Sector Research, Pecs, Hungary, 4–7 July.

—— (1994b), *The Politics of Welfare* (Hemel Hempstead: Harvester Wheatsheaf).

—— and Walsh, K. (1994), 'The Enabling State: The Role of Markets and Contracts', paper presented to the International Seminar on Contracts and Public Services, Sept., University of Birmingham.

—— —— Spurgeon, P., and Thomas, N. (forthcoming), *Contracting for Change* (Oxford: Oxford University Press).

De Board, R. (1978), *The Pychoanalysis of Organizations* (London: Tavistock).

de Jasay, A. (1991), *Choice, Contract, Consent: A Restatement of Liberalism* (London: IEA).

Department of Health (1989a), *Working for Patients*, Cmnd. 855 (London: HMSO).

—— (1989b), *Working for Patients: Contracts for Health Services—Operational Principles* (London: HMSO).

—— (1990), *Working for Patients: Contracts for Health Services—Operating Contracts* (London: HMSO).

—— (1994), *The Operation of the NHS Internal Market*, Health Service Guidance (94) (Leeds: NHS Executive).

DiMaggio. P., and Powell, W. (1991), 'Introduction', in Powell, W., and DiMaggio, P. (eds.), *The New Institutionalism in Organizational Analysis* (Chicago: University of Chicago Press).

Dranove, D., Shanley, M., and White, W. D. (1993), 'Price and Concentration in Hospital Markets: The Switch from Patient-Driven Competition to Payer-Driven Competition', *Journal of Law and Economics*, 36: 179–204.

Dunleavy, P., and Hood, C. (1994), 'From Old Public Administration to New Public Management', *Public Money and Management* (July–Sept.), 9–16.

Edgell, S., Walklate, S., and Williams, G. (eds.) (1995), *Debating the Public Sphere* (Aldershot: Avebury).

Ellis, R. P., and McGuire, T. G. (1986), 'Provider Behavior under Prospective Reimbursement: Cost Sharing and Supply', *Journal of Health Economics*, 5: 129–51.

—— —— (1993), 'Supply-Side and Demand-Side Cost Sharing in Health-Care', *Journal of Economic Perspectives,* 7: 135–51.

Ferlie, E. (1994), 'The Creation and Evolution of Quasi-Markets in the Public Sector', *Policy and Politics*, 222: 105–12.

Fiss, O. (1984), 'Against Settlement', *Yale Law Review*, 93: 1073–90.

Flynn, N. (1992), 'Managing in the Market for Welfare', in Harding, T. (ed.), *Who Owns Welfare: Questions on the Social Services Agenda*, Social Services Forum, Policy Paper No. 2 (London: The National Institute for Social Work).

Flynn, N. (1994), 'Control, Commitment and Contracts', in Clarke, J., Cochrane, A., and McLaughlin, E. (eds.), *Managing Social Policy* (London: Sage).

Flynn, R., Pickard, S., and Williams, G. (1995), 'Contracts and the Quasi-Market in Community Health Services', *Journal of Social Policy*, 244: 529–50.

Flynn, R., Williams, G., and Pickard, S. (1996), *Markets and Networks: Contracting in Community Health Services* (Buckingham: Open University Press).

Foster, M. (1972), 'An Introduction to the Theory and Practice of Action Research in Work Organisations', *Human Relations*, 25: 529–56.

Fox, A. (1974), *Beyond Contract* (London: Faber and Faber).

Francis, A., Turk, J., and Willman, P. (eds.) (1983), *Power, Efficiency and Institutions* (London: Heinemann Educational Books).

Fukuyama, F. (1995), *Trust—The Social Virtues and Creation of Prosperity* (London: Hamish Hamilton).

Fuller, L. (1978), 'The Forms and Limits of Adjudication', *Harvard Law Review*, 92: 352–409.

Furobotn, E., and Pejovich, S. (1972), 'Property Rights and Economic Theory', *Journal of Economic Literature*, 104: 1137–62.

Gabe, J., Kelleher, D., and Williams, G. (eds.) (1994), *Challenging Medicine* (London: Routledge).

Gamble, A. (1988), *The Free Economy and the Strong State* (London: Macmillan).

Giddens, A. (1979), *Central Problems in Social Theory* (London: Macmillan).

—— (1991), *Consequences of Modernity* (Cambridge: Polity Press).

Glennerster, H., Matsaganis, M., Owens, P., and Hancock, S. (1994*a*), *Implementing GP Fundholding* (Buckingham: Open University Press).

—— —— —— —— (1994*b*), 'GP Fundholding: Wild Card or Winning Hand', in Robinson, R., and Le Grand, J. (eds.), *Evaluating the NHS Reforms* (Hermitage: Policy Journals).

Gordon, R. (1985), 'Macauley, MacNeil and the Discovery of Solidarity and Power in Contract Law', *Wisconsin Law Review*, 3: 565–79.

Government Statistical Office, *Health and Personal Social Services Statistics for England* (1995), (London: HMSO).

Granovetter, M. (1985), 'Economic Action and Social Structure: The Problem of Embeddedness', *American Journal of Sociology*, 913: 481–510.

—— (1992), 'Economic Institutions as Social Constructions', *Acta Sociologica*, 353: 3–11.

—— and Swedberg, R. (1992), 'Introduction', in Granovetter, M., and Swedberg, R. (eds.), *The Sociology of Economic Life* (Boulder, Colo. and Oxford: Westview Press).

Greenwood, R., and Hinings, C. R. (1988), 'Organizational Design Types, Tracks and the Dynamics of Strategic Change', *Organization Studies*, 9: 293–316.

Gronbjerg, K. (1991), 'Managing Grants and Contracts: The Case of Four Non-profit Social Service Organisations', *Non-Profit and Voluntary Sector Quarterly*, 201 (spring), 5–24.

Gruber, J. (1992), 'The Effect of Price Shopping in Medical Markets: Hospital Responses to PPOs in California', *NBER Working Paper*, 4190.

Ham, C. (1992), *Health Policy in Britain*, 3rd edn. (London: Macmillan).

—— (1994*a*), *Management and Competition in the New NHS* (Oxford: Radcliffe Medical Press).

—— (1994*b*), 'Reforming Health Services', *Social Policy and Administration*, 284: 293–8.

—— and Hill, M. (1993), *The Policy Process in the Capitalist State*, 2nd edn. (Hemel Hempstead: Harvester Wheatsheaf).

Harden, I. (1992), *The Contracting State* (Buckingham: Open University Press).

—— and Longley, D. (1995), 'NHS Contracts', in Birds, J., Bradgate, R., and Villiers, C. (eds.), *The Termination of Contracts* (London: Chancery).

Harris, J. E. (1977), 'The Internal Organisation of Hospitals: Some Economic Implications', *Bell Journal of Economics*, 467–82.

Harrison, S., and Pollitt, C. (1994), *Controlling Health Professionals* (Buckingham: Open University Press).

Hart, O., and Holmström, B. (1987), 'The Theory of Contracts', in Beuley, T. F. (ed.), *Advances in Economics Theory, Fifth World Congress* (Cambridge: Cambridge University Press).

Hills, J. (1990), 'Introduction', in J. Hills (ed.), *The State of Welfare* (Oxford: Clarendon Press).

Hindle, A. (1995), 'Developing GP Monitoring Systems Guided by a Soft Systems Approach', *Health Services Management Research*, 259–67.

—— Checkland, P., Mumford, M., and Worthington, D. (1995), 'Developing a Methodology for Multidisciplinary Action Research: A Case Study', *Journal of the Operational Research Society*, 46: 453–64.

Hinings, C., and Greenwood, R. (1988), *The Tracks and Dynamics of Strategic Change* (Oxford: Blackwell).

Hood, C. (1991), 'A Public Management for All Seasons', *Public Administration*, 69: 3–19.

—— (1995), 'The "New Public Management" in the 1980s: Variations on a Theme', *Accounting, Organizations and Society*, 20: 93–109.

Hughes, D. (1991), 'The Reorganization of the National Health Service: The Rhetoric and Reality of the Internal Market', *Modern Law Review*, 54: 88–103.

—— and Dingwall, R. (1990), 'Sir Henry Maine, Joseph Stalin and the Reorganization of the NHS', *Journal of Social Welfare Law*, 5: 296–309.

—— Griffiths, L., and McHale, J. (1995), 'Whose Problem?' *Health Service Journal*, 20 (Apr.), 18–20.

—— McHale, J., and Griffiths, L. (1994), 'NHS Arbitration—A Redundant Remedy', paper presented at the ESRC Contracts and Competition Programme Conference, Sept., Robinson College, Cambridge.

Hult, M., and Lennung, S. (1980), 'Towards a Definition of Action Research: A Note and a Bibliography', *Journal of Management Studies*, 17: 242–50.

Hunter, D. (1993), 'The Internal Market—The Shifting Agenda', in Tilley, I. (ed.), *Managing the Internal Market* (London: Paul Chapman).

Hutton, W. (1995), *The State We're In* (London: Jonathan Cape).

Jacob, J. (1991), 'Lawyers go to Hospital', *Public Law*, 255–81.

Joseph Rowntree Foundation (1994), 'Financing User Choice in Housing and Community Care', *Housing Summary* (6 Oct.), Joseph Rowntree Foundation, York.

Jost, T. S., Hughes, D., McHale, J., and Griffiths, L. (1995), 'The British Health Care

Reforms, The American Health Care Revolution and Purchaser-Provider Contracts', *Journal of Health Politics, Policy and Law*, 204: 886–908.

Kerrison, S. (1993), 'Contracting and the Quality of Medical Care', in Tilley, I. (ed.), *Managing the Internal Market* (London: Paul Chapman).

Kets de Vries, M., and Miller, D. (1984), *The Neurotic Organization* (San Francisco: Jossey-Bass).

Kind, P. (1990), 'Issues in the Design and Construction of a Quality of Life Measure', in Baldwin, S., Godfrey, C., and Propper, C. (eds.), *Quality of Life—Perspectives and Policies* (London: Routledge).

Kornai, J. (1989), *Vision and Reality, Market and State* (New York: Harvester Wheatsheaf).

Labour Party (1995), *Renewing the NHS*, July (London: The Labour Party, John Smith House).

Laffont, J. -J., and Tirole, J. (1987), 'Comparative Statics of the Optimal Dynamics Incentive Contracts', *European Economic Review*, 31: 901–26.

—— —— (1993), *A Theory of Incentives in Procurement and Regulation* (Cambridge, Mass.: MIT Press).

Lapsley, I. (1995), 'Costs, Budgets and Community Care', in Clark, C., and Lapsley, I. (eds.), *Planning and Costing Community Care*, Research Highlights in Social Work no. 27 (London: Jessica Kingsley).

—— and Mitchell, F. (eds.) (1996), *Accounting and Performance Measurement* (London: Paul Chapman).

—— and Llewellyn, S. (1995), 'Real Life Constructs: The Exploration of Organizational Processes in Case Studies', *Management Accounting Research*, 6: 223–35.

—— and Mitchell, F. (eds.) (1996), *Accounting and Performance Measurement* (London: Paul Chapman).

Larson, A. (1992), 'Network Dyads in Entrepreneurial Settings', *Administrative Science Quarterly*, 37: 76–104.

Laughlin, R. (1991), 'Environmental Disturbances and Organisational Transitions and Transformations: Some Alternative Models', *Organization Studies*, 12: 209–32.

—— (1995), 'Empirical Research in Accounting: Alternative Approaches and a Case for Middle Range Thinking', *Accounting, Auditing and Accountability Journal*, 8: 63–87.

—— and Broadbent, J. (1996*a*), 'Redesigning Fourth Generation Evaluation: An Evaluation Model for the Public Sector Reforms in the UK?' University of Essex Discussion Paper no. 96.07.

—— —— (1996*b*), 'Evaluating the "New Public Management" Reforms in the UK: A Constitutional Possibility?' University of Essex Discussion Paper no. 96.11.

—— —— and Shearn, D. (1992), 'Recent Financial and Accountability Changes in General Practice: An Unhealthy Intrusion into Medical Autonomy', *Financial Accountability and Management*, 8: 129–48.

—— —— —— and Willig-Atherton, H. (1994), 'Absorbing LMS: The Coping Mechanism of a Small Group', *Accounting, Auditing and Accountability Journal*, 7: 59–85.

—— —— and Willig-Atherton, H. (1994), 'Recent Financial and Administrative Change in GP Practices in the UK: Initial Experiences and Effects', *Accounting, Auditing and Accountability Journal*, 7: 96–124.

Le Grand, J. (1990), *Quasi-Markets and Social Policy*, Studies in Decentralisation and Quasi-Markets, 1 (Bristol: SAUS).

—— (1994), 'Evaluating the NHS Reforms', in Robinson, R., and Le Grand, J. (eds.), *Evaluating the NHS Reforms* (Hermitage: Policy Journals).

Levy, A. (1986), 'Second-Order Planned Change: Definition and Conceptualisation', Organization Dynamics, 15: 5–23.

Lewis, J. (1993), 'Developing the Mixed Economy of Care: Emerging Issues for Voluntary Organisations', *Journal of Social Policy*, 222: 173–92.

—— (1994), 'Voluntary Organisations in "New Partnership" with Local Authorities: The Anatomy of a Contract', *Social Policy and Administration*, 283: 206–19.

Llewellyn, S. (1993), 'Linking Costs with Quality in Health and Social Care: New Challenges for Management Accounting', *Financial Accountability and Management*, 93: 177–94.

—— (1994), 'Where does it Stop on Costs?' paper presented to the conference of the *European Accounting Association*, Annual Congress, Birmingham.

Loveridge, R., Schofield, J., and Smith, P. (1994), 'Is the British National Health Service Trust Still a Nonprofit Organisation?' paper presented to the Association for Research on Non-Profit Organisations and Voluntary Action Annual Conference held on 10–22 Oct., Berkeley Marina, California.

Luhmann, N. (1979), *Trust and Power* (Chichester: John Wiley).

Ma, C.-T. A. (1994), 'Health Care Payment Systems: Cost and Quality Incentives', *Journal of Economics and Management Strategy*, 3: 93–112.

Macaulay, S. (1963), 'Non-Contractual Relations in Business: A Preliminary Study', *American Sociological Review*, 55–67.

—— (1992), 'Non-Contractual Relations in Business', in Granovetter, M., and Swedberg, R. (eds.), *The Sociology of Economic Life* (Boulder, Colo. and Oxford: Westview Press).

McClellan, M. (1995), 'Hospital Reimbursement Incentives: An Empirical Approach', Stanford University (unpublished).

Mahon, A., Wilkin, D., and Whitehouse, C. (1994), 'Choice of Hospitals for Elective Surgery Referrals: GPs' and Patients' Views', in Robinson, R., and Le Grand, J. (eds.), *Evaluating the NHS Reforms* (Hermitage: Policy Journals).

Maynard, A. (1993), 'Creating Competition in the NHS: Is it Possible?' in Tilley, I. (ed.), *Managing the Internal Market* (Liverpool: Paul Chapman).

Melnick, G., Zwanziger, J., Bamezai, A., and Pattison, R. (1992), 'The Effect of Market Structure and Bargaining Position on Hospital Prices', *Journal of Health Economics*, 11: 217–33

Miller, D., and Friesen, P. (1984), *Organizations: A Quantum View* (Englewood Cliffs, NJ: Prentice Hall).

Miller, F. (1992), 'Competition Law and Anti-Competitive Professional Behaviour affecting Health Care', *Modern Law Review*, 55: 453–81.

Montgomery, J. (1997), *Health Care Law* (Oxford: Oxford University Press).

—— and Barker, K. (1996), 'Legal Aspects of the NHS Market', University of Southampton, Faculty of Law.

Morgan, G. (1986), *Images of Organization* (Beverley Hills, Calif.: Sage).

Mullen, P. (1994), *The Organization and Funding of Specialist Health Services in the new NHS*, Discussion Paper 32, Health Services Management Centre, University of Birmingham, Birmingham.

Mumford, M. J. (1996), 'Governance in the National Health Service', in Lapsley, I., and Mitchell, F. (eds.), *Accounting and Performance Measurement* (London: Paul Chapman).

NAHAT (1994), *Developing Contracting*, National Association of Health Authorities and Trusts, Research Paper 15, University of Birmingham.

National Audit Office (1995), *Contracting for Acute Health Care in England* (London: HMSO).

National Health Service Executive (1993), *Purchasing for Health: A Framework for Action* (Leeds: Department of Health).

—— (1994), *The Operation of the Internal Market: Local Freedoms, National Responsibilities* (Leeds: Department of Health).

—— (1996a), Personal communication, 14 Feb. (Leeds: Department of Health).

—— (1996b), *Priorities and Planning Guidance for the NHS: 1996/97* (Leeds: NHS Executive).

National Health Service Management Executive (1991), 'NHS Contracts: Guidance on Resolving Disputes', EL(91)11 (London: Department of Health).

—— (1993), *Review of Contracting 1993–1994* (London: Department of Health).

—— (1994), *The Operation of the NHS Internal Market*, HSG (94) 55 (Leeds: Department of Health).

Neu, D. (1991), 'Trust, Contracting and the Prospectus Process', *Accounting Organisations and Society*, 163: 243–56.

Newdick, C. (1993), 'Rights to NHS Resources after the 1990 Act', *Medical Law Review*, 1: 53–82.

Newhouse, J. P. (1970), 'Toward a Theory of Nonprofit Institutions: An Economic Model of a Hospital', *American Economic Review*, 60: 64–74.

—— (1971), 'Toward a Theory of Non-Profit Institutions: An Economic Model of a Hospital', *American Economic Review*, 63: 64–74.

Nissen, H.-E., Klein, H. K., Hirschheim, R. (eds.) (1991), *Information Systems Research: Contemporary Approaches and Emergent Traditions* (Amsterdam: North-Holland).

Noether, M. (1988), 'Competition between Hospitals', *Journal of Health Economics*, 7: 259–84.

Noorderhaven, N. G. (1992), 'The Problem of Contract Enforcement in Economic Organization Theory', *Organization Studies*, 132: 229–43.

Ouchi, W. (1991), 'Markets, Bureaucracies and Clans', in Thompson, G., Frances, J., Levacic, R., and Mitchell, J. (eds.), *Markets and Hierarchies and Networks* (London: Sage).

Pauly, M., and Redisch, M. (1973), 'The Not-for-Profit Hospital as a Physicians' Cooperative', *American Economic Review*, 65: 87–99.

Perkin, H. (1989), *The Rise of Professional Society* (London: Routledge).

Perrow, C. (1990), 'Economic Theories of Organization', in Zukin, S., and DiMaggio, P. (eds.), *Structures of Capital* (Cambridge: Cambridge University Press).

Polanyi, M. (1951), *The Logic of Liberty: Reflections and Rejoiners* (London: Routledge and Kegan Paul).

Powell, W. (1991), 'Neither Markets nor Hierarchy: Network Forms of Organization', in Thompson, G., Frances, J., Levacic, R., and Mitchell, J. (eds.), *Markets, Hierarchies and Networks* (London: Sage).

Preston, A. E. (1988), 'The Effects of Property Rights on Labour Costs of Non-Profit

Firms: An Application to the Day Care Industry', *Journal of Industrial Economics*, 36: 337–45.

Propper, C. (1993a), 'Quasi-Markets, Contracts and Quality in Health and Social Care', in Le Grand, J., and Bartlett, W. (eds.), *Quasi-Markets and Social Policy* (London: Macmillan).

—— (1993b), 'Quasi-Markets and Regulation', in Le Grand, J., and Bartlett, W., *Quasi-Markets and Social Policy* (London: Macmillan).

—— (1995), 'Agency and Incentives in the NHS Internal Market', *Social Science and Medicine*, 4012: 1683–90.

—— (1996), 'Market Structure and Prices: The Responses of Hospitals in the UK National Health Service to Competition', *Journal of Public Economics*, 61: 307–36.

—— and Wilson, D. (1995), 'Price and Competition in the NHS Internal Market in GP Fundholder Procedure', University of Bristol, Department of Economics (unpublished).

Raftery, J., Mulligan, J., Forrest, S., and Robinson, R. (1994), *The Third National Review of Contracting, 1994* (Leeds: NHSE Purchasing Unit).

Ranade, W. (1995), 'The Theory and Practice of Managed Competition in the NHS', *Public Administration*, 73: 241–62.

Rea, D. (1995), 'Unhealthy Competition', *Policy and Politics*, 232: 141–5.

Reed, M. (1993), Organizations and Modernity', in Hassard, J., and Parker, M. (eds.), *Postmodernism and Organizations* (London: Sage).

Ring, P., and Van de Ven, A. (1992), 'Structuring Cooperative Relationships between Organizations', *Strategic Management Journal*, 13: 483–98.

Robinson, J. C., and Luft, H. (1985), 'The Impact of Hospital Market Structure on Patient Volume, Average Length of Stay and the Cost of Care', *Journal of Health Economics*, 4: 333–56.

Robinson, R. (1994), 'Introduction', in Robinson, R., and Le Grand, J. (eds.), *Evaluating the NHS Reforms* (Hermitage: Policy Journals).

—— and Le Grand, J. (1994), *Evaluating the NHS Reforms* (Hermitage: Policy Journals).

Rogerson, W. (1990), 'Overhead Allocation and Incentives for Cost Minimisation in Defence Procurement', Northwestern University, USA (unpublished).

Royal College of Surgeons in England (1994), *Survey of Surgical Activity in the NHS*, Nov. (London: Royal College of Surgeons).

Sako, M. (1992), *Prices, Quality and Trust* (Cambridge: Cambridge University Press).

Saltman, R., and Von Otter, C. (1992), *Planned Markets and Public Competition* (Buckingham: Open University Press).

Scott, T., and Maynard, A. (1991), 'Will the New GP Contract Lead to Cost Effective Medical Practice', University of York Centre for Health Economics Discussion Paper no. 82.

Shearn, D., Broadbent, J., Laughlin, R., and Willig-Atherton, H. (1995a), 'The Changing Face of School Governor Responsibilities: A Mismatch Between Government Intentions and Actuality?' *School Organization*, 15: 175–88.

—— —— —— —— (forthcoming), 'Headteachers, Governors and Local Management of Schools', to be published in Wallace, G. (ed.), *Schools, Markets and Management* (Bournemouth: Hyde).

Smith, K. K. (1982), 'Philosophical Problems in Thinking About Organizational

Change', in Goodman, P. S. (ed.), *Change in Organizations* (San Francisco: Jossey Bass).

Smith, P. (1994), 'The Nature of Contracts in the British National Health Service', paper presented to the conference of the Association for Research on Nonprofit Organizations and Voluntary Action, Berkeley, Calif.

—— and Thomas, N. (1993*a*), *Contracts and Competition in Public Services*, paper given at the Association of Directors of Social Services Autumn Research Conference, Nov., Bristol.

—— —— (1993*b*), 'Contracts and Competition in the Management of Public Services: A Comparative Study', paper presented at the Research Conference of the Association of Directors of Social Services, University of Birmingham.

Spurgeon, P. (1993), 'Regulation or Free Market for the NHS?' in Tilley, I. (ed.), *Managing the Internal Market* (Liverpool: Paul Chapman).

—— and Smith, P. (1995), 'Living with Contracts', paper presented at the conference on NHS Reforms, May, University of Swansea.

SSI/SWSG (Department of Health Social Services Inspectorate; Scottish Office, Social Work Services Group) (1991*a*), *Care Management and Assessment: Manager's Guide* (Edinburgh: HMSO).

—— (1991*b*) *Care Management and Assessment: Practitioner's Guide* (Edinburgh: HMSO).

Stacey, M. (1988), *The Sociology of Health and Healing* (London: Allen and Unwin).

Stockford, D. (1993), *Purchasing for Health: The Contracting Context*, Keynote address, Conference on Crucial Issues in NHS Contracting, 13–14 Oct., London.

Susman, G., and Evered, R. D. (1978), 'An Assessment of the Scientific Merits of Action Research', *Administrative Science Quarterly*, 23: 582–603.

Taylor-Gooby, P. (1991), *Social Change, Social Welfare and Social Science* (Hemel Hempstead: Harvester Wheatsheaf).

Thompson, G., Frances, J., Levacic, R., and Mitchell, J. (eds.) (1991), *Markets, Hierarchies and Networks* (London: Sage).

Tilley, I. (1993), 'Approaching the Internal Market', in Tilley, I. (ed.), *Managing the Internal Market* (Liverpool: Paul Chapman).

Timmins, N. (1995), *The Five Giants: A Biography of the Welfare State* (London: Harper Collins).

Walsh, K. (1994), 'Contracts for Public Services: A Comparative Perspective', paper prepared for Socio-Legal Studies Association Conference, Nottingham University, 28–30 Mar. 1994.

—— (1995*a*), *Public Services and Market Mechanisms* (London: Macmillan).

—— (1995*b*), 'Working with Contracts', paper presented at the ESRC Quasi-Markets Research Seminar, Mar., School for Advanced Urban Studies, University of Bristol.

Weisbrod, B. A. (1988), *The Nonprofit Economy* (Cambridge Mass.: Harvard University Press).

—— (1991), 'The Health-Care Quadrilemma: An Essay on Technological Change, Insurance, Quality of Care, and Cost Containment', *Journal of Economic Literature* 29: 523–52.

Weitzman, M. (1980), 'The "Ratchet Principle" and Performance Incentives', *Bell Journal of Economics*, 111: 302–8.

Whitehead, M. (1994), 'Is it Fair?' in Robinson, R., and Le Grand, J. (eds.), *Evaluating the NHS Reforms* (Hermitage: Policy Journals).

Whynes D. (1995), 'The Factors Associated with GPFHs' Purchasing Intentions', paper presented at the Industrial Economics Study Group, London Business School, May 1995, University of Birmingham, Department of Economics.

Wilding, P. (1994), 'Maintaining Quality in Human Services', *Social Policy and Administration*, 28/1 (March), 57–72.

Williamson, O. E. (1983), *Markets and Hierarchies* (New York: Free Press).

—— (1985), *The Economic Institutions of Capitalism* (New York: Free Press).

—— (1990), 'The Firms as a Nexus of Treaties', in Aoki, M., Gustaffson, B., and Williamson, O. E. (eds.), *The Firm as a Nexus of Treaties* (London: Sage).

—— (1991), 'Comparative Economic Organization', *Administrative Science Quarterly*, 36: 269–96.

Wistow, G., Knapp, M., Hardy, B., and Allen, C. (1992), 'From Providing to Enabling: Local Authorities and the Mixed Economy of Care', *Public Administration*, 70: 25–45.

Zucker, L. G. (1986), 'Production of Trust: Institutional Sources of Economic Structure, 1840–1920', *Research in Organisational Behaviour*, 8: 53–111.

Zwanziger, J. and Melnick, G. (1988), 'The Effects of Hospital Competition and the Medicare PPOs Programme on Hospital Cost Behaviour in California', *Journal of Health Economics*, 7: 301–20.

INDEX

Index compiled by Frank Pert